Security, Conflict and Cooperation in the Contemporary World

Series Editors

Effie G. H. Pedaliu, LSE Ideas, London, UK
John W. Young, University of Nottingham, Nottingham, UK

The Palgrave Macmillan series, Security, Conflict and Cooperation in the Contemporary World aims to make a significant contribution to academic and policy debates on international history, war and diplomacy since 1900. It evolved from the series Global Conflict and Security edited by Professor Saki Ruth Dockrill. The current series welcomes proposals that offer innovative historical perspectives, based on archival evidence and promoting an empirical understanding of economic and political cooperation, conflict and security, peace-making, diplomacy, humanitarian intervention, nation-building, intelligence, terrorism, the influence of ideology and religion on international relations, as well as the work of international organisations and non-governmental organisations.

Massimo de Leonardis
Editor

NATO in the Post-Cold War Era

Continuity and Transformation

palgrave
macmillan

Editor
Massimo de Leonardis
Faculty of Political and Social
Sciences
Catholic University of the Sacred
Heart
Milan, Italy

ISSN 2731-6807 ISSN 2731-6815 (electronic)
Security, Conflict and Cooperation in the Contemporary World
ISBN 978-3-031-06062-5 ISBN 978-3-031-06063-2 (eBook)
https://doi.org/10.1007/978-3-031-06063-2

Cover photo by maxxyustas

This Palgrave Macmillan imprint is published by the registered company Springer Nature Switzerland AG
The registered company address is: Gewerbestrasse 11, 6330 Cham, Switzerland

Acknowledgments

My collaboration in the field of Atlantic studies with most of the authors commenced many years ago and I am most grateful to them for contributing to this volume. Dr. Davide Borsani was a precious collaborator in all the stages of this endeavour. Simone Zuccarelli much contributed to the final editing of the manuscript.

Dr. Effie Pedaliu deserves my warm gratitude for encouraging me to present the project of this volume for publication in the series of which she is co-editor. Lucy Kidwell followed with great dedication and competence all the phases bringing to the Publisher's acceptance of the volume, while Eliana Rangel took attentive care of the publication.

It is impossible to mention all the archivists, librarians, scholars, diplomats, NATO officials, and top military who over the years contributed with their cooperation and advice to the studies on the Atlantic Alliance on which this volume is based.

My Alma Mater, the Catholic University of the Sacred Heart in Milan, during many decades offered me an ideal place for doing research and financed many of my initiatives. Therefore, I am glad to acknowledge that the Università Cattolica del Sacro Cuore contributed the largest amount to the funding of this research project and to the publication in open access of some of its results. I also thank the Comitato Atlantico Italiano for another important financial contribution to the publication in open access.

Praise for *NATO in the Post-Cold War Era*

"Public awareness of the nature and history of NATO is very limited. This volume brings the organisation, its role, and its future fully into focus. It is a timely reminder in a world of growing dangers of just how significant the alliance still is. It deserves a wide readership on both sides of the Atlantic."

—Richard Overy, *Honorary Research Professor, University of Exeter, UK*

"*NATO in the Post-Cold War Era: Continuity and Transformation* confirms Prof. de Leonardis as one of the most eminent scholars on strategic issues and the North Atlantic Alliance. The essays he edited tackle the current and future challenges for NATO from a variety of key political, historic and geostrategic viewpoints. A must, for anybody involved, or interested in strategic, security, defense policies."

—Claudio Bisogniero, *NATO Deputy Secretary General 2007–2012, Italian Ambassador to Washington 2012–2016, Italian Permanent Representative to the North Atlantic Council 2016–2019*

"In this important volume international experts explain NATO's response to contemporary security challenges in the context of the development of the alliance since its foundation seventy years ago. These essays show how NATO is adapting from a coalition with a European focus to one with global reach, able to respond to the varied range of threats in Eastern and Southern Europe, the Middle East and East Asia that have emerged in the early twenty-first century."

—Prof. William Philpott, *Co-director, School of Security Studies research theme in military and political history, Department of War Studies King's College London, UK*

"A tremendously important collection for our understanding of NATO's present situation and possible development, this volume provides the necessary history, both a deep history back to 1945 and a recent history concentrating on the flux in international relations from 1989. The multi-faceted characteristics and potential of NATO emerges clearly."

—Prof. Jeremy Black, *University of Exeter. Senior fellow of the Center for the Study of America and the West, Foreign Policy Research Institute in Philadelphia. Author of* Military Strategy, a Global History, *UK*

"Massimo de Leonardis has assembled an impressive cohort of colleagues who have produced an equally impressive set of focused studies on the central issues that have faced, and that will continue to face, the Atlantic alliance. Its value inheres not only in the sterling research produced by the de Leonardis team, but also in the intriguing "Mediterranean" perspective of most of the analysts – a perspective often absent in works on the transatlantic alliance. This book will be of value to scholars as well as to policymakers in various NATO member states, as the alliance grapples with the dilemmas of developing a new strategic concept to guide it in coming years. It will be a "must read" for anyone seeking to understand NATO's origins, evolution, and future challenges."

—David G. Haglund, *Professor of Political Studies, Queen's University, Canada*

Contents

Notes on Contributors

Borsani Davide is a Researcher in History of International Relations at the Catholic University of the Sacred Heart, Milan, Italy. He is also an Associate Research Fellow in Transatlantic Studies at the Italian Institute for International Political Studies (ISPI), Milan, and a member of the Bibliography Committee of the International Commission of Military History (ICMH). He has authored books, and contributed to think tanks, journals and co-edited volumes in Italian and English.

Carati Andrea is an Associate Professor of International Relations and Foreign Policy Analysis in the Department of International. Legal, Historical and Political Studies, University of Milan, Italy. Among his recent publications: *R2P, NATO and the Problem of Who Should Intervene: Reassessing the Intervention in Libya*, in *Global Change, Peace and Security*, Vol. 29, no. 3 (2017): 293–309; *No Easy Way Out: Origins of NATO's Difficulties in Afghanistan*, in *Contemporary Security Policy*, Vol. 36, No. 2, 2015, pp. 200–218.

de Leonardis Massimo is a Full Professor [ret.] of History of International Relations and Institutions and currently a Senior Lecturer of History of Treaties and International Politics, Catholic University of the Sacred Heart, Milan, Italy. Coordinator of the History Department at the Master in Diplomacy of the Italian Institute for International Political Studies (ISPI), Milan. President of the International Commission of Military History. Editor of the *Quaderni di Scienze Politiche* and member of the Scientific Boards of various Italian and international institutions and journals. Author or editor of 27 books and other about 280 essays in various languages.

Dobson Alan P. was a Honorary Professor at Swansea University, he has held Chairs at Dundee University and at St Andrews and fellowships at the Norwegian Nobel Institute, (Senior Research Fellowship) Saint Bonaventure University (Lenna) and Baylor University (Fulbright). He has written extensively on Anglo-American relations, international civil aviation, and the Cold War strategic embargo. His most recent book is *A History of International Civil Aviation*, London and New York, Routledge, 2017. Regretfully, in April 2022 Alan died at the relatively young age of 71.

Leonardi Alessandro holds a Ph.D. in History of International Relations from the University of Florence and contributes to the teaching of History of International Relations in the Department of Foreign Languages at the University Rome III and of History of China at the LUMSA University. His research interests lie in the evolution of transatlantic security relations and arms control policies during and after the Cold War.

Marquina Barrio Antonio is Chair in International Security and Cooperation at the Universidad Complutense, Madrid, Spain. He is the author, co-author or editor of more than 120 books in English and Spanish on European Security, Mediterranean Politics and Security, Iran, Middle East, Disarmament, NATO, Spanish Foreign, Security and Defense Policy, Intelligence, Asia–Pacific security. He is a Former Chairman of the Asia–Europe Human Security network, the first President of STRADEMED (Stratégies et Développement en Méditerranée) and Director of UNISCI (Research Unit on International Security and Cooperation).

Marrone Alessandro is the Head of the Istituto Affari Internazionali's Defence Programme and lecturer of Military Policy at the Istituto Superiore di Stato Maggiore Interforze (Joint Staff School) of the Italian Ministry of Defence. He holds a Ph.D. in the History of Europe from Sapienza University of Rome and an M.Sc. in International Relations at the London School of Economics and Political Science.

Mongrenier Jean-Sylvestre is a Doctor in Geopolitics, an Associate Professor of History-Geography and a Researcher at the Institut Français de Géopolitique, Université Paris VII, Vincennes-Saint-Denis. Reserve

Officer in the French Navy, he is attached to the Centre d'études stratégiques de la Marine (CESM) and at the École Militaire. He is the author of several books, including *La France, l'Europe, l'OTAN : une approche géopolitique de l'atlantisme français* (Paris, 2006), *Géopolitique de la Russie* (Paris, 2018) and *Géopolitique de l'Europe* (Paris, 2020).

Pastori Gianluca is an Associate Professor of History of political relations between North America and Europe, Faculty of Political and Social Sciences, Catholic University of the Sacred Heart, Milan, Italy. He collaborates with several public and private research structures; among them, the Italian Institute for International Political Studies (ISPI), Milan, Italy. He is the author or editor of several books and essays, both in Italy and abroad, on the history of international relations, security issues, and military history.

Quanten Kris is a Military professor and head of the Conflict Studies Department at the Royal Military Academy in Brussels (Belgium). He studied Military and Social Sciences, International Relations and History. He obtained his Ph.D. in History at the Catholic University of Leuven and graduated from the NATO Defense College in Rome. He is the author of various books and articles about the Cold War and the role of NATO in it.

Randazzo Francesco is an Associate Professor of History of International Relations at the Department of Political Sciences at the University of Perugia, Italy. He is the Coordinator of the International Center for Research and Eurasian Studies, and the author of several publications that mainly concern Russia, the Soviet Union and their diplomatic relations with Italy.

Ratti Luca is an Associate professor of History of International Relations at the University Rome III, Italy. His works have appeared in journals such as *The Journal of Transatlantic Studies*, *Diplomacy & Statecraft*, *The Journal of Slavic Military Studies*, *The Journal of Middle Eastern Geopolitics*, and *Mediterranean Politics*. His latest volume is *A Not So "Special Relationship": The US, the UK, and German Unification* (Edinburgh, 2017) which explores Anglo-American policy towards Germany during and at the end of the Cold War in Europe.

CHAPTER 1

Introduction: NATO in Its Seventh Decade—A Reappraisal

Massimo de Leonardis

History's Most Successful Alliance Needs Better Publicity

This book wants to provide a full and scholarly assessment of NATO's performance during and particularly after the Cold War. The guiding methodological principle is to evaluate the elements of continuity and the factors of transformation in NATO before and after 1989. The historical approach qualifies this volume among the literature on the Atlantic Alliance, largely dominated by political science and strategic studies.

Good reasons justify a new book on NATO. In 2019 the 70th anniversary of the Atlantic Alliance received comparatively little attention by the general public and also by scholars. Much more attention had been dedicated in 2007 to the 50th anniversary of European Union (EU, born as European Economic Community, EEC), the other key organization

M. de Leonardis (✉)
Faculty of Political and Social Sciences, Catholic University of the Sacred Heart, Milan, Italy
e-mail: massimo.deleonardis@unicatt.it

M. de Leonardis (ed.), *NATO in the Post-Cold War Era*,
Security, Conflict and Cooperation in the Contemporary World
https://doi.org/10.1007/978-3-031-06063-2_1

which shares largely its membership with NATO. In 2012 the EU had been awarded the Nobel Prize for Peace, for contributing 'for over six decades [...] to the advancement of peace [...] in Europe' and some commentators argued that NATO was much worthier of that prize.

Actually, the process of European integration was not the cornerstone of the European peace, on the contrary it was the product of a peace guaranteed by other factors. The bipolar international system and the strategic situation generated the risk of mutual assured destruction (MAD), making a war between the two blocs impossible particularly in the Old Continent, where the existence of NATO deterred a Soviet aggression (de Leonardis 2018). Only in 2007, EU became a collective defence organization, still closely linked to NATO,[1] 'which for those States which are members of it, remains the foundation of their collective defence and the forum for its implementation' (Treaty of Lisbon 2007).

The citizens of EU member states are quite aware that decisions taken in Brussels affect their daily lives, which is not the case for NATO. In 2008, a high ranking NATO official admitted that 'almost 20 years after the collapse of the Soviet Union, significant proportions of most NATO country populations still have vague ideas about the Alliance, its purpose and its roles' (Babst 2008). Twelve years later a think tank analyst wrote that 'indeed, the run-up to the alliance's 70th previously it was 70th anniversary was accompanied by an outpouring of doubts about NATO's future and usefulness' (Sweeney 2020). Since the end of the Cold War, obituaries of the Alliance are periodically written, arousing the ironical comment that NATO has had more resurrections than Dracula (Shea 2002). It would be useless continuing to quote similar remarks, either by those who express pessimistic views or by others who repeat the usual mantra that NATO 'stands as history's most successful alliance'.

Until recently, bashing NATO was an exercise for scholars, but no politician having a governmental role expressed publicly a similar kind of criticism. Then, during the electoral campaign in 2016 future President Donald J. Trump described NATO as 'obsolete', being too much focused exclusively against Russia while largely ignoring international (Islamic) terrorism and the Middle East and North Africa (MENA) region. *No Alternative to Obsolescence*, was a new ironic interpretation of the acronym NATO, which had been circulating in the 1990s. Pinning Trump as the

[1] At the end of 2021, NATO members are 30, while EU numbers 27. Twenty-one States belong to both organizations.

culprit of current NATO problems would be a short-sighted view: saying that NATO 'began to die when the Cold War ended [...] Trump drove the last nail into its coffin' (Traub 2018) is a half-truth.

French President Emmanuel Macron's statement of November 2019 was even more derogatory: 'what we are currently experiencing is the brain death of NATO' (Macron 2019). Traditionally, French Presidents, either from the right or from the left, pose as critics of American hegemony and champion an autonomous EU Defence Policy. Macron is no exception and his criticism and lack of confidence in NATO is the preamble to advocate just that. However, he admits that 'Europe hasn't demonstrated its credibility yet', opens the door to the collaboration with the United Kingdom in the field of defence even after Brexit and recognizes that EU Permanent Structured Cooperation (PESCO) is 'designed to be complementary to NATO'. Complementarity between PESCO and NATO is the last formula to describe the balance between Europeans and Americans within the Euro-Atlantic region, an issue rather marginal during the Cold War but largely debated since the 1990s.

NATO Evolution During the Cold War

In the late 1940s the acute concern about the policies of the Soviet Union was absolutely prominent. The best account written by a protagonist of the negotiations leading to the Atlantic Pact bears the significant title *Time of Fear and Hope* (Reid 1977). Speaking on 29th September 1948 at the General Assembly of the United Nations Organization (UNO), Belgian socialist Prime Minister Paul-Henry Spaak, a future NATO Secretary General from 1957 to 1961, addressed these words to the Soviet delegation: 'do you know which the basis of our policy is? It's fear, fear of you, of your government, of your policy' (Delmas 1965). Thirty years later, the Italian Manlio Brosio, a former NATO Secretary General from 1964 to 1971, remarked that 'for a long time the feeling of danger and the necessity of common defence were enough to keep the Alliance working' (Brosio 1979).

However, NATO survived the disappearance of the enemy, the Soviet Union (USSR), intensifying a process of constant adaptation which had been present also during the Cold War, starting immediately in 1950 and continuing later, albeit on a reduced scale. Actually, the Atlantic Pact was signed on 4th April 1949, but NATO (the North Atlantic Treaty Organization) developed later between 1950 and 1952 as a consequence of the Korean War. In April 1949, even public opinion was aware that the new alliance 'ensures Western Europe's liberation from an invader but does not guarantee it against invasion', as the authoritative weekly *The Economist* wrote (*The Economist* 1949).[2] In his memoirs Secretary of State Dean Acheson (Acheson 1970) recalls that as a tribute to President Truman's wife, Bess, at the ceremony of signature the band of the Marine Corps entertained the guests playing pieces of music from George Gershwin's *Porgy and Bess*. Two of them, *I have got plenty of nothing* and *It ain't necessarily so*, looked to him ironically allusive to the reality of the treaty being signed, an empty shell largely to be filled.

Initially, the Atlantic Alliance was more a political pact of guarantee than an integrated military alliance; its main purpose was deterrence and its mere existence had to prevent a Soviet aggression. If Moscow attacked, the Alliance's initial military plans admitted the impossibility of preventing the Red Army to conquer Western Europe, the liberation of which would follow after at least one year with operations on the model of *Overlord*, the cross-channel invasion of Normandy during the Second World War (de Leonardis 1991; Pedlow 1997). This situation was consciously accepted on the assumption that the USSR had the capability to attack but not the intention. Therefore, no major rearmament effort followed the Atlantic Pact's signature, in order not to endanger economic recovery. The guiding principle of the *Mutual Defence Assistance Program* (MDAP), presented to the American Congress on 25th July 1949 was that 'the military strength of the participating Powers should be developed without endangering economic recovery and the attainment of economic viability, which should accordingly have priority'.[3] Welfare had priority over warfare.

In June 1950, communist North Korea's invasion of South Korea was considered a rehearsal of what might take place also in Europe; pure deterrence was no longer considered sufficient and an effective defence had to be organized. On 26th September 1950 the North

[2] On its part, *The Times* on 11 March 1949 wrote that 'Europe must be defended, not liberated'. Secretary of State Acheson in February 1949 answered in the negative to Norway's Foreign Minister Halvard Lange who had asked if the territorial integrity of signatories would be guaranteed (Acheson 1970).

[3] *Requests from the Brussels Treaty Powers to the United States Government for Military Assistance*, 5 April 1949, in *Foreign Relations of the United States* [FRUS], 1949, *Western Europe*, Volume IV, United States Government Printing Office, doc. 145. See also: The National Archives (TNA), FO 800/460, EUR/49/10, and Kaplan (1980).

Atlantic Council approved the establishment of an integrated military force under centralized commands, which replaced the existing looser committee system with five Regional Planning Groups, coordinated by the Standing Group. Two major commands were created: Allied Command Europe (ACE), for the European theatre of operations, and Allied Command Atlantic (ACLANT) for that ocean. At lower level, subordinate regional Commands were created. Also the Alliance's civilian structure was reformed, creating the office of the Secretary General and establishing a North Atlantic Council in permanent session. An unwritten rule provided that the Secretary General had always to be a European, of course approved by the United States, while the two major commanders had to be American, an Army or Air Force general as Supreme Allied Commander Europe and an Admiral as Supreme Allied Commander Atlantic.[4] So the Alliance was shaped in the mould which lasted until the first post-Cold War years. Incidentally, it should be noted that out of the 13 secretary generals since 1952 only two, an Italian and a Spaniard came from countries of the Southern Front, a clear indication of where NATO strategic focus was placed. Of course, no French secretary was possible while Paris was outside the integrated military structure.

In February 1952, Greece and Turkey joined NATO and the North Atlantic Council endorsed a programme of strong rearmament. After 1950 the solution of the issue of German rearmament became urgent. Following the failure of the project of European Defence Community, sabotaged by France, an Atlantic solution replaced a European one and in 1955 the German Federal Republic was admitted into NATO. The USSR reacted forming the Warsaw Pact, which simply included in a multilateral framework the already existing Moscow's network of military alliances with the satellite states.

The Atlantic Alliance and NATO are interchangeable names referring to the same organization. However, it must be kept in mind that there is an historical, and to some extent conceptual and practical, difference between the two. As just remarked, the Atlantic Alliance was formed in 1949, while NATO was created in the years 1950–1952. The first was mainly a political pact, the second was a full-fledged military alliance.

[4] In 2003 ACLANT ceased to be an operational command and became the Allied Command Transformation (ACT). The first three commanders were Americans; since 2009 it is the prerogative of Air Force Generals from France, which in that year had re-joined the NATO integrated structure, left in 1967.

Some countries, while joining or remaining in the political alliance, did not join at the beginning or left for some years the integrated military structure. France left it in 1967 and re-joined in 2009. It was the result of General de Gaulle's policy, the core of which was the restoration of France's full sovereignty and Great Power status. Greece left in 1974, when democracy was restored, to protest the United States' acquiescence towards the Turkish invasion of Cyprus, and re-joined in 1980. After becoming democratic, Spain entered the Atlantic Alliance in 1982 (the last enlargement during the Cold War), but joined the integrated military structure only in 1999. The Atlantic Alliance dictates the policies and grand strategies to be implemented at military level by the NATO structure. In 2003, a stalemate in the North Atlantic Council was by-passed applying to a military committee.[5]

During the Cold War, NATO's military role was paramount. In this respect, the evolution of NATO was marked by three *Strategic Concepts*, approved in 1952, 1957 and 1967, which reflected different views on the roles of conventional forces and nuclear weapons for the defence in case of Soviet aggression. The first one[6] required a strong increase of conventional forces, which was never attained. A conservative government in the United Kingdom and a Republican administration in the United States considered excessive the military budgets approved by their more progressive predecessors, Labour and Democratic parties, and induced NATO to 'go nuclear', relying much more on nuclear weapons, which seemed to offer 'more bang for the buck', than on conventional forces. Therefore, the conventional rearmament decided in 1952 was shelved and in May 1957 the North Atlantic Council adopted 'massive and immediate [nuclear] retaliation' as official NATO strategy.[7] It meant that even in case of a conventional attack NATO's response would be a massive retaliation not just against the advancing enemy forces but also striking at the Soviet territory.

In that moment, the new strategy presented only advantages for the United States: it allowed a reduction of the defence budget, while

[5] See below p. 19.

[6] Strategic Concept for the Defense of the North Atlantic Area, approved by the North Atlantic Council on 3 December 1952 (Pedlow 1997; de Leonardis 2017).

[7] Overall Strategic Concept for the Defense of the North Atlantic Treaty Organization Area, approved by the North Atlantic Council on 23 May 1957 (Pedlow 1997; de Leonardis 2017).

the American territory seemed safe from a Soviet second strike, since Moscow did not possess intercontinental vectors. The European perspective looked more controversial: the credibility of the American nuclear shield was enhanced and defence budgets could be reduced, but the Old Continent's territory was definitely exposed to the Soviet second strike. The nuclear strategy stressed even more the American hegemony within NATO, since the United States were the only power to possess an adequate atomic stockpile and were not prepared to give the Europeans access to their plans in this field: 'after 1954, both the key weapons and basic strategic decisions for Europe's [...] defense were obviously in the hands of the Americans alone and beyond the purview of the Alliance' (Harrison 1981). Did Washington really think possible to fight a thermonuclear war? According to one interpretation, President Eisenhower, who had been the first Supreme Allied Commander Europe (SACEUR), 'contrived to use the terror of nuclear war as insurance against both general wars and involvement in the regional skirmishes that might lead to them' (Craig 1998). Following a similar reasoning, in 1957 British Prime Minister Harold Macmillan told SACEUR General Lauris Norstad: 'let be under no illusion; military forces today are not designed to wage war; their purpose is to prevent it. [...] today total war can only mean total destruction' (Liddell Hart 1960).

However, a few months later in the same year 1957 two events persuaded Americans to revise the nuclear strategy just approved and to stress also conventional rearmament: in August the Soviet Union tested in the Pacific its first intercontinental missile and on 4th October Moscow put into orbit its first artificial satellite, the *Sputnik.* A situation of 'mutual deterrence' was evolving, in which both sides would be deterred from initiating or risking general nuclear war because of the prospect of mutual nuclear devastation. As a Panel of Consultants of the Department of State had already forecasted in January 1953: 'indeed both the public and the responsible military authorities appear to be persuaded that the important characteristic of the atomic bomb is that it can be used against the Soviet Union; much less attention has been given to the equally important fact that atomic bombs can be used by the Soviet Union against the United States. This situation results partly from [...] an apparent reluctance to face the simple but unpleasant fact that the atomic bomb works both ways'.[8] The United States' territory was going to be no longer invulnerable to Soviet nuclear attack, the 'massive and immediate retaliation' had become risky also for the Americans and not only for the Europeans.

The replacement of the strategy endorsed in 1957 with one of 'flexible response', aimed to raise the nuclear threshold and keep a conflict as much as possible on a conventional level, was not an easy task, and precipitated the crisis with France. Raising the nuclear threshold had as corollary the principle 'one finger on the trigger': only the American President could authorize the use of nuclear weapons. American secretary of defence Robert McNamara stated that national nuclear forces would not strengthen deterrence but only complicate any potential NATO use of nuclear weapons in a war and described as 'dangerous', 'expensive, prone to obsolescence, and lacking credibility' the 'small nuclear capabilities operating *independently* [my emphasis]' (de Leonardis 2017; Stromseth 1988).[9] This last qualification appeased the British, but in France reactions were furious. Paris wanted to have its own nuclear force and was incensed when Washington tried to obstacle it while accepting and actually assuring the survival of the British deterrent.

Described as 'a political compromise, not a military strategy' (Legge 1983), being, for example, open to different interpretations on the employment of tactical nuclear weapons,[10] the new *Strategic Concept* was approved in December 1967 (Pedlow 1997) and remained in effect much longer than the previous ones, being replaced only in 1991. In December 1979 a special meeting of foreign and defence minister of NATO countries took the so called 'NATO Double-Track Decision' in the 'Euromissiles Crisis', the last major confrontation between the two blocs. The Soviet Union had modernized and increased its middle-range (or theatre) nuclear forces creating a situation of imbalance. NATO on one side envisaged the deployment of 574 American middle-range missiles, on the other opened the door to negotiations.

[8] *Report by the Panel of Consultants of the Department of State to the Secretary of State*, January 1953, FRUS, 1952–1954, *National Security Affairs, United States Government Printing Office*, Washington, 1984, Volume II, Part 2, doc. 67.

[9] Even a staunch supporter of the Anglo-American special relationship, the British Prime Minister Harold Macmillan, who in December 1962 obtained to buy the American *Polaris*, in his diary qualified as 'stupid' McNamara's speech (Macmillan 1973).

[10] 'As one German officer expressed it: the Americans say 'as late as possible'; the French say 'as early as possible'; and we say 'as early as necessary'' (Stromseth 1988).

The different strategic scenario after the fall of the Berlin wall changed the nature of the *Strategic Concepts*. While during the Cold War these were classified documents of a military character, the three new ones approved in 1991, 1999 and 2010 were immediately published, being no longer military plans but mainly political analyses of the international situation, an evaluation of the challenges and of NATO's role in facing them. However, the *Concepts* are complemented by military plans which remain secret. This is a sign that NATO's political role has been enhanced. Since the international situation is now much more changeable, these *Concepts* age quickly and may be supplemented by other kinds of documents as the *Comprehensive Political Guidance* of November 2006. The report *NATO 2030*, released in December 2020, recommends the approval of a new *Strategic Concept*.

The 'political' history of NATO during the Cold War was marked by two main documents. In 1956, *The Report of the Committee of Three on Non-Military Cooperation in NATO*[11] tried to re-define the Alliance's role in the phase of the first détente, after the death of Stalin. In 1967, *The Report of the Council on the Future Tasks of the Alliance*, commonly known as the *Harmel report*,[12] performed a similar task in the climate of the great détente. Both documents foreshadowed topics as NATO's role in out-of-area situations which will become key issues after 1989. But, for the time being, the Alliance was not prepared to act on these.

A Flexible Treaty

The Alliance's adaptation after the Cold War was facilitated also by the flexibility of the original treaty, a short text made of a preamble and only 14 articles, unchanged up to nowadays with just some minor amendments due to the admission of Greece and Turkey and the independence of Algeria. A 'liberal' philosophy inspires the treaty: the member states may agree any measures which are not explicitly forbidden by the text. Decisions are taken by consensus, which means that one member may not like a decision, but without a formal opposition that measure is carried out. For example, Greece had many reservations on *Allied Force*

[11] The 'three wise men', so described, were the Norwegian Halvard Lange, the Italian Gaetano Martino and the Canadian Lester B. Pearson, all minister of foreign affairs in their countries.

[12] The Report was prepared by Pierre Harmel, Minister of Foreign Affairs of Belgium.

operation against Serbia in 1999, but did not oppose it formally. More recently, Germany abstained on the UN resolution approving a military intervention in Libya and did not participate to NATO *Operation Unified Protector*.

Of course, it would be naïve to believe that all members carry the same weight. NATO is an unequal or hegemonic alliance and the United States has always managed, more or less easily and quickly, to shepherd it according to its views and interests.[13] Differently from the EU, NATO does not infringe the states' sovereignty nor has a procedure to sanction the members who do not comply with the decisions taken. The great majority of NATO members do not satisfy the pledge entered in 2006 and periodically reiterated to spend for defence at least 2% of their GDP: they just risked President Trump's bashing.

A perusal of the North Atlantic Treaty offers interesting insights and provides a guidance to NATO evolution. Some articles remained dormant during the Cold War, acquiring prominence later. Others became less important, at least one was never implemented. The preamble indicates the determination of the contracting parties 'to safeguard the freedom, common heritage and civilisation of their peoples, founded on the principles of democracy, individual liberty and the rule of law'; this intent is reiterated in art. 2, which talks of 'strengthening their free institutions'. A clear reference to the ideological aspect of the Cold War and to the common values cherished by all the members. Actually, the strategic imperatives of the Cold War compelled also the Atlantic Alliance to compromise. While Francoist Spain's admission to the Pact, desirable from the military point of view, was 'unpalatable politically',[14] no reservations were made on the Portuguese regime of Antonio de Oliveira Salazar, also authoritarian, because the control of the Azores archipelago was indispensable for the Atlantic theatre of operations. According to Salazar, the Treaty's main foundation was (or had to be) anti-communism. Greece and Turkey suffered no serious consequences from NATO when democracy was suspended in Athens and Ankara. However, the common civilizational background was an important bond, as demonstrated by the dissolution of defence organizations similar to NATO, but lacking this

[13] See in particular Chapter 3 of this volume.

[14] *Memorandum of the Sixth Meeting of the Working Group Participating in the Washington Exploratory Talks on Security*. 26 July 1948, 1948, *Western Europe, Volume III*, United States Government Printing Office, Washington, 1974, doc. 130.

kind of tie, like the Southeast Asia Treaty Organization (SEATO) and the Central Treaty Organization (CENTO). On the contrary, the Australia, New Zealand, United States Security Treaty (ANZUS) still survives and thrives also because the members States share a common civilization.

During the Cold War, NATO was neither indifferent to ideology as traditional alliances, nor followed strict ideological guidelines, instead adopted an 'ethical realism' able 'to distinguish clearly between different grades of evil and to choose firmly between them' (Hulsman and Lieven 2005; de Leonardis 2008). After the Cold War, the situation changed; full membership of NATO is open only to democracies. However, through the *Partnership for Peace*,[15] the *Mediterranean Dialogue*[16] and the *Istanbul Cooperation Initiative*,[17] NATO forged links also with authoritarian regimes, the collaboration of which is deemed useful to face the new challenges. Therefore, to some extent remains the old problem of conciliating, with constructive pragmatism and without ideological stiffness, security imperatives and loyalty to democratic principles.

On the importance of culture and ideology scholars have different views. One opinion is that 'allies remained tied together not because they shared the same values, but because they had the same concerns about security' (Colombo 1994). Others maintain that NATO was successful above all because its members belonged to the same civilization (Huntington 1996). An intermediate position is that cultural and ideological factors may contribute to the alliances' stability (Cornish 1997). Certainly, during the Cold War, security was absolutely paramount, but afterwards the common values were important to foster the Atlantic Alliance's survival and evolution.

The preamble and art. 2 mention also the purpose of the members of 'promoting conditions of stability and well-being' in the North Atlantic Area and of seeking 'to eliminate conflict in their international economic policies and [...] encourage economic collaboration between any or all of them'. These sentences express the aspiration of forming not just a

[15] Established in 1994, at the beginning of 2021, includes 20 countries, mostly former republics of the USSR and Yugoslavia, but also six States of Western Europe.

[16] Initiated in 1994 it currently involves seven non-NATO countries of the Mediterranean region: Algeria, Egypt, Israel, Jordan, Mauritania, Morocco and Tunisia.

[17] Launched in 2004, groups four countries of the Arabic peninsula. Bahrain, Qatar, Kuwait and the United Arab Emirates have joined, while so far Saudi Arabia and Oman don't.

military Alliance and creating an Atlantic community. As explained in Chapter 2, this has remained largely an unfulfilled hope; after the creation of the EEC, European countries entrusted to it the coordination of their economies. Since John F. Kennedy's presidency, Washington increasingly resented the economic competition of the EEC and this feeling was aggravated in recent years towards the EU. At least, the common membership of the Alliance prevented that disputes would escalate, as in the case of Greece and Turkey. One of the conditions for joining NATO listed in the *Study on NATO Enlargement* of 1995 was to having previously settled possible disputes on borders, national minorities and economic issues. So perspective members as Hungary, Lithuania, Poland and Romania entered various agreements with their neighbours. Unfortunately, so far NATO was unable to solve the issue of Cyprus' forced partition, which involves two member states, Greece and Turkey.

The Atlantic Pact's core articles are n. 4, 5 (the *casus foederis*) and 6. In art. 5 the 'parties agree that an armed attack against one or more of them in Europe or North America shall be considered an attack against them all' to which they will react assisting 'the Party or Parties so attacked by taking forthwith, individually and in concert with the other Parties, such action as it deems necessary, including the use of armed force'. The final text was a compromise, reached after a tight negotiation, between the Europeans, longing for an automatic military engagement, and the United States, willing to safeguard the constitutional prerogatives of the Congress, the only body empowered to declare war. In effect, art. 5 does not envisage an obligation to use military force. Art. 5 recalls the 'right of individual or collective self-defence recognised by Article 51 of the Charter of the United Nations'.

Art. 5 was activated only once, not during the Cold War but in November 2001, after the terrorist attacks of 11th September, even if Washington rather cold shouldered NATO in the first phase of its intervention in Afghanistan. The 'coalition of the willing' model prevailed over the Atlantic organization, the strategy of coalitions over that of permanent alliances, consistently with the oldest American tradition. Already Henry Kissinger, commenting in 1956 the events of the Korean war, had written: 'the alliances add little to our effective strength or they do not reflect a common purpose, or both […] the attempt to obtain the prior approval by all our allies of our every step will lead not to common action but to inaction […] we must reserve the right to act alone, or with a regional grouping of Powers, if our strategic interest so dictates' (Kissinger 1956).

Rather paradoxically, the other members came to the rescue of the United States, not vice versa, which was the fundamental reason which motivated the creation of the Atlantic Pact. Actually, during the Cold War art. 3, which mentions 'mutual aid', was operating one way.

After the Cold War, the evolution in the scope of the core articles appears particularly relevant. In the early 1990s, art. 5 seemed to have lost some of its importance. The new NATO *Strategic Concept* approved in November 1991 read: 'The threat of a simultaneous, full-scale attack on all of NATO's European fronts has effectively been removed and thus no longer provides the focus for Allied strategy'.[18] Art. 4[19] became prominent, since new challenges and threats appeared, which required not just consultation but action out-of-area, beyond the geographic limits fixed by art. 6.[20]

The territory of the member States looked safe from a traditional attack, but the dissolution of Communist Yugoslavia and the consequent bloody wars between its former republics and within some of them required NATO intervention, after that both UNO and EU had failed to broker a truce. During the Cold War, NATO could just stay 'vigilant and prepared'; 'NATO did a great job, but it never actually did anything except exist' (Fried 2006). A joke said that the real meaning of the acronym SHAPE (Supreme Headquarters Allied Powers Europe) was *Superb Holidays at Public Expenses*. Now NATO had to act to remain relevant. In the context of *Operation Deny Flight*, with a UN mandate, on 28th February 1994 there was the first combat mission in NATO history. Over the skies of Banja Luka in Bosnia-Herzegovina, US F-16 fighters successfully engaged and destroyed several Bosnian Serb warplanes. It was also the first NATO out-of-area intervention and it greatly enhanced NATO credibility. In June 1993, US Senator Richard Lugar (rep.) had said 'NATO will go out of area or out of business' (Asmus et al. 1993)

[18] The Alliance's New Strategic Concept. Part 1, n. 7. https://www.nato.int/cps/en/natohq/official_texts_23847.htm. The following document The Alliance's Strategic Concept, approved in April 1999, rather toned down and qualified this statement: 'notwithstanding positive developments in the strategic environment and the fact that large-scale conventional aggression against the Alliance is highly unlikely, the possibility of such a threat emerging over the longer term exists', n. 20, https://www.nato.int/cps/en/natolive/official_texts_27433.htm.

[19] 'The Parties will consult together whenever, in the opinion of any of them, the territorial integrity, political independence or security of any of the Parties is threatened'.

[20] Art. 6 limits the validity of art. 5 to a geographic area precisely circumscribed.

and NATO Secretary General Manfred Wörner could now boast: 'We are acting out of area and we are very much in business' (Wörner 1994). Conflict prevention and crisis management through various degrees of peace operations (peace-keeping, peace-making, peace enforcement) were now indicated as the new tasks of NATO. While Russia was weak, NATO would also open soon the door of full membership to new States, former members of the Warsaw Pact. Engagement and enlargement were the catchwords of the Clinton administration.

The admission of new members, provided for by art. 10 of the Atlantic Pact, after the Cold War, had a different character from the drafting of the list of founding members in 1948–1949. At that time, military considerations were absolutely prevalent. States admitted had either to be at risk of an attack or the target of specific threats by USSR, like Norway, or able to contribute to common security. No state in danger had to be excluded, but at the same time the membership could not be too wide, making the system unmanageable. The admissions of the post-Cold War, bringing NATO from 16 members in 1989 to 30 in 2020, were increasingly dictated by political reasons and seen as a factor of stabilization and democratization. When NATO tried to move its borders too close to Russia, as in the case of the ventilated admission of Georgia and Ukraine, Moscow, now more assertive, reacted and blocked the process. As explained in Chapter 7, NATO enlargement projected stability, but, pushed too far, became a factor of crisis.

NATO Operations After the Cold War

Since 'the abuse of human rights' was one of the factors which could 'lead to crises affecting Euro-Atlantic stability',[21] the intervention in Kosovo in March-June 1999 marked a step forward a new role for NATO: humanitarian intervention. At least, this was the official motivation given for *Operation Allied Force*. It also signalled NATO's readiness to operate independently: as Secretary General Javier Solana explained, NATO always acted in coherence with UN 'philosophy' but a UN mandate was not legally necessary. After the end of hostilities, UN authorized the Kosovo Force of NATO (KFOR). NATO was confident that the Serbian leader Slobodan Milošević would cave in after a week of aerial

[21] The Alliance's Strategic Concept, approved in April 1999, n. 20.

bombardments; he resisted more than two months.[22] Leaving aside the debate on the ambiguities of 'humanitarian wars' (de Leonardis 2015), two consequences for NATO of the military intervention against Serbia must be mentioned. One was making a dead letter the *Founding Act on Mutual Relations, Cooperation and Security between NATO and the Russian Federation*, signed in May 1997, the preamble of which defined 'the goals and mechanism of consultation, cooperation, joint decision-making and joint action that will constitute the core of the mutual relations between NATO and Russia'. Actually, Russian Prime Minister Evgenji Primakov knew that NATO bombardments on Serbia had started while he was flying to Washington, and, of course, inverted his route.

The second, and more lasting consequence, was to undermine the cohesion of NATO. The Europeans felt compelled to take part in a military operation skilfully planned by the Americans as a test of their loyalty. On the contrary, the Americans resented too many Europeans interferences in the conduct of operations. From the military point of view, air operations revealed the technological gap between the Americans and the Europeans, at exclusion of the British (Kaplan 2004; Bozo 2003; Reichard 2006) Therefore, the intervention in Kosovo was the basis of two subsequent developments: the faster progress of EU towards a military capability and Washington's decision to side-line NATO in invading Afghanistan. If the Americans could accept the Europeans' interferences in the Kosovo conflict, which did not impact on their vital interests, that was inadmissible (and useless from the military point of view) in larger military operations directly affecting US security. Moreover, the only ally who mattered, the British equerry, would participate in any case.

In 2011, the second NATO's 'humanitarian intervention' in Libya had disastrous and lasting consequences. After the collapse of Gaddafi's regime, NATO countries did not bother to deploy a peace-keeping mission and the country remained divided and unstable, a battlefield for internal factions supported by foreign powers. The 'Arabian springs', fostered by the Obama administration, brought turmoil and conflict in the MENA region.

[22] Lawrence Eagleburger, the last Secretary of State of George H. W. Bush, who had been Ambassador to Yugoslavia, watching on television the first bombardment, commented; 'I know my Serbs, it will be a tough affair' (personal recollection at the Salzburg Seminar on The Transatlantic Agenda at the Turn of the Century held on 24 March 1999).

NATO, set aside in the first phase of operations, in August 2003 took the command of the *International Security Assistance Force* (ISAF), with a UN mandate, which operated in Afghanistan alongside the purely American Operation *Enduring Freedom* (active also in the Philippines and in the Horn of Africa, as minor fronts). By far, ISAF was the major combat operation in the history of NATO, employing about 58,300 militaries from 55 countries. Two recurrent leit-motiv characterized NATO engagement in Afghanistan (which is examined in Chapter 10): American requests to the Europeans to send more troops and NATO demands to lift the caveats which limited the combat role of national contingents.[23] In February 2009, NATO Secretary General Jaap de Hoop Scheffer said: 'We cannot afford the price of failure'.[24] In fact, after Korea, Vietnam and Iraq another war engaged by the United States ended without a victory: Korea was a draw, Vietnam a total defeat, in Iraq there is a precarious stalemate.

British Defence Secretary Ben Wallace admitted in October 2021 that 'Nato's political campaign in Afghanistan was a failure', but 'insisted the western alliance had not suffered a military defeat at the hands of the Taliban'.[25] Similar comments were made after the defeat in Vietnam; they may be correct from a strictly military point of view, but they cannot hide the fact that in many cases Western countries lacked the political resolve to eradicate guerrillas. You can win 'battles', but you do not obtain your political goal. At least, Wallace also said, 'we bought counter-terrorism success for 20 years'.

The war against Islamic terrorism led to a honeymoon between Washington and Moscow, which found its institutional framework in the *NATO-Russia Council*, created at the summit of Pratica di Mare (near Rome) on 28th May 2002. Discussions developed on the globalization of NATO, which had to defend its members against global threats such as terrorism, proliferation of weapons of mass destruction and was 'becoming in practice – although not yet in theory – […] an alliance which does not have geographic limits on its operations. […] potentially worldwide in its missions' (Fried 2006). Admission of new members

[23] A joke said that the meaning of the acronym ISAF was 'I Saw Americans Fighting'.

[24] http://news.bbc.co.uk/2/hi/south_asia/7900367.stm, 19 February 2009.

[25] NATO Was a Political Failure in Afghanistan, Says Defence Secretary, *The Guardian*, 26 October 2021, https://www.theguardian.com/politics/2021/oct/26/nato-was-a-political-failure-in-afghanistan-says-defence-secretary.

outside the North Atlantic area was not contemplated, at least for the moment, but in 2006 a new informal group was added to the list of NATO partnerships, the *Contact Countries*[26]: Australia, New Zealand, Japan and South Korea, democratic countries sharing similar strategic concerns and key Alliance values. To some extent it was reminiscent of the origins of the Alliance: Australia and New Zealand, together with the other Old Dominions (Canada and South Africa), had been mentioned in 1948–1949 by the British Secretary Ernest Bevin as potential members of the worldwide coalition against the Soviet Union.

However, in July 2011 President Obama introduced plans to terminate the combat engagement in Afghanistan and in December 2014 ISAF was terminated and replaced, on a much reduced scale, by *Resolute Support Mission*, providing training, assistance and advise to Afghan Security Forces. The *Contact Countries* were re-named *Partners across the globe*, including Afghanistan, Australia, Colombia, Iraq, Japan, the Republic of Korea, Mongolia, New Zealand and Pakistan.[27] This list is at least bizarre, since it includes the former democratic, Western-oriented and trustworthy *Contact Countries* together with others which certainly would be better described as NATO's problems not assets. In general, Obama, with his multiculturalist approach, was not interested in making NATO the pivot of the West.

A brief but major NATO crisis developed in February 2003. Rather contradictorily, after neglecting NATO in the attack to Afghanistan, Washington sought the Alliance's support for the attack to Iraq, in order to obtain political legitimacy. Invoking art. 4, the United States and the United Kingdom, requested to adopt measures in defence of Turkey (which later presented directly itself the request), which might have been targeted by Saddam Hussein's reprisals; Belgium, France and Germany voiced their opposition. For about ten days, in the North Atlantic Council there was a stalemate, which was broken with a procedural cunning, delegating the decision to the *Defence Planning Committee*, a body of which France was no longer a member since 1967. Berlin and Brussels acquiesced (de Leonardis 2016; Gordon-Shapiro 2007). It was another small example of the institutional difference between the political and the military structures.

[26] https://www.nato.int/summit2009/topics_en/12-contact_countries.html.

[27] https://www.nato.int/cps/en/natohq/topics_49188.htm.

In 2014 the so called Islamic State of Iraq and the Levant (ISIL) also known as the Islamic State of Iraq and Syria (ISIS) or Daesh rose to importance and by December 2015 controlled an area containing eight to twelve million people and performed terrorist attacks worldwide. A Global Coalition to Defeat Daesh/ISIS of 83 countries confronted it; in May 2017, NATO joined the coalition as organisation, without engaging in combat. By September 2020 ISIS had lost all its territories.

In the same year 2014, NATO re-discovered its old enemy: Russia, which annexed Crimea and fostered unrest in Eastern Ukraine. The combination of fatigue for the out-of-area missions and aggressive Russian posture re-focused NATO on the core business of art. 5. President Trump criticized this posture as 'obsolete', and pressed to redirect NATO also against terrorism. An assessment of Trump administration's policy towards NATO must carefully distinguish between public rhetoric and reality. Tweets, leaks, documents and facts tell different stories. As a matter of fact, Washington's long standing commitment to NATO remained unchanged. Actually, the number of American troops stationed permanently or temporarily in Europe raised from 63,000 in 2016 to 74,000 in 2018. The official documents of the administration, the *National Security Strategy* released in December 2017 and the *2018 National Defense Strategy*,[28] strongly endorsed NATO, as usual. They pointed out 'inter-state strategic competition' at global level as the main concern of the United States. In December 2019, in the *Declaration* after the summit in London,[29] China was mentioned for the first time ever in an official NATO document: its 'growing influence and international policies present both opportunities and challenges that we need to address together as an Alliance'. Possibly, as in 1950, Asia will again set in motion a new phase of NATO history.

It is understandable to be rather confused by the winding road of NATO after the Cold War. Seen in retrospect, the last decade of the XX century was a rather 'quiet' period. A new world order seemed within easy reach and NATO looked as an important component of it, assuring peace-making and championing human rights. A new and less happy era

[28] https://www.whitehouse.gov/wp-content/uploads/2017/12/NSS-Final-12-18-2017-0905.pdf and https://www.jcs.mil/Portals/36/Documents/Publications/UNCLASS_2018_National_Military_Strategy_Description.pdf. The latter is a summary; the full text being classified.

[29] https://www.nato.int/cps/en/natohq/official_texts_171584.htm.

was inaugurated in 2001. Fighting Islamic terrorism looked as the main task of NATO, which seemed taking the path towards a global alliance for freedom. The decision to scale down and then terminate the engagement in Afghanistan and Russian annexation of Crimea revived the traditional core mission of the Alliance, i.e. the defence of the member states' territory against an external aggression, according to art. 5. It is a role of pure deterrence at regional level. Most of Eastern NATO countries, always fearful of Moscow, staunchly support this role, obtaining the unenthusiastic support of other countries, which do not consider Russia as a threat, being more concerned by instability and mass migrations from Mediterranean Southern shores. Terrorism is still active, but it is no longer NATO's main priority. In view of the unexciting results in Afghanistan and Libya, major missions out-of-area are unlikely in the future.

The various chapters examine the issues which were just sketched in this introduction, while the conclusion will identify possible lines of development. The entire manuscript was completed before the Russian invasion of Ukraine. Apparently, it is not the historians' task to look into the future. Actually, while historians cannot make predictions (I dare say nobody can), they may offer a thorough understanding of the present and indicate possible evolutionary lines of international politics, drawing from past experiences, elements of continuity, permanent factors and identifying turning points. As Jacob Burckhardt remarked, 'it is the historian's function, not to make us clever for the next time, but to make us wise forever' (Howard 1985).

Bibliography

Acheson, Dean. 1970. *Present at the Creation*. New York: W. W. Norton.

Asmus, Ronald D., Richard L. Kugler, and Stephen F. Larrabee. 1993. Building a New NATO. *Foreign Affairs*, September–October.

Babst, Stefanie. 2008. *Reinventing NATO's Public Diplomacy*. Rome: NATO Defense College.

Bozo, Frédéric. 2003. The Effect of Kosovo and the Danger of Decoupling. In *Defending Europe: The EU, NATO and the Quest for European Autonomy*, ed. Jolyon Howorth and John T.S. Keeler. New York: Palgrave Macmillan.

Brosio, Manlio. 1979. *Introduzione. VV. AA., Trent'anni di Alleanza Atlantica*. Roma: Editrice europea.

Calleo, David P. 1999. What Is the Rightful Role of the United States in Europe? In *NATO at Fifty: Perspectives on the Future of the Atlantic Alliance*, ed. Susan Eisenhower. Washington, DC: Center for Political and Strategic Studies.

Colombo, Alessandro. 1994. *Solitudine dell'Occidente*. Milano: Il Saggiatore.
Cornish, Paul. 1997. *Partnership in Crisis: The US, Europe and the Fall and Rise of NATO*. London: Royal Institute of International Affairs.
Craig, Campbell. 1998. *Destroying the Village: Eisenhower and Thermonuclear War*. New York: Columbia University Press.
de Leonardis, Massimo. 1991. Defence or Liberation of Europe: The Strategies of the West Against a Soviet Attack (1947–1950). In *The Atlantic Pact Forty Years Later: A Historical Reappraisal*, ed. Ennio Di Nolfo. Berlin and New York: De Gruyter.
de Leonardis, Massimo. 2008. Realpolitik and Democratic Values in the Atlantic Alliance During the Cold War. In *Regions, Regional Organizations and Military Power, XXXIII International Congress of Military History*, ed. Thean Potgieter. Stellenbosch: Faculty of Military Science.
de Leonardis, Massimo. 2015. *Mito e realtà delle 'guerre umanitarie'. Da Cuba (1898) alla Libia (2011)*. Rivista Marittima, November.
de Leonardis, Massimo. 2016. *Alla ricerca della rotta transatlantica dopo l'11 settembre 2001. Le relazioni tra Europa e Stati Uniti durante la presidenza di George W. Bush*. Milano: Educatt.
de Leonardis, Massimo. 2017. *Ultima ratio regum. Forza militare e relazioni internazionali*. Milano: Monduzzi Editoriale.
de Leonardis, Massimo. 2018. The Atlantic Alliance Between Continuity and Transformation. In *Case Studies in International Security: From the Cold War to the Crisis of the New International Order*, ed. Luca Ratti and Paolo Wulzer. Bern: Peter Lang.
Delmas, Claude. 1965. *L'O.T.A.N.* Paris: Presses Universitaires de France.
Fried, Daniel. 2006. *NATO/Riga Summit Issues Daniel Fried, Assistant Secretary for European and Eurasian Affairs Roundtable with European Journalists*, October 4. https://2001-2009.state.gov/p/eur/rls/rm/73756.htm.
Gordon, Philip H., and Jeremy Shapiro. 2007. *Allies at War: America, Europe, and the Crisis over Iraq*. Washington, DC: Brookings Institution.
Harrison, Michael M. 1981. *The Reluctant Ally: France and Atlantic Security*. Baltimore: Johns Hopkins University Press.
Howard, Michael 1985. The Use and Abuse of Military History. In *The Causes of War and Other Essays*, 215–216. London: Unwin.
Hulsman, John C., and Anatol Lieven. 2005. The Ethics of Realism. *The National Interest*, June.
Huntington, Samuel P. 1996. *The Clash of Civilizations and the Remaking of World Order*. New York: Simon and Schuster.
Kaplan, Lawrence S. 1980. *A Community of Interests: NATO and the Military Assistance Program 1948–1951*. Washington, DC: Office of the Secretary of Defense.

Kaplan, Lawrence S. 2004. *NATO Divided NATO United: The Evolution of an Alliance*. Westport: Praeger.

Kissinger, Henry A. 1956. Reflections on American Diplomacy. *Foreign Affairs*, October.

Legge, Michael J. 1983. *Theater Nuclear Weapons and the NATO Strategy of Flexible Response*. Santa Monica: Rand Corporation.

Liddell Hart, Basil. 1960. *Deterrent or Defense: A Fresh Look at the West's Military Position*. New York: Praeger.

Macmillan, Harold M. 1973. *At the End of the Day 1961–1963*. London: Macmillan.

Macron, Emmanuel. 2019. Briefing. Macron's View of the World. A President on a Mission. *The Economist*, November.

Pedlow, Gregory W., ed. 1997. *NATO Strategy Documents 1949–1969*. Brussels: Historical Office Supreme Headquarters Allied Powers Europe.

Reid, Escott. 1977. *Time of Fear and Hope. The Making of the North Atlantic Treaty 1947–1949*. Toronto, McClelland and Stewart.

Reichard, Martin. 2006. *The EU-NATO Relationship: A Legal and Political Perspective*. Aldershot: Ashgate Publishing.

Shea, Jamie. 2002. *NATO and Terrorism*. Rusi Journal. N. 147.

Stromseth, Jane E. 1988. *The Origins of Flexible Response: NATO's Debate over Strategy in the 1960s*. London: Palgrave Macmillan.

Sweeney, Mike. 2020. *What Is NATO Good For?* Real Clear Defense. https://www.realcleardefense.com/articles/2020/01/06/what_is_nato_good_for_114961.html.

The Economist. 1949. The Atlantic Pact. 13th March, p. 498.

Traub, James. 2018. RIP the Trans-Atlantic Alliance, 1945–2018. https://foreignpolicy.com/2018/05/11/rip-the-trans-atlantic-alliance-1945-2018/.

Treaty of Lisbon Amending the Treaty on European Union and the Treaty Establishing the European Community (2007).

Wörner, Manfred. 1994. NATO's Role in a Changing Europe. VV. AA., European Security After the Cold War, Part I. Adelphi Paper 284.

CHAPTER 2

The Historical Roots of the Atlantic Alliance Between Values and Interests

Massimo de Leonardis

It is taken for granted that the Atlantic Alliance was a product of the Cold War. However, its historical and cultural foundations are much older and this chapter will outline them. There is little doubt that the birth of the Atlantic Alliance owed a lot to the Anglo-American special relationship[1] and, more in general, was the product of an Anglo-American-Canadian *inner group* with a cultural and political background almost exclusively White Anglo-Saxon Protestant (Reid 1977). Still in recent years, we saw a distinct 'Anglo-American West strictly Atlantic' (Barié 2013).

While the Atlantic Alliance proceeds into its seventh decade, it is appropriate to discuss if the Atlantic Alliance and its military arm, NATO,

[1] On the importance of the Anglo-American special relationship as premise and foundation of the Atlantic Alliance there is a very large literature; for a synthesis and bibliographic suggestions, see Ovendale (1998, 2001).

M. de Leonardis (✉)
Faculty of Political and Social Sciences, Catholic University of the Sacred Heart, Milan, Italy
e-mail: massimo.deleonardis@unicatt.it

M. de Leonardis (ed.), *NATO in the Post-Cold War Era*,
Security, Conflict and Cooperation in the Contemporary World
https://doi.org/10.1007/978-3-031-06063-2_2

are still historically relevant. It is not questionable that NATO is still useful, certainly the most effective among international organizations and alliances. But, is the Atlantic Alliance a key player in current affairs, an expression of a rather solid community of purpose as it was during the Cold War? However, even that period, the golden age of NATO, must not be idealized: it was more a rational union of minds than a romance.

In the long run, a question arises about the role of the United States towards Europe: were they a challenge or a resource? Also isolationism needs a re-examination, showing that since its origins the American nation envisaged its future role of world domination. The deep belief in the superiority of the United States' model is expressed by concepts like 'the shining city on the hill', 'the indispensable nation' or 'the last best hope of humanity', frequent in the American political rhetoric. Most Americans believe that adopting their model the entire world would be free, prosperous, peaceful, and, as obvious corollary, would look to Washington as its leader. The United States' interventions in Europe were motivated by the necessity to oppose great powers hostile to their values and interests and offered the opportunity to establish the American model.

The Short Term Path to the Atlantic Pact

The strategic rationale of the Atlantic Pact was indicated by British Prime Minister Winston Churchill already on 12th May 1945, just four days after the end of hostilities in Europe: '1. I am profoundly concerned about the European situation [...] – he telegraphed to President Truman[2] – 2. [...] What will be the position in a year or two, when the British and American Armies have melted and the French has not yet been formed on any major scale, when we have a handful of divisions mostly French, and when Russia may choose to keep two or three hundred on active service? 3. An iron curtain is drawn upon their front'. The future Atlantic Alliance would remedy the strategic situation which put Europe at the mercy of the Red Army.

Less than one year later, on 5th March 1946, Churchill, now leader of the opposition, in his famous speech in Fulton in which he used for the first time in public the expression 'iron curtain', advocated the 'fraternal association of the English-speaking peoples' and in particular 'a

[2] *Churchill to Truman*, 12 May 1945, in *The National Archives* (TNA), CAB 120/186.

special relationship between the British Commonwealth and Empire and the United States'. 'If the population of the English-speaking Commonwealths be added to that of the United States with all that such co-operation implies in the air, on the sea, all over the globe and in science and in industry, and in moral force, – he continued – there will be no quivering, precarious balance of power to offer its temptation to ambition or adventure. On the contrary, there will be an overwhelming assurance of security'.[3]

One month later, the British Chiefs of Staff, in presence of Labour Prime Minister Clement Attlee and Foreign Secretary Ernest Bevin, discussed the first document[4] which pointed out the Soviet Union as the only likely enemy of the United Kingdom. The support of the United States was taken for granted, but there was no certainty as to the moment of its entering the war. The future Atlantic Alliance would assure that Washington were involved immediately, not afterwards, as in the two world wars. That would dissuade Moscow from attacking, also because at that time the United States had the monopoly of the atomic bomb.

At the end of the Second World War, the United Kingdom fully realized that a new American empire was born. In 1944, Harold Macmillan uttered his famous quip: 'We [...] are Greeks in this American empire. You will find the Americans much as the Greeks found the Romans – great, big, vulgar, bustling people, more vigorous than we are and also more idle, with more unspoiled virtues but also more corrupt. We must run AFHQ [the Supreme Command in the Mediterranean] as the Greek slaves ran the operations of the Emperor Claudius' (Sampson 1967). Obtaining the American involvement required the maturation of the events, in order that Washington could become fully aware of the Soviet threat and willing to face it. The constant task of British diplomacy was to 'lecture' and 'influence' the Americans in order that they would take the responsibilities pertaining to their power.

In this respect, 1946 was a transition year. The British deplored the Americans' refusal to coordinate the policies of their two countries towards the Soviet Union: in March a Foreign Office official described

[3] https://winstonchurchill.org/resources/speeches/1946-1963-elder-statesman/the-sinews-of-peace/.

[4] *Strategic Position of the British Commonwealth*, 2 April 1946, D. O. 46/47, in TNA, CAB 131/2.

American foreign policy as an orgy of escape from reality.[5] On their part, initially the Americans courted the idea of remaining aloof from the clash between the British and Russian imperialisms.

In 1947, the roles were rather reversed; the Americans sometimes suspected the British of neutralist tendencies, while London was sceptical on the efficaciousness and opportunity of general declarations challenging the Soviet Union, like the 'Truman doctrine', particularly if not implemented by concrete facts. Through the 'Marshall Plan' the United States demonstrated their willingness to face Europe's problems with economic tools, but the time was not yet ripe for a military engagement. Still in November, the US Policy Planning Staff,[6] while recognizing the necessity to restore a certain balance of power in Europe and Asia, stressed the role of local forces, which had to assume part of the United States' burden. Optimistically, the American ambassador in London pointed out that the evolution of the Commonwealth promised to strengthen the United Kingdom's political and military role.[7] In December a committee of the American Joint Chiefs of Staff stated that the defence of democracy would primarily rely on the leadership and the strength of the United States and of the British Commonwealth (Etzold and Gaddis 1978).

The path leading to the Atlantic Pact entered its decisive phase in November–December 1947 under the initiative of Bevin, who expressed his ideas to the American Secretary of State George Marshall, the French Minister of Foreign Affairs Georges Bidault and the High Commissioner of Canada in London Norman Robertson. These three countries represented the 'three circles' of British foreign policy: The British Commonwealth and Empire, the English-speaking countries, and Europe. In his last meeting with Marshall, Bevin explained that 'his own idea was that we must devise some western democratic system comprising the Americans, ourselves, France, Italy etc. and of course the Dominions. This would not be a formal alliance, but an understanding backed by power,

[5] TNA, FO 371/51606, AN 656, 12 March 1946. The British role is dealt with in detail in de Leonardis (1988).

[6] Report by the Policy Planning Staff, *Résumé of World Situation*, 6 November 1947, in *Foreign Relations of the United States* [FRUS], 1947, *General; The United Nations*, Volume I, United States Government Printing Office, Washington, 1973, doc. 393.

[7] *Douglas to Acheson*, 11 June 1947, *ibi*, doc. 388.

money and resolute action. It would be a sort of spiritual federation of the west'.[8]

This grandiose but vague idea, after many weeks of diplomatic exchanges and events like the Prague coup d'état, found a more precise application on 10th and 11th March 1948. Following the Soviet pressures on Norway, Bevin proposed to Canada and to the United States a plan based on three security systems: '(i) The United Kingdom–France–Benelux system with United States backing; (ii) A scheme of Atlantic security, with which the United States would be even more closely concerned; (iii) A Mediterranean security system, which would particularly affect Italy'.[9] This was the first mention of 'a scheme of Atlantic security', which 'in view of the threat to Norway'[10] had become 'more important and urgent'.

The reactions of Ottawa and Washington were immediately positive. Secret conversations among Canada, the United Kingdom and the United States took place at the Pentagon from 22nd March to 1st April (de Leonardis 1988). Two of the three circles of British foreign policy were therefore represented, but not Europe. France was not invited to the Pentagon talks because in general she had not so intimate relations with the United Kingdom and the United States as these two had between themselves; more specifically, the French state was deemed infiltrated by members of the Communist Party, with consequent risks for secrecy. In any case, French foreign minister Bidault was informed by Bevin that Anglo-Americans military conversations would take place, but considered that their own affair; another indication that vis-à-vis the United States, London enjoyed a privileged position. On 17th March, a purely European organization with American external backing was formed: The Western Union, or Brussels Pact, which was the first mentioned in Bevin's list.

During the Pentagon Talks the idea of an agreement of collective defence of the North-Atlantic area was approved and a treaty was drafted, very similar to the future Atlantic Pact. After other relevant events (notably the Vandenberg resolution and the Berlin's blockade)

[8] Memorandum of Conversation, 17 December 1947, TNA, FO 800/447, CONF 47/9.

[9] TNA, PREM 8/788.

[10] The Soviet Union was making pressures to reduce Norwegian foreign policy to a condition of subjection similar to that imposed by Moscow to Finland. Soviet pressures were renewed at the beginning of 1949.

the *Exploratory Talks on Security* opened in Washington on 7th July with the participation of Canada, the United States and the five members of the Brussels Pact (Belgium, France, Luxembourg, the Netherlands and the United Kingdom) (Barié 1991; de Leonardis 1988; Varsori 1991). France and the United States were initially at loggerheads. Paris requested immediate measures to guarantee her security and territorial integrity, as weapons and equipment to rebuild her army and the prompt deployment of American troops on French soil. Washington was not prepared to move so far and quickly. The United Kingdom, as a power more 'Atlantic' than 'European', gave a fundamental contribution to mediate between the two positions.

Some months after the signature of the Atlantic Pact on 4th April 1949, the Foreign Office elaborated some studies on the long-term perspectives of United Kingdom's foreign policy.[11] The main conclusion was that there was no alternative to a policy of 'Western consolidation', and, in the foreseeable future, also no realistic prospect for the United Kingdom and the Commonwealth to play the role of an independent 'third world power'; the dollar and the atomic bomb were more attractive than the pound and the Royal Navy. The Foreign Office was also aware that the Atlantic Alliance meant some sharing with other countries of the military relations with the United States, which up to that moment had been an exclusive prerogative of Whitehall. London had to accept the inclusion of France in the Standing Group,[12] to avoid the perception of an Anglo-American hegemony within the Alliance.

The United States: 'Necessary but Undesirable'

After briefly sketching the path to the Atlantic Pact, a wider look must be given to its long-term background. This issue drew the historians' attention when in September 1955, in Rome, the X International Congress of Historical Sciences devoted a session to *Le probléme de l'Atlantique*

[11] *A Third World Power or Western Consolidation?*, 9 May 1949, P. U. S. C. (22) Final, *Anglo-American Relations: Present and Future*, P. U. S. C. (31) Final, 24 August 1949, *Cooperation between the United Kingdom and the United States*, 17 August 1949, TNA, FO 371/76386 and 74,187. The documents were prepared by the Permanent Undersecretary's Committee, created at the beginning of 1949 on the model of the American Policy Planning Staff.

[12] The Standing Group was subordinate to the Military Committee, and responsible for the everyday business of the latter, which met very rarely.

du XVIII au XX siècle, with the participation of prominent historians. The introductory report was prepared by Jacques Godechot and Richard Palmer, who both studied the age of 'Atlantic revolutions', which shook Europe and the Americas between the 1770s and the 1820s. Discussing this report, the distinguished British historian Sir Charles Webster maintained that 'the regionalisation of the world had been a theme for discussion since modern historiography began, but the Atlantic was not suggested as a "region" until the Second World War' and added that 'the Atlantic Community might be a temporary phenomenon. It was created by the policy of the USSR and if this changed it might change also' (VV. AA. 1955, 1957).

Another British historian, the Marxist Eric Hobsbawn, agreed with Sir Charles 'that this idea [of the "Atlantic community"] has been brought into historical analysis as a result of the political situation since 1945, which might be a very temporary situation'. A few years later, this vision was contested by the Italian liberal historian Vittorio De Caprariis, a disciple of the famous philosopher Benedetto Croce. In a long term 'cultural history' of the Atlantic Alliance, he wrote about 'a new civilization' which, in Modern age, 'was born indeed on the Atlantic', and identified 'a coherent development of the European and American history'. NATO was 'not only the result of a specific contingent situation, it was also the finishing line of an historical process at the same time manifold and univocal' (De Caprariis 1958). On Webster's opinion, De Caprariis wrote that 'maybe the professional deformation of the scholar of diplomatic virtuosities of the last century had veiled the clarity of the English historian's judgment'. At the end of the XIX century, British historian John Robert Seeley had already described the formation of an Atlantic civilization as the key factor of modern history (Seeley 1895).

The French revolution is usually considered a much more important event in world history than the American one. Actually, this might be true on the general level, but not for international politics. Certainly, the French revolution and Napoleon had a major impact on Europe's international relations, but in the long term France did not change the traditional system of power politics, while the birth of the independent United States of America marked a major break, which became evident more than one century later, but was immediately perceived at the moment by expert observers. For example, in 1794 the Spanish minister in Paris made this comment on the United States: 'this federal republic was born as a pygmy, but a day will come that it will be a giant, even a colossus' (Kagan 2006).

Many founding fathers, from George Washington to James Madison and Alexander Hamilton, envisaged an 'imperial' destiny for the young republic (Ferguson 2004; Kagan 2006). In 1816, Thomas Jefferson, third President of the United States, wrote to his predecessor John Adams that 'old Europe will have to lean on our shoulders, and to hobble along to our side, under the monkish trammels of priests and Kings, as she can. What a Colossus shall we be when the Southern continent comes up to our mark! what a stand will it secure as a ralliance for the reason and freedom of the globe!'.[13] In 1817, the American minister in London and future President John Quincy Adams (son of the above-mentioned John) wrote that 'the universal feeling of Europe in witnessing the gigantic growth of our population and power is that we shall, if united, become a very dangerous member of the society of nations' (Kagan 2006).

In the early 1820s, British Foreign minister George Canning favoured the independence of Portuguese and Spanish colonies in Latin America. The United Kingdom stood alone as a constitutional State among conservative monarchies, and looked for support in Washington, trying to call 'the New World into existence, to redress the balance of the Old'.[14] It was the first example of similar attempts repeated in the XX century, when the balance in Europe will be threatened first by Nazi Germany and then by Soviet Russia. American President James Monroe considered an Anglo-American initiative to support the colonies' independence, but his Secretary of State John Quincy Adams (later successor of Monroe as President), pointing out that also Britain was a colonial power, convinced him that the United States had to act alone. In December 1823 he delivered to the Congress his annual message, known as the 'Monroe Doctrine', which reaffirmed American unilateralism and rejected the *raison d'état* and the European tradition, indicating the republic as the institutional regime most adapted to the American continent. Commenting that doctrine, Prince Metternich, the dominant personality of the Restoration's diplomacy, rightly observed that the United States had 'distinctly and clearly announced their intention to set not only power against power, but, to express it more exactly, altar against altar' (Perkins 1955).

[13] https://founders.archives.gov/documents/Adams/99-02-02-6618.

[14] Speech on 12 December 1826 at the House of Commons, Hansard, XVI [N. S.], 390–398.

Also John Quincy Adams forecasted a great future for the American republic, which 'might become the dictatress of the world',[15] when it would be strong enough to avoid compromising on her principles. That moment seemed coming in 1919, 1945, and after 1989. For the moment, the Monroe doctrine intimated that the gates of the American continent were closed to European colonization. A turning point was marked by the war against Spain in 1898. Cuba, the last Spanish colony in America, came under the control of Washington, together with the Philippines. The de facto protectorate on the Philippines aroused a debate on the creation of an American 'empire'. In 1900 Senator Albert Beveridge, a prominent imperialist, described the United States 'as the arbiter, under God, of the destinies of mankind', the Americans 'as the master organizers of the world', and the 'American people as His chosen nation to finally lead in the regeneration of the world'.[16] More pragmatically, in 1904, President Theodore Roosevelt's corollary to the 'Monroe doctrine' claimed the United States' right to exercise 'an international police power' in the Western Hemisphere.[17]

Since 1815, the United States had completed the conquest of the Western territories up to the Pacific coast, survived a civil war, and, at the end of the XIX century, appeared as a new key protagonist in the international arena. The United Kingdom had to come to terms with the new situation, hoping to control it, but the ground was prepared for Uncle Sam replacing John Bull as 'imperial power' (Watt 1984). In the 1890s, two controversies opposed Washington and London, as capital of the British Empire. One was the dispute between Canada and Alaska about fishing rights and seal hunting. The second and more serious issue was the delimitation of the frontier between the colony of British Guyana (nowadays simply Guyana) and Venezuela, this latter championed by Washington. On that occasion, on 20th July 1895 Secretary of State Richard Olney wrote strong words to the American ambassador in London: 'the United States is practically sovereign on this continent, and its fiat is law upon the subjects to which it confines its interposition [...] That distance and three thousand miles of intervening ocean make

[15] https://www.classicsofstrategy.com/She%20Goes%20Not%20Abroad.pdf.

[16] https://china.usc.edu/us-senator-albert-j-beveridge-speaks-philippine-question-us-senate-washington-dc-january-9-1900.

[17] https://www.ourdocuments.gov/doc.php?flash=falseanddoc=56andpage=transcript.

any permanent political union between an European and an American state unnatural and inexpedient will hardly be denied'.[18] These resonant tones were alarming Latin America, insulting Canada, and challenging the United Kingdom. The Royal Navy was still five times greater than the US Navy, but London adopted a conciliatory stance and Colonial Secretary Joseph Chamberlain ruled out as absurd and criminal any prospect of war between the two Anglo-Saxon countries. Later, London also renounced its rights, established by the Clayton-Bulwer treaty in 1850, to build the inter-oceanic waterway as a joint Anglo-American enterprise, and the new treaty Hay-Pauncefote in 1900 paved the way to the Panama Canal built by Washington only.

An Anglo-American friendship, based also on racial considerations, was established. Famous British imperialist Cecil Rhodes declared 'we happen to be the best people in the world, with the highest ideals of decency and peace, and the more of the world we inhabit, the better it is for humanity' (Faber 1966). On the other side of the Atlantic, the historian and philosopher John Fiske gave a new and wider interpretation of the 'manifest destiny' doctrine,[19] extolling the virtues of the Anglo-Saxon race and forecasting its world domination (Fiske 1895).

In 1906, at the Algeciras conference on Morocco, President Roosevelt, disappointing the German Emperor Wilhelm II, supported the positions of France and Great Britain, described as 'Atlantic powers' in some American despatches. The participation to a conference on a colonial territory in Africa derived from Roosevelt's belief that the United States had to fulfil its duties of Great Power with global interests and responsibilities. The Senate acquiesced reluctantly. During the conference, eight US battleships were stationed in the Mediterranean and from December 1907 to February 1909 a US fleet circumnavigated the world to demonstrate that the United States had become a major sea power.

Walter Lippman, a journalist who was to become the major commentator on foreign policy issues, in February 1917 wrote an article

[18] *Olney to Bayard*, 20 July 1895, in FRUS, 1895, part 1, United States Government Printing Office, Washington, 1896, doc. n. 527.

[19] In 1845, journalist and diplomat John Louis O' Sullivan on the occasion of Texas's annexation had written 'and that claim is by the right of our manifest destiny to overspread and to possess the whole of the continent which Providence has given us for the development of the great experiment of liberty and federated self-government entrusted to us'.

explaining that 'the safety of the Atlantic highway is something for which America should fight. Why? Because on the two shores of the Atlantic Ocean there has grown up a profound web of interest which joins together the western world. Britain, France, Italy, even Spain, Belgium, Holland, the Scandinavian nations, and Pan America are in the main one community in their deepest needs and their deepest purposes. They have a common interest in the ocean which unites them. They are today more inextricably bound together than most even as yet realize'.[20] In April, the United States entered the war on the side of the Entente and against the Central Empires. In order to signify that it was not bound by the treaties signed among the Entente powers, the United States took care to describe itself as an 'associate power' not an 'allied power'.

Plunging into the First World War, Europe committed a 'suicide', as remarked by Pope Benedict XV.[21] At least, the United States aggravated this suicide. In 1917, Washington was prominent in killing the idea of a compromise peace and in 1918 inaugurated the policy that recently has been labelled as 'regime change', when refused to negotiate an armistice with Germany unless the Imperial government was replaced by a republic. The Germans complied, but the Weimar republic got little reward for going fully democratic and dragon's teeth were sown, while Washington plunged into neo-isolationism, or better an 'America first' position. The Wall Street crash in 1929 had serious consequences around the world, in particular reviving the fortunes of Hitler's Nazi party.

Already in the 1930s the Secretary General of the French ministry of foreign affairs Philippe Berthelot penned that 'the Americans are both undesirable and necessary; and think that we went looking for them! Europe will pay dearly for it' (Lenzi 2020). After the Second World War, Americans were even more necessary; it is questionable if they were also liked. The historical studies on the origins of the Atlantic Pact clearly demonstrate that few people in Europe considered the link with Washington something more than a necessity, unpleasant to many, imposed by the political and military confrontation with the Soviet Union. Italian statesman Alcide De Gasperi considered it a 'marriage of convenience'

[20] http://roadstothegreatwar-ww1.blogspot.com/2017/04/americas-road-to-war-did-president.html. See also Steel (2008).

[21] The Pope described the Great War as 'the suicide of civilized Europe' in three subsequent occasions, including his famous Apostolic exhortation *Dès les début* on 1 August 1917, published in French and Italian in AAS (1917).

(Del Pero 2011) and did not share the thesis of the 'big American boys' that the attack in Korea could be a general rehearsal of a similar aggression in Europe. A stinging and similar remark was made years later by the Italian Prime Minister Amintore Fanfani to NATO Secretary General Dirk Stikker: 'Christopher Columbus discovered America but could not bring to the New Continent the wisdom and the experience of the Europeans [...] the United States put into NATO strength, the Europeans experience'.[22]

Already in the early 1950s, the French government feared that the Alliance with the United States might become a kind of Cominform and later General Charles de Gaulle described American President Lyndon Johnson as 'the greatest threat to world peace today', an opinion shared by one third of the French (Kahler 2005). In the aftermath of the Suez crisis, German Chancellor Konrad Adenauer, albeit a staunch supporter of Atlanticism, expressed his solidarity to the French Prime Minister Guy Mollet with these words: 'in this moment, the European countries must unite. It is not a problem of supra nationality. But we must unite against America [...]. The United States is so badly acquainted with the situation in Europe and with European politics that we have to cry' (DDF 1989).

Even the British often expressed, in private, their irritation towards their cousins beyond the Atlantic. For example, Harold Macmillan, in his diary, once labelled as 'stupid' a speech of the American Secretary of Defense Robert McNamara (Macmillan 1973). More significantly, on a previous occasion in September 1952, he lamented 'the most noticeable, and painful, difference between our position now and when we were last in office (1945) is our relationship to US. Then we were on an equal footing – a respected ally. Now we are treated by the Americans with a mixture of patronising pity or contempt. They treat us worse than they do any other country in Europe'. He also gave a very critical description of their character: 'They are really a strange people. Perhaps the mistake is to continue to regard them as an Anglo-Saxon people. That blood is very much watered down; they are a Latin-Slav mixture, with a fair amount of German and Irish. They are impatient, mercurial, panicky. But, while capable of terribly narrow views and incredible breaches of decency and decorum, they are also capable of broad and generous sentiments and really big-hearted generosity ...' (Macmillan

[22] Archivio Fanfani, Senato della Repubblica, Roma, Sez. 1, Serie 1, Busta 14, Fasc. 17. 9 October 1961.

2003). The Anglo-American special relationship knew ups (the Nassau agreement and the Falkland war) and downs (Suez and the American invasion of Grenada), but London and Washington consistently held a similar approach to NATO policies during and after the Cold War.

In the Suez crisis, the Americans humiliated their two major European Allies, France and the United Kingdom, but soon inherited their problems and their imperial responsibilities. When they engaged in Vietnam it was their turn to lament the allies' poor solidarity. Significantly, on the occasion of the Yom Kippur war in 1973, when Portugal was the only NATO country to open its bases to the American aircrafts supporting Israel, Secretary of State Henry Kissinger 'remarked that he was beginning to draw melancholy conclusions about the cohesiveness of the [Atlantic] alliance. It never cohered on anything except the one thing least likely to arise: a military attack on Western Europe'.[23]

Failed Efforts to Create an 'Atlantic Community': The Debate on Art. 2 in the 1950s

The Preamble and art. 2 of the Atlantic Treaty of 1949 expressed the aspiration to building something more than a mere military alliance. As a matter of fact, art. 2 was never put into practice, not even after the Cold War, when there has been much talk about the political role of NATO in respect to the military one; on the contrary, the Atlantic has become 'larger' (de Leonardis 2001, 2016).

In the 1950s efforts were made to foster an 'Atlantic community' (de Leonardis 2017). The agenda of the North Atlantic Council in London on 15th-18th May 1950 included the 'Development of Article 2' in the 'public information activities' and 'in the economic field'.[24] The most ardent supporters of this development were Canada and Italy. The Old Dominion had advocated that article during the negotiations for the Atlantic Pact, both for tactical internal motivations, to facilitate the support of the francophone community, and strategic international reasons. In particular Ottawa was looking for a multilateral counterweight

[23] *Cromer to the Foreign and Commonwealth Office*. 25 October 1973, *Ceasefires in ME War*, TNA. FCO 93/295. Rowland Baring, III Earl Cromer, was Her Majesty's Ambassador to Washington and a grandson of the famous colonial proconsul.

[24] NATO Archives online (NA), https://archives.nato.int/uploads/r/null/1/9/19265/C_4-N-4_1_ENG.pdf.

to the US hegemony on the American continent and was concerned by the initiatives for economic integration among the European countries. Italy, who had not negotiated the treaty and had the strongest Communist party in Western Europe, was eager to play down the purely military character of the Atlantic Alliance and possibly obtain further economic advantages. For the moment, the outbreak of the Korean war directed the Alliance's attention towards more pressing goals.

The huge investments on rearmament re-opened the discussion on the economic aspects. In September 1951, the North Atlantic Council in Ottawa, with the participation of Foreign, Defence and Economy ministers of the member states, deliberated the formation of a five members'[25] ministerial Committee for studying the development of an 'Atlantic Community'. On 30th October, one of the committee's working groups presented a report of 51 pages.[26] The issues considered were the 'co-ordination; and frequent consultation on foreign policy, having particular regard to steps designed to promote peace', a 'closer economic, financial and social co-operation, designed to promote conditions of economic stability and well-being, both during and after the present period of the defence effort, within the North Atlantic Treaty Organization or through other Agencies', and the 'collaboration in the fields of Culture and Public Information'. However, it was remarked that some members of the working group 'were very dubious' whether some of these topics 'ever would or should become matters of active consideration within NATO', but this did not prevent listing a long series of recommendations.[27] Certainly, it was a 'list of wishes', which found a modest realization, as for example the formation on 18th June 1954 of the *Atlantic Treaty Association* and in 1955 of the North-Atlantic Parliamentary Assembly, moreover two bodies formally independent from NATO.

The first détente seemed to provide the great occasion for activating art. 2, since it was believed that the Alliance should play a political role

[25] With representatives of Belgium, Canada, Italy, the Netherlands and Norway.

[26] Atlantic Community Committee. NA. http://archives.nato.int/uploads/r/null/2/5/2581/AC_10-D_1_ENG.pdf. On 16 November was circulated an updated version: http://archives.nato.int/uploads/r/null/2/5/2593/AC_10-D_2_ENG.pdf.

[27] Attachment n° 1 of the document was a list ('in no way exhaustive') of 26 International Organizations (including the Universal Postal Union!) and 13 other non-governmental bodies at world or regional level are the tasks of which were of interest for NATO.

and not just a military one. In December 1955, the North Atlantic Council in Paris recognized that 'recent developments in the international situation made it more necessary than ever to have closer co-operation between the members of the Alliance as envisaged in Article 2 of the Treaty'.[28] The Committee of the 'three wise men', the Italian Gaetano Martino, the Canadian Lester Pearson and the Norwegian Halvard Lange, all foreign ministers of their countries, was tasked to present a report on 'non-military co-operation in NATO'.

During the Committee's works, two crises, the Soviet invasion of Hungary and the Anglo-French military expedition in Egypt (concocted with Israel), attenuated the hopes of détente, stressed the permanent necessity of keeping a high military readiness and marked a very serious break between the United States and his two major European allies.

The Committee's Report[29] noted that 'inter-Allied relations have also undergone severe strains. [...] An Alliance in which the members ignore each other's interests or engage in political or economic conflict, or harbour suspicions of each other, cannot be effective either for deterrence or defence. Recent experience makes this clearer than ever before'. The Report admitted that creating 'a sense of Atlantic Community' had not been 'the decisive, or even the main impulse in the creation of NATO. Nevertheless, it gave birth to the hope that NATO would grow beyond and above the emergency which brought it into being'. This hope had found expression in the preamble and in articles 2 and 4 of the Treaty, which contained 'at least the promise of the grand design of an Atlantic Community [...] because of this insistent feeling that NATO must become more than a military alliance [...]. There is the even more far-reaching question: "Can a loose association of sovereign states hold together at all without the common binding force of fear?" [...] Strengthening the political and economic side of NATO is an essential complement to—not a substitute for—continuous cooperation in defence'. On the 'out-of-area' issue, the Report remarked that 'NATO should not forget that the influence and interests of its members are not confined to the area covered by the Treaty, and that common interests

[28] C–M (55) 128. NA. http://archives.nato.int/uploads/r/null/2/5/25149/C-M_55_128_ENG.pdf.

[29] Report of the Committee of Three. NA. http://www.nato.int/cps/en/natohq/official_texts_17481.htm?selectedLocale=en.

of the Atlantic Community can be seriously affected by developments outside the Treaty area'.

At the North Atlantic Council in Paris of December 1956,[30] discussing the Report, Pearson admitted that perhaps the states with greater responsibilities 'must get a little tired of hearing those of us who represent states without so much power and responsibility talking so much about consultation'. The British Foreign Secretary John Selwyn Brooke Lloyd recalled London's worldwide responsibilities and declared his agreement to consultation if it was aimed to share the burden and not simply to express criticism and give way to obstructionism. This approach was strongly endorsed by Secretary of State John Foster Dulles who stated that, in the light of United States' global commitments, the coordination of all the aspects of foreign policy was impossible, also because sometimes it was necessary to act before consulting. Therefore, he shared the Report's 'vision' and agreed to approve it in general terms, but its concrete application had to be verified on a case by case basis. In May, Dulles had been quite outspoken with President Eisenhower: 'all of our allies are willing to follow the Italian lead and have NATO turned into an economic organization which can probably extract a little more money out of the United States; but when it comes to doing anything to develop Western European unity or any real cohesion with respect to policies vis-à-vis the Soviet Union, then there is very marked evasiveness'.[31]

The result of the North Atlantic Council was a list of good intentions, but in practice little was achieved. During the entire Cold War, NATO continued to remain what had been since its origins, a military alliance with a precise *casus foederis* and a well-delimited geographical outreach. After all, the 'three wise men' themselves had remarked: 'it has not been difficult to make these recommendations. It will be far more difficult for the member governments to carry them into effect'.

Moreover, the European Economic Community (EEC), created in 1957, satisfied the Europeans' aspirations to a community of interests outside the military domain, which remained NATO's exclusive competence.

[30] The minutes of the various sessions of the Atlantic Council in NA. http://archives.nato.int/verbatim-record-of-meeting-final-25;isad.

[31] *Message From the Secretary of State to the President*, 5 May 1956, in FRUS, vol. IV, *Western European Security and Integration*, United States Government Printing Office, Washington, 1988, doc. n. 27.

In the early 1960s, Washington, which had earlier encouraged European integration, started to resent European countries' economic competition. On 22nd January 1963, President Kennedy made these remarks at a National Security Council meeting: 'One effort we must make, the President continued, is to seek to prevent European states from taking actions which make our balance of payments problem worse. For example, we maintain large forces in Germany. We must firmly oppose West Germany if it increases its agricultural production to our detriment. We have not yet reached the point of wheat against troops but we cannot continue to pay for the military protection of Europe while the NATO states are not paying their fair share and living off the "fat of the land". We have been very generous to Europe and it is now time for us to look out for ourselves, knowing full well that the Europeans will not do anything for us simply because we have in the past helped them'.[32]

At the beginning of the Seventies, President Nixon raised forcefully the same problem, deeming unacceptable that Europeans, protected by the Americans, would prosper through the economic competition with the United States. 'The Europeans cannot have it both ways. – He declared at a press conference on 15th March 1974 – They cannot have the United States participation and cooperation on the security front and proceed to have confrontation and even hostility on the economic and political front' (Nixon 1975). A precedent of what Trump declared in a television interview in July 2018: 'I think the European Union is a foe, what they do to us in trade. Now you wouldn't think of the European Union but they're a foe'.[33]

Actually, NATO rarely discussed how 'to encourage economic collaboration between any [member] or all of them' (North Atlantic Treaty, art. 2). When NATO talked about finances, the issue was another: burden sharing. All American Presidents, with more or less energy, repeated the exhortation to the Europeans to spend more for defence, particularly when they felt that Europe was at the same time a US protégé and a growing economic competitor. However, during the Cold War, the American nuclear arsenal was the ultimate assurance of Western Europe's

[32] *Remarks of President Kennedy to the National Security Council Meeting*, 22 January 1963, in FRUS, 1961–1963, vol. XIII, *Western Europe and Canada*, United States Government Printing Office, Washington,1994, doc. n. 168.

[33] https://www.theguardian.com/us-news/2018/jul/15/donald-trump-vladimir-putin-helsinki-russia-indictments.

security, something which made not imperative the appeal to re-balance the burden sharing between Europeans and Americans.

Another Presidential scathing comment is worth mentioning. In December 1981, during the crisis about the imposition of martial law in Poland, Ronald Reagan labelled as 'chicken littles'[34] the European leaders, who were reluctant to adopt his tough line. Margaret Thatcher 'is the only European leader I know with balls', he remarked in another occasion (Moore 2013).

Conclusion: Increasingly Diverging Perspectives After the Cold War, but Still Very Close

The period of the Cold War was a parenthesis between two epochs during which the approach of the European countries and of the United States to international politics has been quite different, since their culture and historical experience are dissimilar. The Cold War was a period with unprecedented characteristics in the field of international relations, which no longer exist. During the Cold War, inside the West, disputes, even bitter ones, between Europe and the United States did not lack, but were downplayed or shelved since there were a complete agreement on the identification of the common enemy and a large consensus on the means to face it. However, even during the Cold War it was impossible to create a real 'Atlantic community' and of course today it is almost completely unrealistic with an Alliance which includes 30, and not 16 members, some of them having different foreign policy agendas.

There is no sign on the horizon that NATO might become a global alliance for freedom, the Western values and interests as advocated in 2006 by former Spanish Prime Minister José María Aznar, in tuning with a good number of personalities inside the Bush Jr. administration. This was a major strategic idea advanced for the future of the Alliance and called for a stronger collaboration, indeed full membership, with non-Atlantic countries belonging to the Western civilization, like Australia, Israel, Japan, New Zealand and South Korea. It might be considered an updated version of Bevin's 'spiritual federation of the West'. However,

[34] Meeting of the National Security Council. 22 December 1981. Margaret Thatcher Foundation: https://c59574e9047e61130f133f71d0fe2b653c4f00f32175760e96e7.ssl.cf1.rackcdn.com/B7FC5FC810694AF59EC862743B4A2FCC.pdf. See Chiampan (2015).

most Europeans were reluctant to extend the guarantees of art. 5 to other areas, while President Obama was not so keen on the 'West', and the idea was put aside.

As already stated, NATO is still the most effective among international organizations and alliances: 'the question for the foreseeable future may not be whether the alliance will persist, but whether or not it will be of increasing or diminishing value to the participants' (Sloan 2010). We must keep in mind the conceptual and practical distinction between the Atlantic Alliance and NATO.[35] The second is in better shape than the first: from the military point of view NATO posture is impressive. The exercise *Trident Juncture*, the most important since many years, which took place in Norway from 25th October to 7th November 2018 involved about 50,000 troops, 250 aircrafts, 65 warships and about 10,000 vehicles from 31 countries (members and partners). NATO is the military arm of a political alliance based on common values and interests. Since the end of the Cold War, these bonds are weaker. The geopolitical situation drastically changed and since many years Europe is no longer the main focus of Washington's attention. However, this does not authorize thinking that the United States are no longer interested in Europe's security. Considering the values, these were never identical and the differences widened, but, from this point of view Europe and North America remain the geopolitical area in the world with the closest interests and affinities.

In 1958 it was augured that NATO might become 'the political brain of the West' (De Caprariis 1958); in 2019 President Macron announced 'the brain death of NATO' (Macron 2019). A realistic view is somewhere between that utopian omen and this unwarranted judgment. Above all we must not forget that multilateralism is a popular but misleading catchword. The Atlantic Alliance is the best example of effective multilateralism; however, she can do only what the (major) members allow.

[35] On 4 April 1949 the Atlantic Alliance was born as a political alliance based on deterrence towards the Soviet Union. As a consequence of the Korean war, between 1950 and 1952 NATO, the political and military organization, was created, putting in place a real defence.

Bibliography

Acta Apostolicae Sedis, Commentarium Officiale [AAS]. 1917. Roma: Typis Polyglottis Vaticanis.

Andrews, David M., ed. 2005. *The Atlantic Alliance Under Stress: US-European Relations After Iraq*. Cambridge: Cambridge University Press.

Barié, Ottavio. 1991. The Final Stage of Negotiations: December 1948 to April 1949. In *The Atlantic Pact Forty Years Later: A Historical Reappraisal*, ed. Ennio Di Nolfo. Berlin-New York: De Gruyter.

Barié, Ottavio. 2013. *Dalla Guerra Fredda alla grande crisi. Il nuovo mondo delle relazioni internazionali*. Bologna: Il Mulino.

Bozo, Frédéric. 2003. The Effect of Kosovo and the Danger of Decoupling. In *Defending Europe: The EU, NATO and the Quest for European Autonomy*, ed. Jolyon Howorth and John T.S. Keeler. New York: Palgrave Macmillan.

Brosio, Manlio. 1979. *Introduzione. VV. AA. Trent'anni di Alleanza Atlantica*. Roma: Editrice Europea.

Chiampan, Andrea. 2015. 'Those European Chicken Littles': Reagan, NATO, and the Polish Crisis, 1981–2. *The International History Review* 37 (4): 682–699.

De Caprariis, Vittorio. 1958. *Storia di un'alleanza. Genesi e significato del Patto Atlantico*. Roma: Editoriale Opere Nuove.

de Leonardis, Massimo. 1988. I 'tre cerchi': il Regno Unito e la ricerca della sicurezza tra Commonwealth, Europa e 'relazione speciale' con gli Stati Uniti (1948–1949). In *L'alleanza occidentale. Nascita e sviluppi di un sistema di sicurezza collettivo*, ed. Ottavio Barié. Bologna: Il Mulino.

de Leonardis, Massimo. 2001. *Europa-Stati Uniti: un Atlantico più largo?* Milano: Franco Angeli.

de Leonardis, Massimo. 2016. *Alla ricerca della rotta transatlantica. Le relazioni tra Europa e Stati Uniti dopo l'11 settembre 2001 durante la presidenza di George W. Bush*. Milano: Educatt.

de Leonardis, Massimo. 2016/2017. L'atlantismo italiano da Alcide De Gasperi a Gaetano Martino: l'art. 2 del Patto atlantico. In *Quaderni Degasperiani per la storia dell'Italia contemporanea*, vol. VI, ed. Pier Luigi Ballini. Soveria Mannelli: Rubbettino.

Del Pero, Mario. 2011. Gli Stati Uniti e De Gasperi (1945–1953). In *Quaderni Degasperiani per la storia dell'Italia contemporanea*, vol. III, ed. Pier Luigi Ballini. Roma: Fondazione Alcide De Gasperi.

Documents diplomatiques français [DDF]. 1989. *Série après 1954, vol. VIII, tome II, 1er juillet–23 octobre 1956*. Paris: Imprimerie nationale.

Etzold, Thomas H., and John L. Gaddis, eds. 1978. *Containment: Documents on American Policy and Strategy, 1945–1950*. New York: Columbia University Press.

Faber, Richard. 1966. *The Vision and the Need: Late Victorian Imperialist Aims*. London: Faber and Faber.
Ferguson, Niall. 2004. *Colossus: The Price of America's Empire*. London: Allen Lane.
Fiske, John. 1895. *Manifest Destiny: Harpers' New Monthly Magazine*, vol. 70, December 1894 to May 1895.
Kagan, Robert. 2006. *Dangerous Nation: America's Place in the World from Its Earliest Days to the Dawn of the Twentieth Century*. New York: Alfred A. Knopf.
Kahler, Miles. 2005. US Politics and Transatlantic Relations: We Are All Europeans Now. In *The Atlantic Alliance Under Stress: US-European Relations After Iraq*, ed. David M. Andrews. Cambridge and New York: Cambridge University Press.
Lenzi, Guido. 2020. *La diplomazia, passato, presente e futuro*. Soveria Mannelli: Rubbettino Focus.
Macmillan, Harold. 1973. *At the End of the Day 1961–1963*. London: Macmillan.
Macmillan, Harold. 2003. *The Macmillan Diaries: The Cabinet Years, 1950–1957*, vol. 1. London: Macmillan.
Macron, Emmanuel. 2019. Briefing. Macron's View of the World. A President on a Mission. *The Economist*, November.
Moore, Charles. 2013. *Margaret Thatcher: The Authorized Biography, Vol. I, Not for Turning*. London: Penguin.
National Security Strategy. 2017. https://www.whitehouse.gov/wp-content/uploads/2017/12/NSS-Final-12-18-2017-0905.pdf.
National Defense Strategy. 2018. https://dod.defense.gov/Portals/1/Documents/pubs/2018-National-Defense-Strategy-Summary.pdf.
Nixon, Richard. 1975. *Containing the Public Messages, Speeches, and Statements of the President—United States. President (1969–1974)*. Washington: United States Government Printing Office.
Ovendale, Ritchie. 1998. *Anglo-American Relations in the Twentieth Century*. New York: St. Martin's Press.
Ovendale, Ritchie. 2001. La NATO e la 'relazione speciale' fra Gran Bretagna e Stati Uniti. In *La nuova NATO: i membri, le strutture, i compiti*, ed. Massimo de Leonardis. Bologna: Il Mulino.
Perkins, Dexter. 1955. *A History of the Monroe Doctrine*. Boston: Little, Brown and Company.
Reid, Escott. 1977. *Time of Fear and Hope: The Making of the North Atlantic Treaty 1947–1949*. Toronto: McClelland and Stewart.
Sampson, Anthony. 1967. *Macmillan: A Study in Ambiguity*. London: Penguin Books.
Seeley, John R. 1895. *The Expansion of England: Two Courses of Lectures*. London: Macmillan.

Sloan, Stanley. 2010. *Permanent Alliance? NATO and the Transatlantic Bargain from Truman to Obama*. London: Bloomsbury.
Steel, Ronald. 2008. Walter Lippmann and the Invention of the Atlantic Community. In *European Community, Atlantic Community?*, ed. Valérie Aubourg, Gérard Bossuat, and Giles Scott-Smith. Paris: Soleb.
Varsori, Antonio. 1991. The First Stage of Negotiations: December 1947 to June 1948. In *The Atlantic Pact Forty Years Later: A Historical Reappraisal*, ed. Ennio Di Nolfo. Berlin-New York: De Gruyter.
VV. AA. 1955. *Relazioni: riassunti delle comunicazioni. Atti a cura della Giunta Centrale per gli Studi Storici e Comitato internazionale di Scienze Storiche, vol. V, Storia contemporanea*. Firenze: Sansoni
VV. AA. 1957. *Atti del X Congresso Internazionale: Roma 4–11 settembre 1955*. Roma: Giunta centrale per gli studi storici.
Watt, Donald C. 1984. *Succeeding John Bull: America in Britain's Place, 1900–1975*. Cambridge: Cambridge University Press.

CHAPTER 3

A Troublesome Relationship: The US Grand Strategy and NATO

Gianluca Pastori

The US grand strategy—the 'intellectual architecture that gives form and structure to foreign policy' (Brands 2014)—has a great deal of historical persistence. The Second World War and Washington's rise to global pre-eminence favoured its elaboration (Leffler 2010); however, its roots date back to the very origins of the country (Hooker 2014). Avoiding any entangling alliance was—and largely remains—one of the pillars of the US's grand strategy. 'American exceptionalism'—the idea that the US is inherently different from any other nation and the belief in the special and unique role that the country plays in world history—goes a long way in explaining this attitude (Restad 2012). On the other

G. Pastori (✉)
Faculty of Political and Social Sciences, Catholic University of the Sacred Heart, Milan, Italy
e-mail: gianluca.pastori@unicatt.it

M. de Leonardis (ed.), *NATO in the Post-Cold War Era*, Security, Conflict and Cooperation in the Contemporary World
https://doi.org/10.1007/978-3-031-06063-2_3

hand, sound political pragmatism supported this position, which translated into the constant effort to free Washington's hands and subordinate its international engagement to the evolution of national interests.

At the end of the XIX century, when the US emerged as a first-class world power, Washington had already established the foundations of its worldview. The overriding aim was to protect the national territory, citizens, constitutional system, and economic well-being in the quickly changing international environment. During the Second World War, this aim was reaffirmed. After the conflict, the US promoted the institutionalisation of public life and the establishment of the present-day international regime. In laying the foundations of the post-war system, these steps led to the emergence of an 'instrumental internationalism [that] played an important role in converting the American political system to global supremacy, and in maintaining its commitment to supremacy ever since' (Werheim 2019).

The same attitude emerges in the US-NATO relationship. Conceived to promote collective security, the Atlantic Alliance soon evolved into a collective defence organisation, a process that the birth of NATO and the development of the US-Europe military cooperation made increasingly evident (Ireland 1984). However, the transformation of the Alliance's nature faced the US with new dilemmas. While the military dimension gained the upper hand, the problem became to balance Washington's expected role as the guarantor of European security with the broader set of its national interests. At the same time, the evolution of the strategic and institutional framework tended to reduce the US's room for manoeuvre and foster the country's commitment worldwide. The Korean War was the turning point in this process, although 'the U.S. policies that transformed NATO were reactions less to the war than to a deeper, systemic crisis that Washington policymakers believed had been developing [...] for more than a year' (Lafeber 1989).

Starting in the 1950s, the different US administrations worked out different approaches to the problem. During the Cold War, the role of nuclear weapons and the weight of the US arsenal allowed Washington to shape the form and extent of the Western military strategy. The idea that 'going nuclear' was the only way to counterbalance the Soviet conventional superiority made the US the almost 'natural' leader in the Western coalition. On the other side, Washington's increasingly global role fuelled diverging security perceptions that, in turn, gradually opened a drift with the European allies. In this perspective, Europe's military subalternity did not prevent its countries from assuming—or trying to assume—sometimes contrasting political and diplomatic postures, raising concerns in the US political circles on the possible implications for the transatlantic bond.

After 1989, the contrast between the US and Europe became more evident. With the end of the Soviet threat, European military expenditure quickly declined, while its ambitions for a more active role grew alongside deeper institutional integration. At the same time, the emergence of a new and often murky world of multi-vector risks prompted NATO's transformation according to the guidelines exposed in its first post-Cold War Strategic Concept (1991). The consequence was a set of decisions addressing complex and interrelated issues: the Alliance's mission in the post-Cold War system, the related questions of its force structure, command structure, and decision-making processes, NATO's membership, and its role in the framework of the interlocking European institutions. However, these changes in NATO's traditional configuration highlighted the contrasting visions that the US and Europe nurtured about its role.

Against this backdrop, the strengthening of the 'unipolar moment' (Krauthammer 1990) reverberated on the complex of US-Europe relations, giving Washington's 'free hand politics' what seemed to be more anti-European undertones. In the wake of the US-led military intervention in Iraq (20 March 2003), a wave of anti-Europeanism hit the US, with 'Anti-European sentiment [...] well-entrenched in the higher echelons of the [George W.] Bush administration, including the White House, the Department of Defense and the traditionally pro-Atlanticist State Department' (Chamorel 2004). In parallel, the belief in an inherent difference between the US 'coming from Mars' and Europe 'coming from Venus' (Kagan 2003) gained strength on both shores of the Atlantic. In this context, the European allies increasingly perceived Washington's adherence to its grand strategy as worrisome and possibly dangerous, making the call for a 'new transatlantic bargain' aimed to re-founding the US-Europe relationship on a sounder and more equitable basis a widespread—although ambiguous—cry in the second part of the decade.

The Cold War: An Age of Consensus?

From the US perspective, the period spanning between 1945 and 1989 roughly includes two main sub-periods: the first one, roughly coinciding with the Truman and Eisenhower administrations (1945–1961), was marked by the complex acceptance of Washington's role as guarantor of the European security; the second one, roughly spanning from John F. Kennedy's inauguration to the end of the second Reagan administration (1961–1989), was marked by the equally complex management of this role. The consolidation of the European geopolitical balance, the evolution of nuclear strategy, and the emergence of the 'Global Cold War' (Westad 2007) impacted these dynamics, favouring the shift of the US attention from Europe to the Third World and promoting the search for greater political and strategic autonomy on the European side.

Both the Truman and the Eisenhower administrations conceived the US involvement in terms of support provided to the European partners in guaranteeing the Old Continent's security. In 1947, while the idea of a formal security agreement with the US was growing popular in Europe, the priority of the Truman administration was 'not providing military aid, let alone joining a Western federation, but securing congressional approval for the Marshall Plan' (Kaplan 2007). Equally, the Joint Chiefs of Staff (JCS) feared that excessive US involvement in the European theatre could jeopardise the country's security in a time of looming economic difficulties (Condit 1996). Within this framework, '[s]upport for West European unity [was] a consistent theme of US foreign policy since the early post-World War II period' (Cromwell 1992: 1). However, the efforts to establish some form of permanent security cooperation between the two shores of the Atlantic were mainly a product of the European (especially British) initiative, supported by the most sensitive elements of the US establishment.

The militarisation of the Soviet strategy following the Prague coup (21 February 1948) and the Berlin blockade (24 June 1948) was pivotal in changing this attitude. On 17 March, with the Brussels Treaty, Great Britain, France, and the Benelux countries gave birth to the Western Union. In the same month, the US new Defense Secretary James Forrestal asked Congress to add three billion dollars to the 9.8-billion-budget in FY 1949 to meet the Soviet buildup. Between 22 March and 1 April, the US, Great Britain, and Canada joined the Pentagon talks on security. However, neither the talks nor the congressional approval of the Vandenberg resolution (11 June) entangled Washington into the formal guarantee that Europe was asking for. The same distance emerged in the Exploratory talks, which started on 6 July.

The most critical bone of contention was the automatism of the mutual defence clause. The European countries would have preferred a stringent formula, similar to the provisions of Article 4 of the Brussels Treaty, stating that an attack on one member required the others to provide 'in accordance with the provisions of Article 51 of the Charter of the United Nations [...] all the military and other aid and assistance in their power'.[1] Instead, the final version of the North Atlantic Treaty embodied in Article 5 a 'weaker' guarantee, shaped on the Inter-American Treaty of Reciprocal Assistance (signed: 2 September 1947; in force: 3 February 1948).[2] Thus, while agreeing that an attack against one member 'shall be considered an attack against them all', Article 5 just required that the allies 'will assist the Party or Parties so attacked by taking forthwith, individually and in concert with the other Parties, such action as it deems necessary, including the use of armed force, to restore and maintain the security of the North Atlantic area'.[3]

This 'open' security guarantee fit into the US perception of the imbalance existing between the two blocs and the 'psychological' role Washington could play in addressing it. In US eyes, the risk that Moscow's initiatives could drag the country into a conflict was a deterrent strong enough to contain the Soviet threat while avoiding a large-scale American presence overseas. The end of the nuclear monopoly (29 August 1949), the adoption of NSC-68, and the revision of the containment

[1] Treaty of Economic, Social and Cultural Collaboration and Collective Self-Defence. 17 March 1948. Brussels. https://www.nato.int/cps/en/natohq/official_texts_17072.htm.

[2] Inter-American Treaty of Reciprocal Assistance. 2 February 1947. Rio de Janeiro. http://www.oas.org/juridico/english/treaties/b-29.html.

[3] The North Atlantic Treaty. 4 April 1949. Washington, DC. https://www.nato.int/cps/fr/natohq/official_texts_17120.htm?selectedLocale=en. According to paragraphs 1 and 2, Article 3 of the Rio Treaty: '1. The High Contracting Parties agree that an armed attack by any State against an American State shall be considered as an attack against all the American States and, consequently, each one of the said Contracting Parties undertakes to assist in meeting the attack in the exercise of the inherent right of individual or collective self-defense recognised by Article 51 of the Charter of the United Nations. 2. On the request of the State or States directly attacked and until the decision of the Organ of Consultation of the Inter-American System, each one of the Contracting Parties may determine the immediate measures which it may individually take in fulfillment of the obligation contained in the preceding paragraph and in accordance with the principle of continental solidarity. The Organ of Consultation shall meet without delay for the purpose of examining those measures and agreeing upon the measures of a collective character that should be taken'.

doctrine that it entailed raised the level of the confrontation and 'provided the blueprint for the militarisation of the Cold War from 1950 to the collapse of the Soviet Union at the beginning of the 1990s' (May 1993). However, Truman's aim remained to enhance Europe's military preparedness and sustain its military capabilities, an aim that the Mutual Defense Assistance Act (6 October 1949) had started promoting (Kaplan 1980). At the same time, the strain that Korea placed on the US military instrument (whose budget raised from 14 billion dollars in 1950 to 44 billion in 1952) re-launched the debate over the role of deterrence in influencing Soviet decisions.

President Eisenhower's adoption of massive retaliation as the new US nuclear doctrine was a product of this debate and the supposed shortcomings of the previous approach. Its emphasis on a 'massive retaliatory power' to be used 'by means and at places of our [US] choosing' (Dulles 1954) confirmed both the US strategic autonomy regarding Europe and the role of the US arsenal in guaranteeing Western security. At the same time, the administration pushed forward with the idea of enhancing European military capabilities. The successful test of the first US low-yield nuclear bomb (April 1953) supported this process. The consequence was a more flexible use of this class of weapons and the development and deployment 'of a range of ballistic missiles [...] and projectiles, which could be employed for distances of a few dozen to a few hundred kilometers' (Heuser, 1995) and which—in Eisenhower's own words—'virtually achieved conventional status' within the US armed services.[4]

At the Lisbon summit (20–25 February 1952), the Atlantic Alliance 'agreed to [...] the most impressive non-nuclear force goal ever in its history', viz the creation of 50 active and 46 reserve divisions by 1954. Although the target was never reached, in the early 1950s, NATO's conventional forces in the Central theatre grew from 16 to 20 divisions, and by 1955 the Alliance was able to deploy 25 active and 25 reserve divisions in Europe (Bitzinger 1989; on the evolution of NATO's conventional force structure: Duffield 1995). Partly a product of West Germany's remilitarisation, this surge enhanced Europe's ability to contribute to the common security, lifting part of the burden from the US shoulders. The

[4] Press Release, 'Atoms for Peace' Speech. 8 December 1953. Dwight D. Eisenhower Presidential Library. Online Documents. https://www.eisenhowerlibrary.gov/sites/default/files/file/atoms_Binder13.pdf.

Eisenhower administration also showed interest in promoting greater US-Europe cooperation in the nuclear field: an approach that the Atomic Energy Act of 1954 favoured, revising the principles of the McMahon Act (Atomic Energy Act of 1946), and permitting the sharing among the allies of more atomic information than in the past.

However, it took John F. Kennedy's years (1961–1963) to scale up the US involvement. Adopting the flexible response as the new US nuclear doctrine required better coordination among the allies and made Washington's role pivotal in steering the European partners' posture. SACEUR General Lauris Norstad (1956–1963) warned US Defense Secretary Robert McNamara 'not to exaggerate the ability of NATO "to enforce a gradual, controlled development of the battle and ... the extent to which we can dictate the Soviet response"' (Freedman and Michaels 2019). The reliance on tactical nuclear weapons to protect the Fulda and Gorizia gaps made the outbreak of a limited nuclear conflict plausible. At the same time, while the deployment of tactical nuclear weapons in several NATO countries fostered a sense of shared responsibility, the withdrawal of the *Jupiter* missile from Italy and Turkey after the Cuban missile crisis (16–28 October 1962) was widely perceived as a proof of the subordination of the European interest to the US ones already emerged at the time of the Suez crisis (Petersen 2010).

The escalation of the Vietnam conflict and the shifting of Washington's attention to the Asian theatre fostered this sense of estrangement. During the 1970s, the nuclear umbrella remained the primary bond between the US and Europe. However, the feelings of the European allies grew increasingly mixed (Schultz and Schwartz 2010). Although the Soviet threat remained strong enough to make a stable US military presence on the Old Continent desirable, the flexible response almost ensured that an eventual nuclear showdown would have occurred on European soil. Moreover, the beginning of the 'long détente' and the emergence of a multi-pillar nuclear control regime widened the gap between nuclear and non-nuclear powers. On the one hand, the emergence of such a regime contributed to reducing regional tensions; on the other, the European countries feared that the final agreement could reflect the interests of the two superpowers more than those of their allies and that—once again—the promotion of a US-Soviet political convergence could be reached at the expenses of European security (Tal 2017; Dietl 2013, 2016).

From 11/9 to 9/11: The Legacy of a 'Lost' Decade?

It needed the so-called 'Second Cold War' to partially revive the transatlantic bond. The US decision to deploy a new generation of IRBMs and cruise missiles (*Pershing II* and *Tomahawk*) partly aimed to meet the European fears that SALT I and SALT II agreements had raised. However, Washington remained the driving force in both the rearmament during the first Reagan mandate (1981–1985) and the détente started after 1985. The debate on the so-called 'zero option' and the signing of the INF Treaty (8 December 1987) emphasised Europe's dependence on US guidance. While the declining importance of nuclear weapons encouraged discussions about a European defence community less reliant on the US, neither Britain nor France was eager to take over Washington's role, nor were the other countries (who had previously sheltered under the US umbrella) interested in a European alternative. Against this backdrop, both the Reagan and the George H.W. Bush administrations kept on providing Europe with the 'traditional' US guarantee, even if the events in Mikhail Gorbachev's Soviet Union and their impact at the international level were making the 'old' deterrence architecture increasingly obsolete.

The Soviet crisis posed the US and NATO the challenge of redefining their role also in other dimensions. The experience of the Gulf War (2 August 1990–28 February 1991) seemed to provide Washington with a new global role, emphatically outlined in George H.W. Bush's 'new world order' speech (11 September 1990).[5] The prospect of long-term US-USSR cooperation at one time offered the overall stability that the Cold War had granted without the risk of an East–West armed confrontation. On 5–6 July 1990, NATO extended 'the hand of friendship' to the Soviet Union and the Warsaw Pact countries, stating the need to 'profoundly alter the way we think about defence'.[6] On 3 October, Germany's reunification redefined the continent's security landscape, pushing NATO's borders eastward for the first time since 1955. Between November and June 1991, the Treaty on Conventional Armed Forces in Europe and the

[5] Bush, G. H. W. 11 September 1990. Address Before a Joint Session of Congress. https://millercenter.org/the-presidency/presidential-speeches/september-11-1990-address-joint-session-congress.

[6] Declaration on a Transformed North Atlantic Alliance. Issued by the Heads of State and Government participating in the meeting of the North Atlantic Council. 5–6 July 1990. https://www.nato.int/cps/en/natohq/official_texts_23693.htm.

START I Treaty dented two pillars of the Cold War regional balance. In November 1991, adopting its first post-Cold War Strategic Concept, NATO paved the way for its future 'out-of-area' activism. Significantly, it pointed out how, in the new strategic environment, '[r]isks to Allied security are less likely to result from calculated aggression against the territory of the Allies, but rather from the adverse consequences of instabilities that may arise from the serious economic, social and political difficulties, including ethnic rivalries and territorial disputes, which are faced by many countries in central and eastern Europe'.[7]

The impact of these events on US-Europe relations was manifold: on the one hand, the new role of the US as the sole 'global policeman' widened the gap between its security perceptions and the European ones; on the other, the end of the Cold War made less urgent—in European eyes—the need to preserve a strong security tie with Washington. In the dominant rhetoric, the disappearance of the Soviet threat should have opened a new and more peaceful age, allowing the European countries to capitalise on the 'peace dividend' while playing a more active role in the regional scenario. Some US political circles somehow supported these ambitions. For instance, in the first part of the Yugoslav crisis, Washington's aloofness mirrored this attitude, while George H.W. Bush's decision to deploy US troops in support of the UN humanitarian efforts in Somalia confirmed his commitment to the 'new world order' model.

Bill Clinton's administration (1993–2001) broke the stalemate. Since the mid-1990s, embracing the so-called 'assertive multilateralism', it re-nationalised the US foreign policy, partly abandoning the previous emphasis on multilateralism as a pillar of the country's international posture. At the same time, it redefined the balance between national and international priorities, explicitly placing Washington's interests at the top of the list. Assertive multilateralism 'posited that if the United States no longer had the political will or the resources to act as a global policeman, it should form coalitions to do so. It meant "that when America acted with others, [America] should lead in establishing goals and ensuring success." Vitally, this did not preclude unilateral action in self-defense or in safeguard vital interests' (Boys 2015).

[7] The Alliance's New Strategic Concept. 1990. Agreed by the Heads of State and Government participating in the Meeting of the North Atlantic Council. 7–8 November 1990. https://www.nato.int/cps/en/natohq/official_texts_23847.htm.

Despite the criticisms several authors have raised about Clinton's record in the international realm (Dumbrell 2010), the President's more assertive approach (especially during his second term in office) positively reverberated on NATO, providing the Atlantic Alliance with a more robust political guidance. This attitude was sometimes resented in the European capitals, for instance, in 1993, when the US administration proposed to adopt a 'lift and strike' policy to promote a diplomatic solution to the then-ongoing Bosnian crisis.[8] However, since the mid-1990s, two initiatives tackled the main issues facing the Alliance: the relationship with the former Warsaw Pact countries and the role of military power in the post-Cold War age.

The Partnership for Peace (PfP) program offered the Central European countries and the former Soviet republics a forum for collaboration while defusing the potentially divisive problem of NATO enlargement, deferred to an indefinite future. Almost in parallel, NATO military intervention in Bosnia-Herzegovina (Operation Deliberate Force: 30 August–20 September 1995) contributed to re-drawing the role and image of the organisation, with a growing emphasis on its technical-military role. Europe's internal divisions and the failure—at both national and multinational levels—to deal with the Yugoslav crisis largely explain why Washington could—de facto—impose its agenda. The US driving role in the adoption of the Dayton agreements (December 14, 1995) shed light on Europe's lack of unity and the limits of any alternative to a US-led NATO as an instrument of regional security.

The Kosovo experience (Operation Allied Force: 24 March–10 June 1999) confirmed the role that the US had assumed in shaping the process of NATO transformation. On the eve of the air campaign, Clinton himself explicitly recalled how 'Europe was slow to recognise the dangers' at the time of the First and the Second World War and how 'the United States waited even longer to enter the conflicts', thus allowing the original crisis to escalate. In this perspective, and after the Bosnian experience, 'if we [United States] and our allies [...] decided just to look the other way as

[8] The idea behind the 'lift and strike' policy was to lift the United Nations arms embargo imposed on both parts of the conflict to provide the Bosnian Muslims with US weapons and strike the Bosnian Serbs if they tried to stop that move. Initially suggested by Bosnian President Alija Izetbegović and supported by several US senators during George H. W. Bush's administration, Clinton endorsed this policy during the 1992 presidential campaign but abandoned it the following year, after his inauguration, in the face of the opposition from the United Kingdom, France, Germany, Italy, and Russia.

these people were massacred on NATO's doorstep. That would discredit NATO, the cornerstone on which our security has rested for 50 years now'.[9]

However, in the conduct of the operation, the different visions existing between Washington and the European countries often emerged, hampering—from a US perspective—the effectiveness of NATO's action. The decision to focus on a pure air campaign raised several criticisms. The same happened to the decision to stage a phase-articulated campaign, which became 'a means for exerting tight political control over any decision to escalate' (Nardulli et al. 2002). The military establishment—including SACEUR, General Wesley Clark (1997–2000)—resented the extent to which they could not act upon purely military objectives and called for an examination of the Alliance's decision-making processes after the end of the mission.[10] In any case, Kosovo confirmed the role of NATO as the 'strong arm' of the international community. Worth noting that, on the same days of Operation Allied Force, this role found its formal recognition in NATO's new Strategic Concept, which included, among the Alliance's tasks, the possibility of conducting non-Article 5 crisis response operations 'to prevent conflict, or, should a crisis arise, to contribute to its effective management, consistent with international law'.[11]

The Clinton administration was instrumental also in pushing forward the issue of NATO enlargement. The US decision to support the admissions of the new members was the product of different pressures: from the European allies, engaged in the parallel EU enlargement process; of the same Central and Eastern European countries, fearful of a possible Russian comeback and eager to consolidate their bonds with Washington; from parts of the US administration, who saw enlargement as a win-win strategy to project stability in Central and Eastern Europe

[9] Transcript: Clinton addresses nation on Yugoslavia strike. 24 March 1999. https://edition.cnn.com/ALLPOLITICS/stories/1999/03/25/clinton.transcript/.

[10] Report to Congress—Kosovo/Operation Allied Force After-Action Report. 31 January 2000. Department of Defense. https://webharvest.gov/peth04/20041027022740/www.defenselink.mil/pubs/kaar02072000.pdf.

[11] The Alliance's Strategic Concept. Approved by the Heads of State and Government participating in the meeting of the North Atlantic Council in Washington, DC. 24 April 1999. https://www.nato.int/cps/en/natolive/official_texts_27433.htm.

and contain possible Moscow's hostile initiatives. In any case, the decision broke the fragile balance of US-Russia relations. On 5 December 1994, the Clinton-Yeltsin summit in Budapest had already turned into a confrontation on NATO Foreign Ministers' decision to speed up the enlargement process. Adding to the tensions that Operation Allied Force generated, the Alliance's enlargement fueled the sense of encirclement in the Russian leadership and confirmed its belief in NATO's hostile attitude. In turn, Moscow's new posture became another element that pushed the former Warsaw Pact countries to ask for NATO membership, negatively impacting the dialogue between Washington and its 'old' allies, who feared a possible deterioration of their relations with Russia.

In this perspective, the 1990s pulled NATO in two different directions, on the one hand emphasising its military dimension and extending its 'physical' presence into new theatres, on the other promoting the assumption of new political profiles. Beyond acting as an 'agent of international socialisation' for Central and Eastern Europe countries (Gheciu 2005), the Alliance engaged in a troublesome political dialogue with Russia, the Mediterranean countries, and the European Union. The decision reached during the Franco-British summit in Saint-Malo (4 December 1998) to provide the EU with the capacity for autonomous decision-making and action, backed up by credible military forces, to respond to international crises when the Atlantic Alliance is not involved,[12] met stubborn US and NATO resistance. Its terms revolved around the clauses that State Secretary Madeleine Albright listed for any European Security and Defense Initiative (the so-called 'three Ds'): no decoupling from NATO, no duplication of assets and structures; no discrimination against NATO members who are not EU members (Albright 1998). The Berlin Plus agreement (16 December 2002) only partially solved the stalemate, subordinating the EU intervention to the Alliance's decision not to intervene first ('right of first refusal') and linking the access to NATO assets to the unanimous approval of the NATO members.

[12] Joint Declaration on European Defence. Joint Declaration issued at the British-French Summit at Saint-Malo. 4 December 1998. https://www.cvce.eu/content/publication/2008/3/31/f3cd16fb-fc37-4d52-936f-c8e9bc80f24f/publishable_en.pdf.

The Age of Disenchantment: 9/11 to 11/9

Despite the limits that the advocates of greater European operational autonomy pointed out, the Berlin Plus agreement's implementation added an essential degree of flexibility to the transatlanic relationship. Between 2003 and 2004, the EU launched its first two military missions—Operation Concordia in the Former Yugoslav Republic of Macedonia and Operation Althea in Bosnia-Herzegovina—replacing NATO in its stabilisation efforts. Moreover, from a US perspective, the framework that the Berlin Plus agreement offered was consistent with the aim of its assertive multilateralism, viz to disengage Washington from the theatres where it had no or few issues at stake. On the negative side, in a period of rising tensions, it contributed to widening the political gap between the US and the European allies, affecting the transatlantic solidarity, and questioning the role of NATO as a negotiation forum.

In the 2000s, 'variable geometry coalitions' emerged as a possible alternative—both in US and NATO strategies—against the 'permanent cooperation' enshrined in the Atlantic Alliance. The 'coalition of the willing' that supported George W. Bush's intervention in Iraq was widely perceived as a more effective tool than NATO. At the same time, its adoption highlighted the different positions existing among the European allies. In the wake of the US military intervention, Defence Secretary Donald Rumsfeld's remarks on the existence of an 'old' and a 'new' Europe, with different visions of what military cooperation was, shed light on the fracture existing within the Alliance. In the same vein, the US focus on the fact that it was 'the mission to define the coalition' gave new evidence to a deeply seated US mistrust towards the perceived operational weakness of the post-Cold War NATO (Jung 2012).

The 9/11 terrorist attacks on New York and Washington, DC, speeded up the process that transformed the 'assertive multilateralism' of the Clinton age into George W. Bush's unilateralism and led to the redefinition of NATO's role in the US strategy (Kraus et al. 2004). After the first emotional rally around the American flag and the favour that accompanied the beginning of Operation *Enduring Freedom* (OEF: 7 October 2001–28 December 2014), the rhetoric and praxis of the US 'Global War on Terror' (GWOT) started meeting increasing criticisms. The day after the attacks (12 September), NATO invoked the Article 5 defence guarantee[13]; however, the Alliance remained on the sidelines in the American-led military campaign in Afghanistan. The US administration decided not to ask for NATO cooperation for military and political reasons: only the US could project its military forces halfway worldwide, and Washington did not want political interference during the campaign. On the other side, the logistic and operational needs of the new military effort highlighted the limits of NATO's force structure, promoting a more thorough, structural adaptation process (Terriff 2013).

The assuming of control over ISAF (International Security Assistance Force; 11 August 2003–28 December 2014) fuelled the process, while the decline in OEF strength on the eve of the Iraqi campaign in 2003 resulted in enhanced operational pressure on a mission whose original tasks were the training of the Afghan security forces and the assistance to the Afghan authorities in rebuilding the country's government institutions. Despite its positive impacts on NATO's assets, force structure and capabilities, the Afghan experience confirmed, on the political side, the distance existing both between the US and the European allies and among the European allies themselves. Many countries adopted restrictions ('national caveats') to 'tailor' their engagement and appease their public opinions, impacting ISAF's effectiveness and producing resentment within the Alliance (Saideman and Auerswald 2012). Against this backdrop, the shift of the US priority from Afghanistan to Iraq and the growing relevance of the 'coalition of the willing' model raised concern about NATO's ability to deal with the new international threats.

Unsurprisingly, national caveats were on the forefront in the NATO summits held in Riga (2006) and Bucharest (2008), and again in 2009, the newly elected President Barack Obama elliptically raised the point in a speech at the margin of the NATO sixtieth anniversary summit, remarking that 'Europe should not simply expect the United States to shoulder that

[13] On 12 September, the North Atlantic Council (NAC) formally declared that if there were evidence that the terrorist attack on the United States had been directed from abroad, Article 5 of the Washington Treaty would have come into force. On 2 October, after the US delegation offered the requested evidence that the al-Qaida terrorist network carried out the attacks with the support of the Afghan Taliban regime, NATO's Secretary-General, Lord Robertson of Port Ellen, confirmed that the *casus foederis* had been triggered.

[Afghan military] burden alone'.[14] However, not even Barack Obama's Democratic administration promoted greater cohesion in the now twenty-eight-strong Alliance.[15] On the opposite, the admission of new Central and Eastern European countries highlighted their different visions and positions vis à vis the Western European allies, especially on NATO-Russia relations. Filling the vacuum between Russia and the Alliance's eastern border, enlargement fuelled, in fact, the re-emerging of Russian assertiveness and confirmed its role as one of the thorniest issues in the dialogue between Washington and Moscow.

The political retrenchment of the Obama administration fostered these developments. During its first term, Washington refocused on Afghanistan, adapting its strategy in the light of the Iraqi experience. ISAF Commander General Stanley McChrystal (in office: 2009–2010) and his successor, General David Petraeus (in office: 2010–2011), adopted relevant changes at the strategic, operational, and tactical levels. A new surge in troops' presence supported these changes. Following a trend started in 2009, in May 2011, ISAF forces totalled 132,400, out of which some 90,000 were US (Scheer 2012). However, this effort, far from being resolutive, put NATO under further stress. The widespread opinion that Afghanistan had become a testbed of the transatlantic alliance overloaded the mission with expectation at a moment when the effects of the 2007–2008 financial crisis reduced NATO's available resources. The apparent lack of results and the growing number of casualties challenged ISAF's support in several NATO countries, while the outbreak of the Arab Springs posed more immediate problems to the Southern European countries, and Russian activism raised concerns in Poland and the Baltic republics. Finally, the US tilt toward the Pacific—trumpeted in State Secretary Hillary Clinton's *America's Pacific Century* (Clinton 2011)—seemed to confirm Washington's willingness to re-elaborate its geopolitical priorities and return to a relentless pursuit of national interests with the consolidation of its Eastern Asian presence.

[14] Remarks by President Obama at Strasbourg Town Hall. 3 April 1999. https://obamawhitehouse.archives.gov/the-press-office/remarks-president-obama-strasbourg-town-hall.

[15] After the Czech Republic, Hungary and Poland in 1999, NATO membership was extended to Bulgaria, Estonia, Latvia, Lithuania, Romania, Slovakia and Slovenia in 2004, and Albania and Croatia in 2009.

The consequence was a parallel redefinition of NATO's standing. Operation Unified Protector (OUP: 23 March–31 October 2011), mandated under UN Security Council resolutions 1970 and 1973 to protect the Libyan population from the regime's large-scale violence, saw the US for the first time 'leading from behind', according to Washington's new political mantra. On both shores of the Atlantic, critical voices contested this posture (Dueck 2015; Kaufman 2016). Poor US guidance was blamed for the lack of long-term planning, which left Libya's security, in the aftermath of OUP, in the hands of the militias that proliferated after the death of Muammar Qhadafi (20 October 2011). The US contribution was fundamental for the success of the kinetic part of the operation. Washington provided the bulk of the precision-guided munitions used during the attacks. In the first days of the campaign, US firepower was essential to disable the Libyan air control system and guarantee to NATO forces the superiority they enjoined throughout the whole mission. However, the lack of shared vision coupled with Washington's unwillingness to commit to a long-term stabilisation effort favoured the crisis' internationalisation and transformed Libya into a battlefield of competing influences. In its turn, this power struggle opened the door to the Russian and Chinese interests and led to conflicts among the European allies, who split on the issue of which part to support in the clash between the UN-backed Government of National Accord in Tripoli and the Tobruk-based government led by General Khalifa Haftar.

These dynamics also affected other theatres and issues. The Strategic Concept adopted at the NATO Lisbon summit (19–20 November 2010),[16] while reaffirming the value of the Alliance's three core tasks (collective defence, crisis management, and cooperative security), expanded its interests to new fields, conveying 'a collective intention to push NATO further in the direction of global engagement' (Ringsmose and Rynning 2011). However, in a time of financial constraints and diverging political visions, this program contrasted with the allies' competing attitudes about NATO's role and fuelled the divergences that the outbreak of the Ukraine crisis would have pushed to the forefront. The events of 'Euromaidan', the Russian annexation of Crimea, and

[16] Active Engagement, Modern Defence. Strategic Concept for the Defence and Security of the Members of the North Atlantic Treaty Organization. Adopted by Heads of State and Government at the NATO Summit in Lisbon, 19–20 November 2010. https://www.nato.int/strategic-concept/pdf/Strat_Concept_web_en.pdf.

the outbreak of violence in Donetsk and Luhansk re-launched the long-coveted concerns of the Eastern European countries about a resurgence of the Russian threat. At the same time, the need to deploy assets to oppose the Kremlin's encroachment speeded up ISAF's disengagement and the adoption of a low-profile posture with the beginning of Operation Resolute Support (1 January 2015).

While the US renounced playing their traditional balancing role, these evolutions led to new rifts between 'old' and 'new' allies and between Eastern and Southern European countries. Once again, these rifts revolved around the nature and task of the Atlantic Alliance, seen on the one side as an essentially political structure aimed at promoting security at a global level, on the other as a primarily military player aimed a guaranteeing the physical protection of the European continent. Obama's decision to deploy a US rotating contingent in Poland in the very last days of his mandate, although aimed at bolstering NATO's eastern flank, actually weakened the Alliance's position, highlighting the role of the bilateral dimension and the importance of a 'privileged' link with Washington to promote one country's security.

The US 'Pivot to Asia': Another Challenge to the Atlantic Alliance?

Since October 2011, the 'pivot to Asia' significantly altered the US-Europe strategic relationship. China's economic and political strengthening, coupled with Europe's relative stability, was the main reason behind the US interests' rebalancing and the redefinition of Washington's European commitment. From a long-term perspective, it was a sort of 'back to the roots'. At the beginning of the nineteenth century, a mix of separation and interdependence from Europe allowed the US to focus on its internal expansion and spread its influence in the Pacific (Mariano 2013). Albeit resented in some quarters, this new posture somehow fit the European ambitions to assume a more independent role. Two years earlier, the Lisbon Treaty had already created the EU High Representative for Foreign Affairs and Security Policy figure, foreshadowing the possibility of a 'true' European foreign policy. Between 2009 and 2010, the development of the Common Security and Defence Policy (CSDP) and the establishment of the European External Action Service (EEAS) followed the same path. The ambition of the President of the European Commission, José Manuel Barroso (in office: 2004–2014), to promote the Union's evolution toward a federation of nation-states[17] required the assumption of a higher political profile. In this perspective, US policy opened the EU a window of opportunity, which relatively good West-Russia relations widened.

European expectations went somehow frustrated. During Obama's presidency, the 'pivot' largely failed to materialize, a victim of a 'conceptualization and implementation [...] piecemeal, inconsistent, and poorly coordinated' (Green 2017: 539). It took the Trump administration to reach some qualifying Obama's targets, such as allocating to the Pacific theatre more than fifty per cent of the US military assets (Kolmaš and Kolmašová 2019). At the same time, the EU faced growing difficulties in defining and implementing meaningful international actions. The long-term consequences of the subprime crisis (which hit Europe with some delay compared to the US) and the poor management of Greece's debt crisis deeply affected Brussels's political credibility, fuelling widespread criticisms and feeding the already vociferous 'Eurosceptic' front. Also, in the oft-turbulent balance among the different EU priorities, the shifting attention toward the economic and financial issues pushed foreign and security policy out of the spotlight, affecting both High Representative Catherine Ashton's (in office: 2009–2014) actual performance and its assessment. Finally, the outbreak of the Arab Springs and the management of their regional effects further exposed the limits of intra-European diplomatic and military cooperation, showing how 'the hour of crisis is still the hour of the [EU] member states' (Helwig and Rüger 2014).

In this context, the US efforts to play an active role in both the European and Asian theatres proved increasingly tricky due also to the shrinking US military expenditure[18] and the partial erosion of President Obama's political favour, which in 2014 reached its lowest point before rebounding in 2015 and (more clearly) on the eve of the 2016 elections. Within NATO, uncertainties dented Washington's leadership and reverberated in tensions among members. On the Asian front, the

[17] José Manuel Durão Barroso, President of the European Commission, State of the Union 2012 Address, Plenary session of the European Parliament, Strasbourg 12 September 2012. https://ec.europa.eu/commission/presscorner/detail/en/SPEECH_12_596.

[18] According to SIPIRI—The Stockholm International Peace Research Institute, between FY 2008–2009 and FY 2015–2016, US military expenditure dropped, in constant (2019) US dollar, from 841,220 to 681,580 million (SIPRI Military Expenditure Database. https://www.sipri.org/databases/milex).

shortcomings of the US strategy failed both to contain China's political rise and engage the country in a long-term, mutually beneficial strategic dialogue. These elements offered fertile ground to Donald Trump's attack on the Democratic experience and NATO, dubbed a costly anachronism, 'obsolete and disproportionately too expensive (and unfair) for the U.S.'. In turn, Trump's attacks on the Atlantic Alliance confirmed European concerns about a possible US-Europe strategic decoupling. The new attention that the issue of Europe's strategic autonomy attracted since mid-2016 is a clue of its growing discomfort facing Washington's changing attitude. In the following years, this discomfort assumed sharper tones, culminating in French President Emmanuel Macron's declaration about the need to create 'une vrai armée européenene' to protect Europe 'sans dépendre seulement des Etats-Unis et de manière plus souveraine'.[19]

Building on a deepening distrust, Donald Trump's aggressive (albeit erratic) Chinese policy widened the US-Europe gap. The President's openly anti-European posture did not compensate for the tilt of the US focus on Asia as Obama's actively advertised commitment to Europe had done in the previous years. Moreover, the search for new partners pushed several Central-Eastern and Southern European states to tighten their economic and commercial relations with the People's Republic, especially in the framework of Beijing's Belt and Road Initiative (BRI) and '16 + 1' program (Góralczyk 2017). Just in the second part of the mandate, the US administration tried to redress the situation partly, for instance, lobbying to contrast the Chinese presence in the US and European TLC sectors and emphasizing the threat that China's involvement in port building and management posed to the Mediterranean maritime security. On some occasions, such an approach proved quite effective; however, it did not structurally alter the status quo nor evolve into an actual US-Europe rally point. Instead, growing US-China tensions spurred Brussels to speed up the elaboration of a formal EU Indo-Pacific strategy, to 'pursue its multifaceted engagement with China, engaging bilaterally to promote solutions to common challenges, cooperating on

[19] Emmanuel Macron: son interview par Nikos Aliagas sur Europe 1 (INTEGRALE), 6 November 2018. https://www.youtube.com/watch?v=ilggBgh8Lhw.

issues of common interest and encouraging China to play its part in a peaceful and thriving Indo-Pacific region'.[20]

Coherently with Donald Trump's vision, NATO received little attention. From the Alliance's point of view, it was a mixed blessing. On the positive side, the political retrenchment allowed it to deal with troublesome internal aspects (such as the convergence to the Celtic Manor targets) and soothe East/South tensions. On the negative side, the same idea of an Atlantic Alliance came under attack. Quite paradoxically, NATO's supposed inability to adapt to the new security needs became the target of both Trump's attacks and the European replies, forcing the Alliance to struggle to preserve its role in member countries' security perceptions and control the increasing centrifugal tensions. State Secretary Mike Pompeo (in office: 2018–2021) was probably the most active figure in promoting NATO's re-orientation toward China, which the 2017 National Security Strategy depicted (together with Russia) as a 'challenge [to] American power, influence, and interests, attempting to erode American security and prosperity'.[21] Unsurprisingly, China first appeared in a NATO official document in the 2019 London summit final declaration.[22] Since then, it returned in both the report of the Reflection Group established as part of the #NATO2030 program (November 2020)[23] and the 2021 Brussels summit final communiqué.[24] As a common ground for the US and Europe, the concerns that Beijing's new

[20] Joint Communication to the European Parliament and the Council. The EU Strategy for cooperation in the Indo-Pacific. Brussels. 16 September 2021. https://ec.europa.eu/info/sites/default/files/jointcommunication_indo_pacific_en.pdf.

[21] National Security Strategy of the United States of America. December 2017. https://trumpwhitehouse.archives.gov/wp-content/uploads/2017/12/NSS-Final-12-18-2017-0905.pdf.

[22] London Declaration. Issued by the Heads of State and Government participating in the meeting of the North Atlantic Council in London 3–4 December 2019. https://www.nato.int/cps/en/natohq/official_texts_171584.htm.

[23] NATO 2030: United for a New Era. Analysis and Recommendations of the Reflection Group Appointed by the NATO Secretary General. 25 November 2020. https://www.nato.int/nato_static_fl2014/assets/pdf/2020/12/pdf/201201-Reflection-Group-Final-Report-Uni.pdf.

[24] Brussels Summit Communiqué. Issued by the Heads of State and Government participating in the meeting of the North Atlantic Council in Brussels 14 June 2021. https://www.nato.int/cps/en/natohq/news_185000.htm.

international role raised proved helpful in blunting Trump's criticisms of the Alliance and shaping a new consensus within NATO.

However, although the issue entered NATO's agenda, it is doubtful whether a shared vision of its nature and how to deal with it exists, both between the US and Europe and within Europe itself. Such a lack of shared vision emerges at different levels. While recognizing the 'systemic challenge' that China's 'stated ambitions and assertive behaviour' poses to the Atlantic Alliance, the Brussels Summit Communiqué provided scanty details about a specific NATO's China policy: a situation that the post-summit statements of several European leaders highlighted. Different approaches among NATO allies and EU members are another divisive element, which EU-US lingering distrust makes critical. Washington's 'Pacific tilt' widened the structural gap in US relations with Europe, confirming—from the European perspective—the US willingness to 'scrap the contract' signed at the beginning of the Cold War. The Trump administration overemphasized this aspect, but the underlying continuity with its predecessors was clear, especially to international observers (Brands 2018). In this perspective, countries like Great Britain, France, Germany, and The Netherlands have adopted or revised their Indo-Pacific national strategies to promote their regional interest better. It is another proof of how China's emergence in the international arena and its impact on the global geopolitical balance has put the transatlantic bond under strain and given prominence to the distance separating Washington from the European allies.

Concluding Remarks

The election of Donald Trump as the forty-fifth US President focused the spotlight on the many problems affecting the system of US-Europe relations. However, the relevance that Trump himself placed on the economic and financial aspects (the 'burden sharing' issue) contributed to hiding other troublesome dimensions. Since the mid-1990s, the evolution of the US geopolitical priorities has triggered structural changes in both NATO and the transatlantic relationship. With the end of the Cold War and the decline of Europe's geostrategic relevance, Washington is less and less ready to 'pay the political bill' of European cohesion. Within this framework, Bill Clinton's adoption of 'assertive multilateralism' did not only reshape the terms of the US-UN relationship. It also started a renationalisation of the US foreign policy that Donald Trump pushed to the extreme.

Under both George W. Bush and Obama administrations, the process evolved, despite the two Presidents' different visions and narratives. In this perspective, both George W. Bush's decision to embrace the model of the 'coalition of the willing' and Barack Obama's adoption of the 'leading from behind' approach as the pivot of the US strategy reflected the declining value that Washington seems to place on the 'old' Cold War's imperative of keeping the West united. On the other shore of the Atlantic, the US disengagement made NATO less and less important for many European countries, which reacted, on the one hand, stressing the need for greater strategic independence to achieve through the establishment of a 'truly European army', on the other looking for privileged, bilateral ties with Washington based on some form of patron/client relationship.

A consequence of these evolutions is the growing focus—on both shores of the Atlantic—on short-term strategies to cope with the dynamism of the international system and the US willingness to return to the 'free hands politics', partially abandoned during the Cold War. In this perspective, assertiveness and restrain—the symbolic pillars of US foreign policy in the post-Cold War age (Onea 2013)—are the two sides of the same coin, viz the effort of the US political establishment—both Republican and Democratic—to define viable new strategies replacing the patterns of action that the end of the Soviet threat made obsolete. The apparent decline of the US-led post-Second World War international liberal order pushes in the same direction, making permanent structured cooperation within the international organisations seemingly obsolete.

The ambiguous US-NATO relationship mirrors a similar logic. The weakening of the previous instrumental relation has left a gap that impacts the Alliance's efficiency and forces the members to redefine the meaning of their relationship. Competing visions on NATO's current role are the product of this process and find their most evident expression in the proliferation of the tasks included in the Alliance's Strategic Concept. The same idea of the 'West' faces unexpected challenges both as a meaningful geopolitical construct and as a product of shared values. As a cultural artefact of the US-Europe relationship, the idea of 'West' witnessed a gradual degradation in recent years, which impacted the idea of Alliance as a 'spiritual federation', embodied in the well-known formula of British Foreign Minister Ernest Bevin.

It is not surprising that the difficulties that NATO faced, especially since the early 2000s, went hand in hand with the debate on the presumed widening of the 'transatlantic drift' and the emergence of new competitors to the US global hegemony. In this period, a transformation in the coordinates of the US political landscape has made Washington's assumption of an active international role increasingly contested at the domestic level. President Trump's recurrent criticisms of NATO and US-Europe solidarity mirror a structural change in the US approach to the issue and an overall change in the attitude of the US public opinion. A similar change took place on the European side, too, due to NATO's perceived inability to deal with the multi-faceted challenges of the present-day regional security environment.

From a long-term perspective, this is probably the most dangerous consequence of the 'free hands politics' that the US has pursued regarding NATO. The diverging security visions between the two shores of the Atlantic have opened a drift that the US relative decline contributes to widening. None of these elements regards NATO directly. However, leading to a gradual US disengagement, they contribute to the surfacing of the many cleavages of a seventy-year-old structure. Unsurprisingly, 'the critical need for reviving strong, reliable American leadership' has been recently highlighted as '[t]he single greatest challenge NATO faces today' (Lute and Burns 2019). A situation that somehow resembles the first years of the transatlantic relationship .

Bibliography

Albright, Madeleine K. 1998. The Right Balance Will Secure NATO's Future. *Financial Times*, December 7.

Bitzinger, Richard B. 1989. *Assessing the Conventional Balance in Europe, 1945–1975*. Santa Monica: RAND.

Boys, James D. 2015. *Clinton's Grand Strategy: US Foreign Policy in a Post-Cold War World*. London and New York: Bloomsbury.

Brands, Hal. 2014. *What Good Is Grand Strategy? Power and Purpose in American Statecraft from Harry S. Truman to George W. Bush*. Ithaca: Cornell University Press.

Brands, Hal. 2018. Foreign Officials See Bush and Obama in Trump. *Foreign Policy*, 23 February.

Chamorel, Patrick. 2004. *Anti-Europeanism and Euroscepticism in the United States*. Florence: European University Institute—Robert Schuman Centre for Advanced Studies.

Clinton, Hillary. 2011. America's Pacific Century. *Foreign Policy*, October 11. https://foreignpolicy.com/2011/10/11/americas-pacific-century.

Condit, Kenneth W. 1996. *The Joint Chiefs of Staff and National Policy, II, 1947–1949*. Washington, DC: Office of Joint History—Office of the Chairman of the Joint Chiefs of Staff.

Cromwell, William C. 1992. *The United States and the European Pillar: The Strained Alliance*. New York: St. Martin's Press.

Dietl, Ralph L. 2013. *Equal Security: Europe and the SALT Process, 1969–1976*. Stuttgart: Franz Steiner.

Dietl, Ralph L. 2016. *Beyond Parity: NATO Europe and the SALT Process in the Carter Era, 1977–1981*. Stuttgart: Franz Steiner.

Dueck, Colin. 2015. *The Obama Doctrine: American Grand Strategy Today*. Oxford: Oxford University Press.

Duffield, John S. 1995. *Power Rules: The Evolution of NATO's Conventional Force Posture*. Stanford: Stanford University Press.

Dulles, John F. 1954. The Evolution of Foreign Policy. *Department of State Bulletin* 30: 107–110.

Dumbrell, John. 2010. President Bill Clinton and US Transatlantic Foreign Policy. *Journal of Transatlantic Studies* 8 (3): 268–278.

Freedman, Lawrence, and Jeffrey Michaels. 2019. *The Evolution of Nuclear Strategy*, 4th ed. London: Palgrave Macmillan.

Gheciu, Alexandra. 2005. *NATO in the 'New Europe': The Politics of International Socialization After the Cold War*. Stanford: Stanford University Press.

Góralczyk, Bogdan. 2017. China's Interests in Central and Eastern Europe: Enter the Dragon. *European View* 16: 153–162.

Green, Michael J. 2017. *By More Than Providence: Grand Strategy and American Power in the Asia Pacific Since 1783*. New York: Columbia University Press.

Helwig, Niklas, and Carolin Rüger. 2014. In Search of a Role for the High Representative: The Legacy of Catherine Ashton. *The International Spectator: Italian Journal of International Affairs* 49 (4): 1–17.

Heuser, Beatrice. 1995. The Development of NATO's Nuclear Strategy. *Contemporary European History* 4 (1): 37–66.

Hooker, Richard D., Jr. 2014. *The Grand Strategy of the United States*. Washington, DC: National Defense University Press.

Ireland, Timothy P. 1984. *Creating the Entangling Alliance: The Origins of the North Atlantic Treaty Organization*. Westport: Greenwood.

Jung, Karsten. 2012. Willing or Waning? NATO's Role in an Age of Coalitions. *World Affairs* 174 (6): 43–52.

Kagan, Robert. 2003. *Of Paradise and Power: America and Europe in the New World Order*. New York: Knopf.

Kaplan, Lawrence S. 1980. *A Community of Interests: NATO and the Military Assistance Program, 1948–51*. Washington, DC: Office of the Secretary of Defense—Historical Office.

Kaplan, Lawrence S. 2007. *NATO 1948: The Birth of the Transatlantic Alliance*. Lanham: Rowman and Littlefield.

Kaufman, Robert G. 2016. *Dangerous Doctrine: How Obama's Grand Strategy Weakened America*. Lexington: University Press of Kentucky.

Kolmaš, Michal, and Šárka Kolmašová. 2019. A 'Pivot' That Never Existed: America's Asian Strategy Under Obama and Trump. *Cambridge Review of International Affairs*. https://doi.org/10.1080/09557571.2018.1553936.

Kraus, Jon, Kevin J. McMahon, and David M. Rankin, eds. 2004. *Transformed by Crisis: The Presidency of G.W. Bush and American Politics*. New York: Palgrave Macmillan.

Krauthammer, Charles. 1990. The Unipolar Moment. *Foreign Affairs* 70 (1): 23–33.

Lafeber, Walter. 1989. NATO and the Korean War: A Context. *Diplomatic History* 13 (4): 461–477.

Leffler, Melvyn P. 2010. The Emergence of an American Grand Strategy, 1945–1952. In *The Cambridge History of the Cold War, I, Origins*, ed. Melvyn P. Leffler and Odd Arne Westad. Cambridge: Cambridge University Press: 67-89.

Lute, Douglas, and Nicholas Burns. 2019. *NATO at Seventy: An Alliance in Crisis*. Cambridge: Harvard Kennedy School—Belfer Center for Science and International Affairs.

Mariano, Marco. 2013. *L'America nell' "Occidente". Storia della dottrina Monroe (1823–1963)*. Rome: Carocci.

May, Ernest R. 1993. *American Cold War Strategy: Interpreting NSC 68*. Boston: Bedford.

Nardulli, Buce R., et al. 2002. *Disjointed War: Military Operations in Kosovo, 1999*. Santa Monica: RAND.

Onea, Tudor A. 2013. *US Foreign Policy in the Post-Cold War Era: Restraint Versus Assertiveness from George H. W. Bush to Barack Obama*. New York: Palgrave Macmillan.

Petersen, Tore T. 2010. Suez 1956: European Colonial Interests and US Cold War Prerogatives. In *European-American Relations and the Middle East: From Suez to Iraq*, ed. Daniel Möckli and Victor Mauer. London and New York: Routledge: 11-25.

Restad, Hilde E. 2012. Old Paradigms in History Die Hard in Political Science: US Foreign Policy and American Exceptionalism. *American Political Thought* 1 (1): 53–76.

Ringsmose, Jens, and Sten Rynning. 2011. Introduction: Taking Stock of NATO's New Strategic Concept. In *NATO's New Strategic Concept: A*

Comprehensive Assessment, ed. Jens Ringsmose and Sten Rynning. Copenhagen: Danish Institute for International Studies: 7-22.

Rynning, Sten. 2021. Deterrence Rediscovered: NATO and Russia. In *Netherlands Annual Review of Military Studies 2020: Deterrence in the 21st Century—Insights from Theory and Practice*, ed. Frans Osinga and Tim Swijis. The Hague: Asser Press: 29-45.

Saideman, Stephen M., and David P. Auerswald. 2012. Comparing Caveats: Understanding the Sources of National Restrictions Upon NATO's Mission in Afghanistan. *International Studies Quarterly* 56 (1): 67–84.

Schreer, Benjamin. 2012. The Evolution of NATO's Strategy in Afghanistan. In *Pursuing Strategy: NATO Operations from the Gulf War to Gaddafi*, ed. Håkan Edström and Dennis Gyllensporre. Basingstoke: Palgrave Macmillan: 139-156.

Schultz, Matthias, and Thomas A. Schwartz, eds. 2010. *The Strained Alliance: US-European Relations from Nixon to Carter*. Washington and Cambridge: German Historical Institute and Cambridge University Press.

Tal, David. 2017. *US Strategic Arms Policy in the Cold War: Negotiation and Confrontation over SALT, 1969–1979*. New York: Routledge.

Terriff, Terry. 2013. 'Déjà vu All over Again'?: 11 September 2001 and NATO Military Transformation. In *NATO Beyond 9/11: The Transformation of the Atlantic Alliance*, ed. Ellen Hallams, Luca Ratti, and Benjamin Zyla. Basingstoke and New York: Palgrave Macmillan: 91-117.

Werheim, Stephen. 2019. Instrumental Internationalism: The American Origins of the United Nations, 1940–3. *Journal of Contemporary History* 54 (2): 265–283.

Westad, Odd Arne. 2007. *The Global Cold War: Third World Interventions and the Making of Our Times*. New York: Cambridge University Press.

CHAPTER 4

Russia-NATO-US: From Detente to Impossible Cooperation

Francesco Randazzo

Among the international political events that have most contributed to the deterioration of relations between Russia and NATO since the late 1990s, several scholars agree on identifying two concomitant issues: the armed intervention of the Atlantic Alliance against Yugoslavia in March 1999 and the start of the process of NATO enlargement in Eastern Europe, including the former Democratic People's Republics of Central and Eastern Europe. Nevertheless, the early years of the Yeltsin presidency had seemed to be the precursor to a new, unprecedented climate of distension and cooperation between Russia and the West. The needs and objectives of the new post-Soviet Russia had been summarized in 1993 by General Sergei V. Stepashin, then-chairman of the Defence and Security Committee of the Supreme Soviet of the Russian Federation,

F. Randazzo (✉)
Department of Political Sciences, University of Perugia, Perugia, Italy
e-mail: francesco.randazzo@unipg.it

M. de Leonardis (ed.), *NATO in the Post-Cold War Era*, Security, Conflict and Cooperation in the Contemporary World
https://doi.org/10.1007/978-3-031-06063-2_4

in an article for *The RUSI Journal*: internal stabilization and restoration of economic ties with the former Soviet countries, accompanied by the intensification of scientific, economic and technological cooperation with Western nations; the establishment of a relationship of trust with NATO member states, so that they could provide Russia with technical, financial and humanitarian support in the very delicate phase of transition to democracy and market economy; close coordination with the North Atlantic Alliance in order to safeguard the global military balance, prevent the emergence of aggressive powers and avert the proliferation of nuclear weapons; the transformation of Russia into a geopolitical bridge between the Euro-Atlantic and Asian-Pacific security systems (Stepashin 1993). The appeal culminated in the proposal for a 'Marshall Plan for a post-communist revival': a coordinated, long-term effort with which the West would support the laborious conversion of the Russian militarized economic system into market economy.[1]

In the aftermath of the Paris agreement, which in May 1997 gave birth to the *Founding Act on Mutual Relations, Cooperation and Security between NATO and the Russian Federation*, Kissinger went so far as to say that Russia had obtained a preponderant status in NATO compared to any candidate for admission (Piontkovsky and Tsygichko 1998). Among the requirements of the treaty were cooperation in the fields of nuclear security and missile defence, Russian participation in multilateral conferences and peacekeeping operations in Europe, and the exchange of information. However, the Kosovo crisis perturbed this reconciliation and dealt it a blow from which it would never fully recover.

A better understanding of the parable of relations between Russia and NATO can be traced back to the beginning of the 1990s, when the European balance suffered a major setback following the fall of the Berlin Wall. Moscow was forced to backtrack the centre of gravity of its military force, leaving room for the strengthening not only of the Atlantic Alliance but also for the explosion of new nationalisms in Central and Eastern Europe. Centuries of 'advancement' westward swept away in the space of a few years with a low-profile political leader in power, Boris Yeltsin, who took

[1] Although this wish was not fulfilled, two-way initiatives for conciliation and normalization of relations multiplied: the 1992 US-Russian Charter for Partnership and Friendship was followed in 1994 by the Partnership for Peace with the countries of the former Warsaw Pact and the Founding Act on Mutual Relations, Cooperation and Security between NATO and the Russian Federation, signed in Paris on 27 May 1997.

over the leadership of the country after Mikhail Gorbachev's dismissal. It was Gorbachev himself—the architect of a tightrope waltz from the 'old' to the 'new' Soviet style—who had reopened a glimmer of optimism in the global stage following the Reykjavík summit (11 October 1986) and the subsequent INF (Intermediate-Range Nuclear Forces) Treaty, signed in Washington on 8 December 1987: a convention which not only took a step forward in the reduction of missile arsenals, but laid the foundations for a lasting and unreserved detente between the two major world powers. These steps were taken by the Secretary of the Soviet Communist Party with the expectation that the United States would not allow NATO to threaten the areas of Soviet 'influence', thus avoiding interference in Moscow's strategic interests in Eastern Europe. The agreement was finalized by a subsequent meeting of the two leaders six months later in Moscow. In 1991, the superpowers adopted the first Strategic Arms Reduction Treaty, after which nearly 2,700 warheads were disposed of. The demilitarization programme launched in the early 1990s would soon give way to a return of the Russian ambition to exert a hegemonic role in an area that, for about half a century, had seen Moscow play an undisputed leadership over the local Communist regimes.

Reconstructing relations between Russia and NATO over the last thirty years, i.e. from the 'facts' of Berlin in 1989, requires any historian, or political analyst, to reflect carefully on the starting conditions of this relationship and on the phases that have marked the gradual departure from the starting positions determined by the progressive change in the international scenario. But, above all, it is necessary to make a clear distinction between Russia's relations vis-à-vis the United States and the European Union, which cannot be superimposed—even in a condition of obvious and profound reciprocal influence.

Russia joined NATO's Partnership for Peace in 1994, in the wake of its admission into the North Atlantic Cooperation Council (1991). At the time, the country was dealing with a state of economic collapse and political unrest; add in the humiliation of a former superpower, now reduced to asking for help from nations that had been labelled as a mortal enemy for seven decades. Therefore, the starting point saw Yeltsin's Russia facing an unprecedented and unpredictable turn in its relations with the outside world, during which the political elite looked for 'allies' capable of helping it out of the dangerous tunnel into which the new post-Soviet society was entering. The constitutional crisis experienced between 2 and

4 October 1993 (with the Army besieging and then storming the Parliament by Yeltsin's order) made the world realize that a fateful game was being played in Russia, while the political declaration signed by the Presidents of Russia, the European Council and the European Commission in Brussels the following November provided 'the basis for permanent political dialogue and a system of regular consultations at different levels on all political, economic and other issues of common interest'.[2] In 1996, a Russian contingent took part in the NATO SFOR-led peacekeeping mission in Bosnia and Herzegovina, and in 1997 the Founding Act on Mutual Relations, Cooperation and Security was signed and the Joint Permanent Council (JPC) established. This moment can be considered the *zenith* in the history of cooperation between the two former rivals. However, at the end of the second Yeltsin Presidency, the international framework had changed radically as compared to the early 1990s. The abrupt halt to successful cooperation was partly due to NATO's intervention in the Yugoslav wars and partly to the enthusiasm with which Russia welcomed the political rise of Vladimir Putin, a politician of a completely different temperament from the now 'worn-out' and 'embarrassing' Boris Yeltsin—whose drunken TV appearances alongside world leaders had weakened the image of a new and competitive Russia.

The following years saw plenty of opportunities for cooperation between Moscow and the Western bloc: the intervention of the Russian military peacekeeping forces in Kosovo in 2000 alongside NATO troops, the granting of the use of Russia's airspace to the international coalition during the campaign in Afghanistan in 2002, the establishment of the NATO-Russia Council (NRC) to replace the Joint Permanent Council in 2002, the Joint NATO-Russia Action Plan against terrorism in 2005, and the repeated Russian contributions to NATO Active Endeavour naval counter-terrorism operation between 2004 and 2008. Yet, relations between the Atlantic Alliance and Russia suffered a severe blow when the permanent members in Brussels launched the process of integration of the former Warsaw Pact countries into the Atlantic Alliance, with the professed aim of speeding up their transition to democracy. In the words of its advocates, the inclusion of all the Eastern countries in a single alliance was also meant to 'defuse potential tensions between them' (Alvaro and Briani 2008). At the Madrid summit in 1997, it was

[2] I rapporti tra l'Ue e la Russia. 31 May 1995. https://ec.europa.eu/commission/presscorner/detail/it/MEMO_95_85.

announced that the Czech Republic, Hungary and Poland would have joined NATO in two years. In 2004, the Alliance was enlarged to include Bulgaria, Estonia, Latvia, Lithuania, Slovenia, Slovakia, and Romania. Moscow did not welcome this eastward expansion, as it perceived it as hostile to Russian national security interests—a perception exacerbated by the intervention in Yugoslavia in 1999, implemented without a UN mandate.

Putin's ascension as Head of State, the attack on the Twin Towers and the fight against international terrorism, which in Russia had forged an alliance with the separatist Chechen guerrillas, led to a new phase in relations between Moscow and Brussels, with both sides having a compelling interest in arresting the rampant and elusive enemy that threatened Christian civilizations in Europe and around the world. The need, therefore, to establish a common front meant that the management of the Kosovo crisis, the raw nerve of Russian diplomacy in Europe, was overshadowed.

The psychological impact produced in Russia by the bombings on Serbia had been in fact disruptive, a geopolitical trauma whose implications on East-West relations were compared to those of the dual crisis of Berlin and Cuba in the early 1960s. As pointed out by several authors, the Russian government, Parliament, the major political parties and public opinion in general found themselves united and unanimous—a rare occurrence—in condemning the Western initiative against Slobodan Milosevic's regime and in favour of the self-determination of the Kosovar people.

At that time, Milosevic's Yugoslavia was the only ally—with the possible exception of Belarus–Moscow still could count on to the west of the Dardanelles and the Ural. More importantly, Belgrade was the last Russian bridgehead in Europe—the guarantee of its presence in European dynamics, of its participation in economic development and in the construction of a new European security system, at a time when Russia, following the collapse of the Warsaw Pact, was experiencing the unsettling feeling of being progressively squeezed out of the continent (Gobarev 1999).

'The tragic error of the American leadership', in Yeltsin's words, came at the moment of maximum agreement between Russia and the Atlantic Alliance: only two years after the signing of the Russian-NATO Founding Act, whose achievements in terms of cooperation at the highest levels between Moscow and the West were immediately frustrated by the unilateral suspension announced by the Russians.[3] The sudden march of the Russian mechanized units on the Pristina airport was a reflection of Moscow's sudden disenchantment with NATO, whose aggressiveness, offensive rather than defensive vocation and arrogance towards Russia suddenly became manifest in the eyes of the Russians. If, until then, in the doctrine of national security of the Federation NATO occupied the fifth and last place in the ranking of possible threats, following the events in Belgrade it was immediately recognized as the primary menace not only to Russian national interests, but to the very survival of the state. The rampant conviction was that NATO had treacherously attacked Serbia (without a declaration of war, as Nazi Germany had done with the USSR in 1941) only as a show of strength to humiliate Russia; that the main candidates for further 'humanitarian intervention' by NATO at that point were the former Soviet republics, some of them torn apart by separatist upheavals, and even Chechnya and Dagestan themselves; that, finally, the old doctrine of nuclear deterrence should have been recovered as a fundamental guarantee of Russia's sovereign independence and its status as a global power. Already at the time, political observers theorized that NATO's hostility or indifference towards Moscow, and the latter's willingness to find a place of its own in the Euro-Atlantic stage, would push the Kremlin to seek new allies outside the Slavonic world and the old Soviet borders: that Moscow could turn, therefore, to the People's Republic of China (Gobarev 1999).

The Kosovo crisis contributed decisively to dispel all the illusions and 'myths' of the years of the Yeltsin-Kozyrev administration (the latter being Foreign Minister from 1990 to 1996), heir to the mirage of a 'common European home' of Gorbachevian memory. Faced with an Alliance perceived as expansionist and militaristic—as demonstrated by the emphasis placed by the NATO leadership on the new concept of out-of-area operations (1999), the indifference shown by the Western powers to the repeated appeals for the joint elaboration of a new security system, and

[3] The agreements between Russia and the West in the mid-1990s had partly reassured the Muscovite leaders of the goodwill of the Europeans not to betray Russia's security concerns. The main example being the Founding Act of 1997, seen hopefully as the cornerstone of a new system of balance between the expectations of NATO countries and the Kremlin's will to preserve a sort of 'curtain' in defence of Russian interests in Eastern Europe (Oznobishev 2018).

the inefficiency of the 'palliatives' offered by them (Partnership for Peace, Permanent Joint Council)—the old beliefs and slogans of the Cold War regained credibility, to the point of persuading the Russians that NATO was nothing more than an instrument of 'war, murder and aggression' (Antonenko 1999, 2000). With Yevgeniy Primakov now at the new head of the Foreign Ministry, the waving East-West partnership gradually gave way to a new multipolar doctrine, aimed at reviving old relations—or establishing new ones—with non-European nations relatively hostile to the US: China, Iran, Iraq, and Syria.

Particularly disturbing for the Russians was the parallelism, maybe plausible or perhaps a product of the psychoses of the time, between the Kosovo and Chechen issues: in both cases, from the Russian point of view, a separatist Muslim majority aimed at exercising unconditional power over an oppressed Slavic minority, using terrorism as a weapon and thriving in the chaos generated by the dissolution of a multinational federation. There was the fear that the Kosovo crisis, settled by Western military intervention on the side of the Albanian secessionists, could encourage centrifugal drives in the CIS member states and in Russia itself. Even more unsettling was the thought that Kosovo would serve as a precedent for future NATO intrusions inside the Russian sphere of influence (for example, in the case of the Armenian-Azerbaijani conflict) or on the periphery of the Federation itself. This is why, during the Second Chechen War, the Kremlin refused any Western intervention, even in the form of mediation or access by humanitarian organizations to help refugees. Even if joint participation in the Kosovo peacekeeping mission (KFOR) served to re-establish a minimum of cooperation and mutual trust between the two sides, the process was not clear of disputes and misunderstandings. The involvement of the Russian forces, far from disinterested, served to reaffirm Moscow's military presence in the area, to protect the Slavonic component from the persecution of the Albanian 'terrorists', and to guarantee the disarmament of the Army of Liberation of Kosovo as provided for by the United Nations. And yet, the unsatisfactory complacency (at least from a Moscow point of view) shown by the West to the Kremlin's demands for the territorial integrity of Yugoslavia and the preservation of Milošević's regime led to the outraged reaction of the Russians, who threatened the unilateral withdrawal of their contingent. The repeated misunderstandings and mutual provocations ended up jeopardizing almost any possible step towards a restoration of dialogue and cooperation between the recalcitrant partners (Antonenko, 1999, 2000).

Such was the indelible imprint left by the Kosovo issue on politics and public opinion in Russia: an act of aggression against a sovereign nation carried out in violation of the United Nations Charter, the Helsinki Accords and the NATO-Russia Founding Act. In the eyes of the Russians, the bombings on Belgrade had revealed the true face of the Alliance: an expansionist bloc, with armed forces and military plans aimed at offence, and unable to survive without an external enemy—today, Yugoslavia; tomorrow, probably, Russia. The lesson that the Kremlin has learned from the experience was that no one would have taken into account the demands of the weak: be it Yugoslavia or post-Soviet Russia, whose genuine opposition to the military operation against its historical partner fell on deaf ears in Brussels and Washington. The USSR, for its part, had inspired fear: and as long as it had continued to disturb the sleep of the West, no one could have so candidly ignored the will of the Kremlin (Arbatova 2001). Asked about the future of relations between Moscow and the West, Russian political observers pointed out that NATO had now lost the opportunity to evolve into a pan-European security system extending from the Atlantic to the Urals: the only hope that the geopolitical achievements of two decades of *perestroika* would not be irremediably lost was, therefore, the deepening of the partnership between Russia and the European Union, building on the already well-established ties in the fields of economy and commerce. A partnership to be built around a number of clearly defined pillars: a common inclination towards multipolarism, in contrast to the dominant American monopoly of power, and the absence of strident antinomies in security and defence, but rather a shared interest in containing the emerging Islamic radicalism. The enlargement of the EU was not perceived as threatening in Moscow, unlike the expansion of NATO; and yet, this cooperation between the European Community and Russia lacked long-term strategic objectives that went beyond trade relations and good intentions (Arbatova 2001)—the latter being periodically frustrated by the allegiance of those same EU nations to the Western Alliance.

Nevertheless, the new millennium seemed to open with positive notes. The principles of the Founding Act of 1997 were revived and reaffirmed in the Declaration of Rome of 2002, which explicitly stated the areas Russia and NATO would concentrate their efforts in. Among them, the fight against terrorism and the proliferation of WMDs; the elaboration of joint plans in the field of missile defence; the organization of joint military exercises, etc. The military conferences at the highest levels, organized in increasing numbers following the war in Afghanistan, did indeed produce important results in the field of intelligence sharing; the emergency drills in which NATO and Russian troops had to respond to humanitarian crises or terrorist attacks were also particularly fruitful. Nothing more, however, could be obtained: the reciprocal phobias, the scarce interest of the Russian military ranks in such a partnership, and, finally, the new wave of expansion of the Atlantic Alliance in the East (2004) remained as insurmountable obstacles on the road to further goals (Polikanov 2004).

In fact, if the Yugoslav crisis had proved capable of coagulating the opinions of the various strata of Russian society in open opposition to the Western initiative, the same can be said of the process of expansion of NATO in Central and Eastern Europe. The process was regarded as a violation of the balance of power in Europe, suppressing the 'security buffer' which separated Russia from NATO and potentially bringing the latter's military presence to the borders of the Federation itself; questioning the status of Ukraine and Moldova as neutral nations; undermining the foundations of the CFE Treaty (Treaty on Conventional Armed Forces in Europe 1990), and emptying of meaning the role of OSCE as the backbone of the European security system; and, finally, provoking Russia into an arms race and consequently strengthening of the 'war party' in Moscow (Sergounin 1997). The firmly critical attitude towards the enlargement of NATO united, therefore, the different schools of foreign policy that had been flourishing among the Russian intelligentsia in the years following the Soviet collapse; a symptom of the decline of the 'Atlanticist' instances, which had seemed triumphant in the years in which the Russian leadership (including Yeltsin himself) went as far as foretelling a future Russian adhesion to the Atlantic Pact. The ranks of those who looked at NATO not as a militarist and totalitarian front, but as an alliance between democracies and the viaticum to Russia's full integration into the Western economy were already rapidly shrinking. Already in the second half of the 1990s, therefore, the majority of the Russian intelligentsia had disdainfully abandoned the tortuous path of amity with NATO, trying other ways so that Russia would not remain marginalized in its new, reduced borders. Some advocated progressive integration into a renewed European Community, provided that this process was inspired by the principle of protecting multilateralism in international relations and preserving the cultural and political specificities of Russia as a Eurasian nation ('democratic Eurasianists'). Others were strongly opposed to such a project of integration into the Western system, advocating instead the remilitarization of the Western borders ('Slavophiles') or substantial isolationism and the adoption of a low profile in international affairs, in order to focus on domestic issues ('neo-isolationists'). Among the political parties, the most extreme position was embodied by the ultranationalists of the Liberal Democratic Party of Russia—nowadays, the third-largest party in the Duma; they advocated the rescission of the treaties with the West (a move supported by the Communists as well) and the use of economic sanctions and even military force against those Eastern European nations which would have applied for membership of NATO (Sergounin 1997). Famous scholar A. Arbatov has nevertheless highlighted the implicitly complacent position of Russian reactionaries towards NATO: their hope was, in fact, that the expansion of the Alliance would lead to a new escalation with the West, creating ideal conditions for the suppression of democracy in Russia and the restoration of the empire in the former Soviet space (Arbatov 1995).

As far as relations between NATO and Russia were concerned, Arbatov believe that the accession of the former Warsaw Pact countries to the Alliance—and the latter's very survival after the end of the Cold War—had to be explained mainly with the uncertainty that characterized Russia and the ex-Soviet area throughout the 1990s. For the same reason Russia, in spite of the goodwill repeatedly expressed by its rulers, could never have become a full member of NATO: the *raison d'être* of the Alliance was precisely to revive its former deterrent role, in the event that the chaotic situation in Russia had cleared the way for an authoritarian and imperialistic resurgence. Conversely, a solidification of democracy in Russia could have led, in the future, to the dissolution of NATO and its replacement by a more complex, multilateral security mechanism. For a future normalization of NATO-Russia relations, able to reconcile the desire of the Eastern European countries to join NATO with Russia's security concerns, the author foresaw first and foremost a slower and more gradual extension of the Alliance, and possibly the introduction of restrictions such as a commitment not to station troops and nuclear weapons in the territory of the new member states; the promise to encourage, in parallel, a deepening of economic, political and military cooperation between the two sides; a radical reform of NATO that would make peacekeeping and humanitarian action the main focus of collective action, as part of a more inclusive multilateral action under the auspices of the UN and the OSCE (Arbatov 1995). A number of observers and political scientists in Russia have indeed stressed the central role played by the Organization for Security and Cooperation in Europe in the projects of the Russian government (Polikanov 2008), with the aim of establishing a new pan-European security system based on the Helsinki principles of 1975. The OSCE was, moreover, one of the few European international institutions of which Russia was a member: hence the hope of subordinating NATO to the OSCE as the military arm of the organization, entirely dedicated to safeguarding peace on the continent through peacekeeping operations. Great was the disappointment when, by 2004, the failure of the plan became evident. Moscow's hopes for the preservation of some form of multilateralism also turned, in the early 2000s, towards a new tripartite organization for security in Europe, with its pillars being the defence structures of Russia, the Atlantic Alliance, and the European Union—thus advocating a clear separation between NATO and the EU. Nevertheless, what emerged from vague bilateral approaches on the matter were mainly political declarations without binding force, as complained on several occasions by Russian observers (Pushkov 1997).

Further factors of concern about NATO's continued expansion towards Eastern Europe and the Balkans may be highlighted. The admission of countries such as Poland and the Baltic republics is a cause for particular disturbance in Moscow: not only because of their proximity to the borders of the Federation, or by virtue of the presence of significant Russian minorities in Estonia, Lithuania and Latvia, or as a consequence of the Kremlin's concerns on the future of Kaliningrad. More prosaically, Russian politicians and analysts have emphasized the historical hostility and deep-rooted grudges that these nations have against Russia, deploring their contribution in perpetuating fault lines dating back to the Cold War (Krickovic 2016). The empirical consequence being, among others, the perennial exclusion of Moscow from the processes of European economic integration. As far back as 1997, in a harsh commentary for the magazine *Die Friedens-Warte*, General Makhmut Gareev denounced the 'cultural and psychological mentality' that bound the countries of Eastern Europe to the West and fostered their enmity towards Russia; going so far as to affirm that 'on the eve of World War II the ruling circles of Poland were prepared to let the fascists tear their country to bits, rather than accept the Soviet Union's help' (Gareev 1997).

The admission of the Baltic Republics into NATO (2004) pushed Moscow to progressively exacerbate its manifestations of dissent over the expansion of the Alliance, to the extent that the entry of Georgia and Ukraine was labelled as the red line which, if crossed, would have triggered a massive military reaction. The occupation of the Crimea and the support given to the separatists in Ukraine can be explained as well, according to Russian observers, not as manifestations of Russia's neo-expansionism, but with the ultimate objective of generating such instability in the country that the effective start of the process of admittance to NATO would be categorically excluded. Likewise, the Ukrainian crisis also serves the purpose of exerting pressure on Europe in the direction of a long-desired reform of the European security system, such as to guarantee Russia its own sphere of influence: this also in view of the limited scope and authority granted to the organs of consultation and cooperation between the parties, such as the NATO-Russia Council (Krickovic 2016)—the 'palliatives' mentioned above.

Among the factors contributing to the coldness and hostility between NATO and Russia, one author in particular (Tsyganov 2013) has theorized the existence of an 'Anti-Russian Lobby' in the United States, formed at the beginning of the twentieth century and established as a powerful force in the aftermath of World War II. Although variegated in its composition, it would have brought together a number of easily identifiable groups: the assertors of American hegemony, according to whom the real enemy to be overthrown was not just Soviet communism, but Russia as a whole; agencies and organizations born with the aim of promoting democracy and human rights, but soon turned into instruments of a propaganda war against the USSR, such as Freedom House and Human Rights Watch; and, finally, those Eastern European nationalist emigres who had managed to carve out influential roles in the American intelligentsia. According to the author, the Lobby has counted among its ranks names of the calibre of Prof. Richard Pipes (2005), who thus provided an academic justification for the anti-Russian doctrine, and Zbigniew Brzezinski (2009), Jimmy Carter's national security adviser, often labelled as the architect of NATO expansion to the East during the Clinton administration. Both Pipes and Brzezinski were Polish emigrants. In more recent times, Sen. John McCain—the main proponent of Georgia's admission to NATO—would have figured as well among the prominent members. Ideologically, the members of the lobby advocate a vision whereby Russia would be alien to—and incompatible with—European and Western civilization; in empirical terms, they demand unconditional support for Washington's foreign policy from the governments of Eastern Europe, in return for the guarantees given to them against the Russian threat. The actual support shown by some of these countries to initiatives such as the Iraqi War and the admission of Georgia and Ukraine into NATO would theoretically demonstrate the validity of this argument.

When looking at Moscow's 'global resurgence', many political analysts inside and outside Russia have correlated the assertive foreign policy of the ruling political elite with the country's long imperial history. A sort of historical continuity that imposes on the Kremlin the search for internal legitimacy through the recovery of imperial identity and 'the obsessive use of the figure of an external enemy threatening that very integrity and the enormous natural wealth of the country, exploited primarily as resources of power' (Vitale and Romeo 2009). The expectations of *grandeur* of the Russian State apparatus, the paternalism of the ruling class, and the strong nationalism are elements which end up conditioning international relations and hindering regional 'aggregative' processes, whose socio-political-territorial nature contrasts with two fundamental elements of state-imperial Russia: the *imperskoe myshlenie* (imperial ways of thinking) and the *imperskaya ideya* (imperial idea). This kind of *weltanschauung* 'imply a recurrent appeal to the strong state as a source of political-territorial security for the nation and its wealth, to an authoritative personal guide with whom to identify and to whom to entrust one's entire individual destiny' (Vitale and Romeo 2009).

Dealing with such a political vocabulary, proper to an old 'superpower', a mention has at least to be made about the relationship between the state and the military. At the sunset of the Tsarist era, the support of the military for the Revolution had been decisive, as demonstrated by the tradition according to which the first shot of the Revolution was fired on the Winter Palace by the cruiser *Aurora*. After the Soviet period, in which the military apparatus played a decisive role in subjugating external and internal threats to the stability of the Union and the Warsaw Pact, the Yeltsinian era was marked by a gradual loss of prestige of the armed forces: in the span of ten years, a much-needed reform of the now-defunct and splintered Red Army was repeatedly announced, but never actually implemented. The Army regained its centrality under Putin: in line with a long militarist tradition, the typical Russian values were reaffirmed as 'the needs of defense and security, entrusted to a precise military-political leadership, held to be the exclusive depositary of the technology and doctrine on the subject and of the possibility of disposing entirely of the citizens, even at the cost of great sacrifices, for the defense of the territorial State' (Vitale and Romeo 2009). The armed forces have thus regained their role, above all, as protectors of the status quo, crystallized by the de facto uninterrupted monopoly of political power exerted by Vladimir Putin. The game played since then on the international chessboard has seen Russia re-emerge from the 'humiliation' of the Cold War and impress in relations with NATO and the world with a new acceleration, in the direction of greater involvement in international crises. An example of this is provided today by the recent Syrian and Libyan crises. Russia, therefore, returns to re-evaluate its military capacity through an authentic Revolution in Military Affairs, launched in the early 2000s.

In conclusion, we have seen how relations between Russia, NATO, and the European Union are largely influenced by factors that are endogenous to Russian society, factors that affect the peculiarity of Russian history, society and politics and suffer constant and never-ending prejudices, deriving from a past that Russia carries around like a heavy burden. It is very complicated to objectify these relations. We have taken into consideration a series of points of view deriving mainly from Russian historians and intellectuals, who look 'from a distance' at the processes underway in their country in the years close to the new Putin era, particularly regarding Russia's geopolitical doctrine and ambitions. Many other readings and interpretations could have been counted, even by apologists of 'Putin's System' and supporters of the rebirth of 'Greater Russia': just think of the series *Proekt 'Putin'*, containing the writings of many Russian political scientists and historians, including Yuriy Mukhin (*Putin i Naval'nyy. Geroi nashchego vremeni*), Vitaliy Tretyakov (*Vladimir Putin 20 let u vlasti*), Vladimir Bolshakov (*Putin v 2018 godu*), Vladimir Bushin (*Pyatnadtsat let Putina. Kuda bredet Rossiya*).

Relations between Russia and the West, and the Kremlin's approach to international diplomacy in general, continue to be based on shows of strength, spheres of influence, deterrence, and occasional proxy wars, thus supporting the thesis that the Cold War has never ended but, if anything, has undergone a clear repolarization. For most of the last century, the confrontation between East and West was conceived and presented to the respective public opinions as a struggle between two models of social 'democracy', between two different ideas of economic evolution, and between two different concepts of civil coexistence. Nevertheless, since the collapse of the Communist bloc the actual, more empirical motives and priorities have overwhelmingly emerged from behind the shadow of ideology—economic and financial supremacy, hoarding and exploitation of energy resources, national security, control and influence over strategic sectors and countries in Eurasia and beyond. Surely, the ongoing pandemic will impose the elaboration of new agendas and new objectives, with a focus on the protection of public health and the defence of borders—objectives that some will use as a pretext to revive nationalist policies and restrictions on personal liberties. All this will be combined with diplomatic cynicism, which certainly does not help relations with the West and the United States, not to mention sinusoidal relation with China. The future, at the moment, does not reserve Russia particular merit in having been able to face the so-called 'internal' crises, while in the international sphere its assertiveness has proved to be decisive in stopping the escalation of Middle Eastern conflicts. Perhaps, in a not-too-distant future, the US itself will realize that NATO is an anachronistic instrument of pressure against Russia—its sole existence representing, as we have seen, an insurmountable obstacle on the path to build, if not a full reconciliation, at least a *modus vivendi* of peaceful coexistence between East and West. Europe, for its part, can only benefit from a relationship of peaceful coexistence with Russia, since, once the barriers of communist ideology have fallen, the greatest obstacle to the encounter between the two worlds has been definitively removed.

Bibliography

Alvaro, Riccardo, and Briani Valerio. 2008. Le relazioni della Russia con la Nato e l'Unione europea. *Dossier Senato della Repubblica* 103 (10): 5–15.

Antonenko, Oksana. 1999–2000. Russia, NATO and European Security After Kosovo. *Survival* 41 (4): 124–144.

Arbatov, Alexei. 1995. NATO and Russia. *Security Dialogue* 26 (2): 135–146.

Arbatova, Nadia A. 2001. European Security After the Kosovo Crisis: The Role of Russia. *Southeast European and Black Sea Studies* 1 (2): 64–78.

Baranovsky, Vladimir G. 1995. La Russie et la sécurité européenne. *Politique Étrangère* 60 (1): 33–55.

Baranovsky, Vladimir G. 2002. 11 septembre: Une vision russe. *Politique Étrangère* 67 (1). 9–20.

Bettanin, Fabio. 2018. *Putin e il mondo che verrà. Storia e politica della Russia nel nuovo contesto internazionale*. Roma: Viella.

Brzezinski, Zbigniew. 2009. *The Choice: Global Domination or Global Leadership*. New York: Basic Books.

Danilov, Dmitriy A. 2005. Russia and European Security. In *Russia and European Security*, ed. D. Lynch, 79–98. European Union Institute for Security Studies (EUISS).

Gareev, Makhmut A. 1997. The Expansion of NATO Does Not Solve, But Aggravates Security Issues. *Die Friedens-Warte* 72 (3): 297–303.

Gianotti, Lorenzo. 2014. *Putin e la Russia. Irresistibile e anacronistico ritorno all'autocrazia*. Roma: Editori Riuniti.

Gobarev, Vicktor. 1999. Russia-NATO Relations After the Kosovo Crisis: Strategic Implications. *The Journal of Slavic Military Studies* 12 (3): 1–17.

Krickovic, Andrej. 2016. When Ties Do Not Bind: The Failure of Institutional Binding in NATO Russia Relations. *Contemporary Security Policy* 37 (2): 175–199.

Lebed, Alexandre. 1997. La Russie entre elle-même et l'Europe. *Politique Étrangère* 62 (1): 167–176.

Oznobishev, Sergey. 2018. Otnoshenya Rossiya-Nato: Ot deklarativnogo partnerstva k glubokomu krizisu. *Mirovaya Ekonomika i Mezhdunarodnye Otnosheniya* 62: 5–16.

Ping-kuei, Chen. 2009. *Menace of Power: Russia-NATO Relations and Balance of Power in Europe*. Saarbrücken: Verlag Dr Mueller E K.

Piontkovsky, Andrey, and Vitali Tsygichko. 1998. Russia and NATO After Paris and Madrid: A Perspective from Moscow. *Contemporary Security Policy* 19 (2): 121–125.

Pipes, Richard. 2005. *Russian Conservatism and Its Critics: A Study in Political*. New Haven, CT: Yale University Press.

Polikanov, Dmitry. 2004. Nato-Russia Relations: Present and Future. *Contemporary Security Policy* 25 (3): 479–497.

Polikanov, Dmitry. 2008. Russia and NATO: Implacable Partners. *The RUSI Journal* 146 (5): 27–31.

Pushkov, Alexey K. 1997. Don't Isolate Us: A Russian View of Nato Expansion. *The National Interest* 47: 58–63.

Roubinski, Youri. 1997. La Russie et l'Otan: Une nouvelle étape? *Politique Étrangère* 62 (4): 543–558.

Savelyev, Alexander G. 1995. La non-prolifération vue de Russie. *Politique Étrangère* 60 (3): 597–608.

Sergounin, Alexander A. 1997. Russian Domestic Debate on NATO Enlargement: From Phobia to Damage Limitation. *European Security* 6 (4): 55–71.

Stepashin, Sergey. 1993. Russia and NATO: A Vital Partnership for European Security. *The RUSI Journal* 138 (4): 11–17.

Tsyganov, Andrey P. 2013. The Russia-NATO Mistrust: Ethnophobia and the Double Expansion to Contain 'the Russian Bear.' *Communist and Post-Communist Studies* 46 (1): 179–188.
Vitale, Alessandro, and Giuseppe Romeo. 2009. *La Russia postimperiale. La tentazione di potenza*. Soveria Mannelli: Rubbettino.

CHAPTER 5

The Anglo-American Special Relationship and NATO: The Past and the Present as Indicators of What Might Come Next?

Alan P. Dobson

Introduction

> Trump is not the first president to complain about insufficient European defence spending, but he is the first to tie the defence spending levels of allies to a willingness to defend them if they are attacked. Strangely, he also appears to believe that allies pay the United States directly, as if NATO collected membership dues rather than members contributing to their own national defence as part of their alliance obligations. (Goldgeier, 2019)

Alan P. Dobson: Deceased

A. P. Dobson (✉)
Swansea University, Swansea, Wales, UK
e-mail: a.p.dobson@swansea.ac.uk

M. de Leonardis (ed.), *NATO in the Post-Cold War Era*, Security, Conflict and Cooperation in the Contemporary World
https://doi.org/10.1007/978-3-031-06063-2_5

These comments by James Goldgeier raise important issues for NATO. First, they point to a level of disruptive animosity between the US and its European allies arising from differing values. Secondly, they illustrate the growing prevalence of misunderstanding and poor communication. They are both equally worrying. Communication between allies is always crucial, but it is even more so for NATO because it is not simply a traditional alliance. NATO has never been grounded solely on security needs, but also on values, attitudes and a sense of community. For those qualities to thrive animosity of a kind recently in evidence in Washington needs to be absent and good communication enjoyed, otherwise the transatlantic community and its sense of 'we-ness' will fracture and, with it, NATO (Dobson and Marsh 2013).

And so, there are problems, but this is far from being a novel scenario. Recently Sten Rynning (2019) noted that in 1956 there was sufficient concern about the quality of transatlantic dialogue that NATO commissioned Lester Pearson of Canada, Halvard Lange of Norway and Gaetano Martino of Italy to consider how appropriate habits of transatlantic consultation could best be nurtured in NATO.[1] Ironically, its prescriptions largely failed, because of the Anglo-American Special Relationship and French understandable truculence over that, but at least there was a rich bilateral Anglo-American transatlantic dialogue that helped keep NATO effective. But then President Nixon and Henry Kissinger posed problems for that conduit of communication by championing secret and exclusive great power diplomacy, which caused massive problems in the 1970s. In part, it prompted revitalisation of the Western European Union, that had developed from the Brussels Treaty signed by the Benelux countries, Britain and France in 1948. It was a defence alliance that preceded NATO but for many years became somewhat dormant once NATO was formed. However, it remained institutionally intact over the years and provided a forum for renewed thinking in Europe about how it might take care of its own defence without such reliance on the US, but the results were hardly commensurate with needs. The end of the Cold War and the refocusing of NATO on more global concerns exacerbated problems of dialogue as NATO searched for a new rationale for its existence and new strategy. It came through that process intact and with a revised remit,

[1] Report of the Committee of Three on Non-Military Cooperation in NATO. 13 December 1956. http://www.nato.int/cps/en/natohq/official_texts_17481.htm. See also Milloy (2006).

though one that did not convince everyone and there was a growing realisation of both Europe's continuing dependence on US military capability and the paucity of European military muscle (Dobson and Marsh 2013). More recently, especially in the aftermath of the 2008 global financial crisis, these issues have caused a real strain in the alliance compounded by US nationalist unilateralism and its concerns about costs, free-riding and diverging values and interests all of which have started to corrode the idea of an Atlantic Community (Dobson and Marsh 2013).

It is these kinds of things that Karl W. Deutsch noted as important many years ago in his study of the transatlantic community. And the community was a word chosen carefully to encapsulate a sense of 'we-ness' as opposed to 'otherness'. What is clear today is that the Atlantic Community is under threat with the nation states that make up the alliance in danger of losing their sense of 'we-ness'. There are a host of complex reasons for this: President Donald Trump's celebration of hyper-nationalism, resurrection of protectionism and his view that NATO is a bad deal for the US; Brexit; political divergences over multilateralism and the Liberal world order; failure of European allies to craft viable defence capabilities; diverging political doctrines within the alliance, most notable in Turkey; NATO's recent global ambitions and a serious down-blip in the Anglo-American Special Relationship (Deutsch et al. 1957).

Within this wide context, Anglo-American relations have traditionally been of considerable importance and an outstanding exemplar of internationally felt we-ness. One only needs to go back to their experience in World War Two and its legacy to appreciate how closely they often worked. They fought side by side and shoulder to shoulder, but in an effort integrated like no other. The system of Combined Boards and the Combined Chiefs of Staff ensured efficient strategy and command, production and distribution of goods, services, armaments and munitions. US Lend-Lease delivered $27 billion worth of goods without payment to the UK and the UK in return delivered $6 billion to the US in reverse Lend-Lease (Allen 1946). American and British officers commanded each other's servicemen. There was widespread sharing of intelligence and technology, including the development of the atom bomb, and close political, social and family friendships were forged, including up to 70,000 British GI war brides who returned with their husbands to the US at the war's end. In 1944 that great Anglo-American, Winston Churchill, fulsomely asserted that Anglo-American relations amounted to a *Special Relationship*.

A complex system of cooperation developed during and after the war not just at the highest political level, but also at institutional levels that often proved resilient when relations at the top became tense. It is important to note that after heated disputes about the future of Palestine and the Jewish State in the 1940s, Suez in the 1950s, Skybolt in the 1960s, Britain and the IMF crisis in the 1970s and the US invasion of Grenada in the 1980s relations soon returned to normal, or were actually strengthened. Much of those renewals had to do with what is sometimes referred to the coral reef of relationships at the military, nuclear, intelligence, economic and cultural levels as well as political moves at the summit level to repair things. Most notable here are two formal agreements. First, the UKUSA intelligence agreements of 1946/1947 involving not just the US and Britain but also Australia, New Zealand and Canada and from which came the use of Menwith Hill in Yorkshire by the US National Security Agency, claimed by some to be the largest US 'spy station' outside the US. And second, the 1958 Agreement for Cooperation on the Uses of Nuclear Technology for Mutual Defence Purposes and the 1962 Nassau Agreement, both of which facilitated military nuclear cooperation and the latter enabled Britain to purchase Polaris Missiles—an agreement that has been periodically renewed ever since.

So, let me turn to these relationships and how they impacted on Anglo-American relations within NATO, which could be seen as something of a bellwether for the future. If the British and the Americans suffer divergence of values and talk past each other in a fog of mutual distrust and misunderstanding as they have done during the presidency of Donald Trump, then that would amount to the demise of a closer sense of 'we-ness' than enjoyed generally in NATO. In that event then what hope for the rest of the allies?

The Most Equal

At the end of the 1980s, in the glow of the Thatcher-Reagan years, one commentator on NATO wrote the following.

> Within the web of consensus, all the USA's NATO allies are equal, but some are more equal than others. Most equal of all is Britain. (Smith, 1989)

And one could support that by noting that the Deputy Commander SACEUR has always been British, that the Channel Command was held by Britain from 1952 to its disbandment in 1994, that the first General Secretary and two later ones were British, namely Lord Ismay, Carrington and Robertson, and between them held office for over 13 years. One could elaborate this further with evidence of close collaboration between Britain and the US over time with the conclusion even more compelling that: 'Most equal of all is Britain'. But this needs nuance, especially at a time when we are possibly on the cusp of radical change. The impact of Brexit, the presidency of Donald Trump and its legacy could be so extensive that configurations in NATO could be transformed. But to know what transformation means here it is important to know what the change is from. In other words, we need an accurate appreciation of what it meant for Britain to be described as the most equal partner of the US in NATO, before we can assess how things might have changed or are changing. However, it is worth making the point now that being the most equal partner did not entail an absence of strong differences of opinion and bitter arguments. Paradoxically, the overall strength of the Special Relationship between Britain and the US allowed just such things to happen and the two case studies that follow amply illustrate that. It would be overambitious of me to try to unravel all of the complexities involved here, but I think that two episodes from the past cast light on the quality of Anglo-American relations, particularly within NATO, and I shall sketch them out in order to achieve a more nuanced sense of what being the most equal partner has meant in the past. Once that has been achieved then we can briefly review the post-Cold War years and then try to read the runes of the present. The two case studies are taken from 1952 and 1989.

SACLANT and Anglo-American Relations

When Winston Churchill returned to power in 1951 as prime minister he was confronted with a NATO agreement, that had been insisted upon by the Americans and accepted by the Labour Government of Clement Attlee. In it, the NATO Supreme Allied Commander of the Atlantic (SACLANT) was to be an American. Churchill felt that Britain's power, prestige and status had all slipped badly and unwarrantedly so under the Attlee government. And he was determined to reverse that trend as much as he could, which included trying to overturn the decision to have an

American SACLANT. His opportunity to try came in January 1952 at a summit meeting with President Truman in Washington and he briefed his delegation accordingly (Dobson 1997; Dobson and Marsh 2010).[2]

At an Anglo-American Chiefs of Staff meeting on 6 January initial exchanges were between General of the US Army, Omar N. Bradley and US Admiral William M. Fechteler, who was SACLANT designate, on one side and the British First Sea Lord, Admiral Sir Rhoderick R. McGrigor from the other. McGrigor argued, as instructed by Churchill, for the division of the Atlantic between the Royal and US navies, which effectively meant side-lining NATO. Bradley responded that while he was aware of British difficulties he did not feel 'the problem of the Atlantic was one which could be dealt with outside NATO'.[3] The Americans tried to be accommodating within that principle but then Chief of the Imperial General Staff, Field Marshall William Slim, intervened and placed the Americans on the spot. Essentially the British wanted to control their own defence destiny and there was a danger of that being compromised if British forces in NATO could not be used to what the British and not NATO thought would be to best effect. But instead of continuing to make a direct argument for that, Slim asked: 'what the comparable situation was in the Western Atlantic and the coastal waters of the United States eastern seaboard'.[4] Fechteler felt obliged to explain:

> ... all United States naval officers were under the orders of the Chief of Naval operations, the latter could, and would, intervene if in his judgment operations vitally affecting the United States, whether in the Western Atlantic or coastal waters, were not being properly conducted. If necessary, and in emergency, he could withdraw United States forces from the control of SACLANT.[5]

Not surprisingly, as the official record blandly put it, there followed 'a general discussion on the principles involved'. The outcome was:

[2] For more detail on the summit see Dobson (1997); Dobson and Marsh (2010).

[3] Minutes of British and US Chiefs of Staff Meeting. 6 January 1952. TNA. CAB 21/3057.

[4] Ibid.

[5] Ibid.

a. Although it was agreed that it was an inalienable right of any Government or Head of a national Service to withdraw from NATO to control his national forces if national interests were being vitally affected this struck at the whole root of the NATO concept. Although we should recognise this right undoubtedly existed its existence should not be stressed in any written document, particularly since similar arguments could be applied to air forces.
b. In the same way as US Chief of Naval Operations maintained a right to intervene in matters vitally affecting the US there could be no doubt that the First Sea Lord could exercise a similar right in regard to vital UK interests.[6]

After the conference McGrigor clearly spelt out to colleagues what the Americans had conceded.

> ... the First Sea Lord should be able to instruct Commander-in-Chief, East Atlantic to divert British naval and air forces into the United Kingdom coastal waters in emergency but there was anxiety that this should not be published or discussed in N.A.T.O. circles.[7]

This episode is instructive in three ways. First, it demonstrates the more equal status of Britain than others in its relationship with the US in NATO. Between them they came to understandings, which were not to be discussed or even mentioned among other NATO members. Secondly, it demonstrates that the relationship, while clearly one of junior to senior partner, was not hegemonic. Churchill bemoaned the facts of reality on his journey to the US when he lamented: 'They [the Americans] have become so great and we are now so small. Poor England!' (Wilson 1966). But that did not mean that the Americans always got their own way on everything. They did on the major point—they retained SACLANT for an American commander, but they had to make concessions. Thirdly, anyone who looks in detail at the discussions and the way Churchill harangued the Americans over SACLANT at the summit in Washington will realise just how turbulent things could be between these two closest of allies.

[6] Ibid.

[7] First Sea Lord Chief of Naval Staff to various CI Chiefs. 24 January 1952. ADM 205/85.

Such turbulence was not uncommon and was possible because it was contained within parameters of mutual respect derived from shared values and common interests.

The SNF Crisis and Anglo-American Relations[8]

In 1989 the world changed dramatically. The Cold War gradually wound down to closure and change always brings challenges. For Anglo-American relations a major one came in May immediately after the 40th anniversary summit meeting of NATO leaders in Brussels where US President George H.W. Bush had to cope with serious difficulties, namely his and Britain's wish to modernise short range nuclear weapons deployed in Europe and the political difficulties that posed for his West German ally Chancellor Helmut Kohl. Kohl depended on a coalition partner to sustain him in power whose party was strongly opposed to SNF modernisation and there was wide popular support, including from opposition political parties, which were gaining ground, for a de-nuclearised West Germany. All this was very difficult for Kohl with domestic general elections looming close. In the end Bush pushed through a controversial compromise agreement, which in its making and its effect was not palatable to British Prime Minister Margaret Thatcher. Bush ruled out any zero option for SNF, but there was also uncertainty about SNF modernisation. However, in some ways even worse was to come for Thatcher. Speaking immediately after the summit to a West German audience in the Rheigoldhalle in Mainz, Bush said that:

> The United States and the Federal Republic have always been firm friends and allies. But today we share the added role – partners in leadership. (Bush 1989).[9]

Thatcher was furious. Compromise on SNF had been bad enough but where did this statement leave the Anglo-American Special Relationship?

[8] This section is taken from a work in progress, Dobson, A.P. 'How Special is Special?' Prime Minister Margaret Thatcher and President George H. Bush's Visit to London in May–June 1989, paper presented at a one-day conference Manchester Metropolitan University, 7 December 2018 on US presidential visits to the UK.

[9] For some general coverage of the Anglo-American relationship and Bush's foreign policy see: Pugh and Williams (1990) and Dumbrell (2001).

The next day Bush travelled to London where journalists were quick to pounce on the perceived threat to Britain's specialness. The first question posed at a press conference in 10 Downing Street after talks between Thatcher and Bush was: 'Is Britain America's most important ally in Europe?' (Bush and Thatcher 1989). Thatcher fielded the question diplomatically pointing out that Britain had many friends but '... we pride ourselves at being among the foremost of the United States friends, and we will always be'. 'Very Good answer', opined Bush before being asked whether West Germany and France would now soon join in the Special Relationship. He replied to that in part by saying 'I've always felt – that we have a very, very special relationship. But it needn't be at the expense of our friendship with other countries' (Baker and DeFrank 1995).

About all of this rather laboured language Thatcher later recalled in her memoirs:

> When the President came to London he sought to deal with the problems those remarks [about Germany as partner in leadership] had caused by saying that we too were partners in leadership. But the damage had been done. (Thatcher 1993)

However, the key to understanding why Bush did what he did lay in two facts. First, the Americans knew that Thatcher's priority, as she herself put it: '... is agreement between the US and Britain' (Thatcher 1993). In other words, the last thing that she wanted was a public schism between the US and the UK. Secondly, the Americans assessed that unlike Kohl, Thatcher had no domestic political constraints and could be flexible if she wanted to. On 19 May, well ahead of the NATO Summit, Secretary of State Baker met Bush and told him 'You've got to lead the alliance and that means getting Margaret to compromise'. And that is what the Americans did, knowing that it would cause anger and resentment from Thatcher, but that at the end of the day there would be no irreparable harm to Anglo-American relations: there would be no rift. It was largely, though not entirely, about managing perceptions. Both Kohl and Thatcher had publicly expressed their positions strongly before the summit took place in attempts to pre-empt matters. Bush did not care too much for that and was especially irritated by the series of statements and leaks that set out the West German position. That said, he knew Thatcher's inflexibility well and he and his entourage of advisers therefore came forward with a compromise without prior consultation with her. In many ways that was the most galling thing for Thatcher and it left a bitter taste in her mouth that lingered on till she wrote her memoirs. And the bitterness was sharpened by Bush's description of the US–West German relationship as partners in leadership. But if one looks at the actual nature of the compromise Thatcher actually achieved far more of her substantive objectives than Kohl: the only one she failed to achieve was a clear commitment to and timetable for SNF modernisation. Maybe Bush sensed that the reality of the compromise benefited Thatcher and that was why he felt the need for the flattery of 'partners in leadership' in Mainz. The interweaving of perceptions and substantive goals created a complex dilemma for Bush at the NATO Summit. He resolved it the best way he could, even though that meant acting unilaterally over composing the compromise, which hurt Thatcher, and cosying up to Kohl, which aggravated the hurt. All this contrasted starkly with how most affairs had been dealt with by Thatcher and Bush's predecessor Ronald Reagan and that also added nuance to perceptions. Bush did what he felt he had to do for the good of the Western Alliance and that temporarily meant side-lining the Special Relationship, but he soon set about trying to repair it, recover its quality and re-position it centre stage while in London. Bush's perspective was that the ties that bind the Anglo-American relationship were so strong they would not break. And he knew that Thatcher thought likewise. So, the overriding likelihood was that the Special Relationship would endure. And it did as events in the First Gulf War amply demonstrated.

What can we draw from this episode? Firstly, the relationship between the US and the UK in NATO was not as exclusive as it had been in the early 1950s. Secondly, it was increasingly difficult for Germany and France to be treated as outliers in key decisions as they had sometimes been in the 1950s: this was especially the case after 2009 with regard to France after it reintegrated into NATO's military command structure. And thirdly, both Britain's Special Relationship with the US in NATO and its overall standing and importance to the US had diminished. Notwithstanding those changes and the differences in chemistry between Thatcher and Reagan compared with Thatcher and Bush, both sides still perceived of the Special Relationship as resilient and important and both sought outcomes compatible with the good health and welfare of the NATO Alliance and as in 1952 crafted compromises accordingly. Also, as in 1952, there was a robustness to the Anglo-American relationship which allowed frank and sometimes angry exchanges because of policy differences and yet the ties that bound them within a Special Relationship continued not just at the broad and deeply integrated institutional levels of defence and intelligence cooperation, but at the top political and diplomatic levels as well. The parameters of common values and interests still contained the disagreements and allowed for a constructive outcome.

Post-Cold War Relations

Of course, relations did not end in 1989 either for the Special Relationship or within NATO, but many thought that the end of the Cold War would bring significant changes. Relations had been special indeed during the Reagan-Thatcher political affair, but the end of the Cold War brought radical change and for a while it looked as if both NATO and the Special Relationship with Britain might be casualties. But the war in the Middle East changed perspectives again. Barely four weeks after air strikes began Operation Desert Storm to liberate Kuwait from its Iraqi invaders, President George H.W. Bush expressed his gratitude for British military support. At the White House, he requested of the British Defence Secretary Tom King:

> Please tell John Major [British Prime Minister] I appreciate the cooperation of the United Kingdom and his personal role. .... The British military is doing extremely well. The British briefs help show that the United States is not going it alone. The American people find it reassuring when they see we are not in this by ourselves. This is terribly important.[10]

Before the Gulf War Bush had looked increasingly to Chancellor Kohl's Germany, finally reunified in October 1990, for his main European ally and partner in leadership, but standing shoulder to shoulder in conflict soon reversed the down-blip in the Anglo-American Special Relationship and yet again it arose Lazarus-like and flourished.

After John Major and with Tony Blair entering office as prime minister in 1997 the Special Relationship blossomed even more, underpinned by parallel developments of political doctrine in the US and the UK often

[10] Memorandum of conversation between President Bush, British Defence Secretary Tom King, US Defense Secretary Dick Cheney, UK Ambassador Acland, Brent Scowcroft et al. 12 February 1991. George H. W. Bush Library. Scowcroft Papers. Presidential Correspondence File, box 2, folder: 91, 108–004.

referred to as The Third Way. In effect it was a revival of Keynesian social democracy with more emphasis on the importance of government provision of health, education and welfare to enable citizens, in the words of the British social welfare Liberal Thomas Hill Green, 'to make the best of themselves'. It came as of little surprise that President Bill Clinton and Blair got on well together, though there were some tetchy differences, for example over Kosovo and NATO military intervention there, but what amazed many was the close bonding that took place between Blair and Clinton's successor George W. Bush.

That bonding was largely due to developments in the Middle East and the Second Gulf War triggered by the 9/11 outrage. If the First Gulf War helped to underline the importance of the Special Relationship, its military component the Second Gulf War did so even more. Following 11 September 2001, Blair positioned himself 'shoulder to shoulder' with the Americans and strove to show how useful Britain could be. Blair engaged in a form of Kissingeresque mediating between the US and European allies who were doubtful about US policies and provided strong British military support for the invasion of Iraq. Blair's actions produced dividends for the Special Relationship, if not for his longer-term political reputation. After Bush's successful re-election a conservative think-tank in Washington declared:

> British Prime Minister Tony Blair will be the first foreign head of state to visit George W. Bush following his re-election victory. The November 11 and 12 Washington summit between the world's two most powerful leaders will take place against the back-drop of a major U.S.-led offensive against insurgents in Fallujah and just months ahead of national elections across Iraq. (Gardiner and Hulsman 2004)

This was the first time in decades that anyone had intimated that a British prime minister was the second most powerful man in the world. A more measured, but equally revealing comment came from Lincoln P. Bloomfield, US Assistant Secretary of State for Political-Military Affairs: 'The U.S.-U.K. political-military partnership has produced today the closest and most capable bilateral military alliance in the world' (Bloomfield 2004). All this clearly had implications for Anglo-American relations within NATO.

As NATO changed with the end of the Cold War and sought new priorities Britain worked closely with the US on crisis after crisis supporting NATO enlargement and helping to consolidate ex-Soviet Bloc East European countries within the Western family of nations by promoting EU enlargement. The fact that Lord Robertson was Secretary General of NATO from 1999 to 2004 facilitated good Anglo-American relations within NATO and in the wider Special Relationship as he oversaw the response to 9/11 and the first ever invocation of Article 5 in a move of alliance solidarity with the US. Generally, under the premiership of Tony Blair Anglo-American relations stayed special even though Blair moved closer to Europe on some issues. At the same time Britain still self-excluded itself from the euro zone, collaborated closely with the US on monetary, defence and intelligence policies, and, while it pursued the development of the European Security and Defence Policy (ESDP), it was with the aim of making it compatible and complementary to NATO. One could say that the British saw the ESDP as a way to increase Europe's military capability and get even closer to the Americans, make themselves more significant militarily and help close the inter-operability gap with the US.

Even after Bush and Blair left office, while relations seemed less warm, they nevertheless continued to be constructive and mutually supportive in NATO and the wider Special Relationship. When a direct and challenging threat to NATO came when David Cameron was in 10 Downing Street and Barack Obama in the White House, they both responded firmly and in tandem. The problem was with Vladimir Putin's Russia and the crisis in the Ukraine as the Crimea broke away. Both Obama and Cameron tried to do what they could without provoking direct hostilities. Cameron took the lead in the EU in calling for sanctions against Russia for its takeover of the Crimea (Watt 2014). And Obama led the move to strengthen NATO forces in Eastern Europe (Crowley 2016). The tradition of close Anglo-American cooperation seemed well-embedded and set to continue even when relations at the top were not of the warmest. The institutionalised links that bound the US and the UK together as allies and within NATO seemed indeed to be like a coral reef of long endurance providing mutual benefit in nuclear weapons, intelligence gathering and sharing and joint military operations such as the invasion of Iraq in 2003 and operations under the auspices of NATO in Afghanistan. While Britain's capabilities have relatively declined, asymmetry in its relations with the US grown, the importance of the Special Relationship declined and NATO's role has been a source of debate and controversy since the end of the Cold War, that sense of we-ness between the US and Britain seems to have endured and with overall benefit to NATO: at least one could say that with a considerable degree of confidence until the arrival of Donald Trump in the White House in 2017.

Conclusions

The specialness of Anglo-American relations continues to wax and wane over time and the latter condition seemed evident in President Obama's pivot to Asia, which raised questions over the status of Anglo-American relations as well as the NATO alliance. One could plausibly suggest that NATO has suffered a long-term trajectory of decline in importance since the end of the Cold War, but it has been neither precipitous nor terminal at any point up to the entry of Donald Trump into the White House (Deni 2019). It would be premature to hazard a final judgement on what the overall impact of Trump's term in office has and will continue to have on Anglo-American relations and the consequences for relationships more widely in NATO, but the auguries are not encouraging.

Both the SACLANT and SNF controversies within Anglo-American relations help indicate a more realistic starting point to assess how relations have shifted between the two allies within NATO during the last few years. One can see the limitations of being the most equal partner and that the concept of 'the most equal' has diminished over time. That is one thing, but it is quite another to sum up the problems of the Anglo-American relationship while Trump was in office as follows. This is how ex-UK Ambassador to the US Sir Peter John Westmacott put it.

> ...at the government level, the facts are pretty clear that on a number of issues that are important for Britain and where we've traditionally seen eye-to-eye with the Americans — like climate change and free trade, like the Middle East and Arab-Israeli issues, like the Iran nuclear deal... the EU and NATO. Those are all areas where President Trump has up-ended the normal way of seeing things and the normal ways Britain and America have seen eye-to-eye. ... So, on those things we're not in the same place and I very much hope we'll get back to it. (Ellyatt 2018)

While Britain has arguably been the most equal of America's partners in NATO, their relationship has always been asymmetrical and increasingly so; it has often been robust in terms of differences and exchanges;

but there has been a closeness that warrants the use of Special Relationship. That relationship has changed over time, with rises and declines in its intensity and closeness, but with Trump in the White House for the first time since World War Two there appeared to be a real danger of sustained and irreparable divergence at the top political level. One might argue that this was no different than disputes over the Palestine issue in the 1940s, Suez in the 1950s, Skybolt in the 1960s and the US invasion of Grenada in the 1980s, but there was now a rather new development. The long existing parameters, formed of common values and interests, within which robust but productive negotiations could take place, were eroded or even cast aside. Having said that, many times and oft has the demise of the Special Relationship been predicted in the past only for it to rise Phoenix-like to prosper again and with Biden's victory in November 2020 that opportunity at least offers itself once again: as Westmacott put it maybe Biden will allow the two countries to 'get back to it', to return to their long-term parallel thinking and sharing of perspectives. However, in the meantime the Anglo-American axis so often influential in NATO appears to be in abeyance. The kinds of robust and honest exchanges over both SACLANT and SNF taking place with Trump as president were just implausible. Mutual respect and a concordance of overall policies are needed to enable such exchanges and such qualities were singularly lacking between Trump and Prime Minister Theresa May and transpired to be little better between Trump and May's successor Boris Johnson, particularly in the light of the British decision to allow significant participation by the Chinese company Huawei in developing its G5 network. Even though Johnson later back-tracked, partly at least because of pressure from the US, the whole episode left sour taste in the mouths on both sides. Trump's relations with NATO leaders have been fraught to say the least. And NATO in recent years could no longer rely on Anglo-American consensus for supporting the alliance and that is largely symptomatic not just of a decline in the Special Relationship under Trump, but also dislike and contempt of NATO by the president. It is difficult to build consensus in NATO when the president of the US questions the value of its existence. Things are promising to be very different in tone and content with President Joe Biden. Relations are certainly more tranquil and already there is a return to a familiar normality. But NATO has serious issues to contend with whether Trump is there or not and just how constructive the Anglo-American relationship can be to help address them is difficult to assess at this early stage of the Biden presidency. Biden and Prime Minister

Johnson are hardly naturally paired, Brexit could seriously muddy the waters here—for many reasons including the new Irish border issue—and it may be more difficult than in the past for the Special Relationship to play a constructive role in NATO.

Brexit is an important component in all this, but perhaps not a controlling one. While specialness has remained a factor in Anglo-American relations, with Trump and Brexit its status has down-spiralled rapidly at the highest political level, and that also has negative consequences for NATO. First of all because of Trump's hostile attitude towards the alliance; secondly because bilateral Anglo-American relations are struggling and cannot be relied upon to help stabilise NATO's uncertain future and thirdly because the time of the British government for nigh on three years has been consumed by the politics of, preparation for and negotiations about Brexit to the cost of policy-making elsewhere, including foreign and defence policy. All British policy-making has suffered from the time and energy that has had to be focused on Brexit, and in the last eighteen months on the Covid-19 pandemic, but both will pass. While there will be difficulties ahead for both the EU and Britain, even with the 'Christmas Eve Agreement', their mutual commitment to NATO and their sense of collegial defence is unlikely to diminish. In 2017, Britain was one of only 6 NATO members who spent 2% or more of their GDP on defence, but France's was substantial at just over 1.7%, and it is the Anglo-French defence axis upon which Europe would have to rely for its collective defence if NATO were to become dysfunctional. Even before President Trump arrived on the scene Britain and France had moved into closer defence cooperation through the 2010 Lancaster House Treaties and that was later reaffirmed by President Macron and Theresa May at the Sandhurst Summit in January 2018. Macron has expressed some controversial opinions on NATO, most notably his dubbing of it as 'brain dead' in an interview for *The Economist* in November 2019, but he is clearly committed to strengthening Europe's defence capability.[11] Brexit will probably not affect these relationships. And even though it would be a rather frail replacement for NATO with the US at its heart, Franco-British cooperation within a continuing close overall relationship with the EU's Common Security and Defence Policy might be the best road ahead if

[11] The Economist (7 November 2019). Emmanuel Macron warns Europe: NATO is becoming brain-dead. https://www.economist.com/europe/2019/11/07/emmanuel-macron-warns-europe-nato-is-becoming-brain-dead.

NATO were to weaken or unravel. The trick for Britain here might be to ensure that Macron's expressed desire for more European strategic autonomy does not undermine NATO, an agenda Britain has pursued consistently with US support and approval since ESDP took shape.

Throughout all of these considerations of what has happened over the last few years runs President Trump and his attitude towards NATO and Europe in general including the UK. At the moment there is a distinct possibility of a return to normality in NATO and the Special Relationship because of the resilience of coral reefs of institutionalised cooperation that go on below the highest political levels and the success of Joe Biden in the 2020 presidential election. The institutional framework in both the Special Relationship and NATO is wonderfully robust. It would take a long and dedicated effort to unravel the depth of intelligence and defence cooperation that is carried on at an extensive Anglo-American institutional level. Similar considerations apply to NATO and importantly, US military leaders have repeatedly differed with Trump over his statements on NATO. If Trump had won re-election then the coral reefs could have decomposed through hostility and neglect from the top in Washington over a more extended period of time. NATO, the Special Relationship, the longstanding character of the US–EU relationship—they could all have been things of the past or rendered irrelevant to world affairs.

Perhaps it was with these thoughts in mind that the NATO Reflection Group in its 2020 report concluded that:

> ... it is essential that all Allies recommit to the spirit as well as the letter of the Washington Treaty, reaffirm their political commitment to one another, sustain their commitment to democratic values, and glean the benefits that come from the projection of collective strength.[12]

With Biden in the White House these essentials of the alliance of 'we-ness' might be possible of realisation once again. There is also an opportunity to renew the Special Relationship, though it will probably not be repaired to what it was before. Whatever form it takes, it will undoubtedly be a constructive if diminished co-worker with NATO, hopefully with the

[12] NATO 2030: United for a New Era. Analysis and Recommendations of the Reflection Group Appointed by the NATO Secretary General, 25 November 2020. https://www.nato.int/nato_static_fl2014/assets/pdf/2020/12/pdf/201201-Reflection-Group-Final-Report-Uni.pdf.

ability for both British and American partners to speak truly and robustly to each other. All of which might once again empower NATO to tussle with its ongoing problems and challenges in a more positive and collegial manner.

Bibliography

Allen, Roy G.D. 1946. Mutual Aid Between the US and the British Empire, 1941–45. *Journal of the Royal Statistical Society* 109: 243–271.

Baker, James A., and Thomas M. DeFrank. 1995. *Politics of Diplomacy: Revolution, War and Peace 1989–1992*. New York: Putnams.

Bloomfield, Lincoln P. Jr. 2004. Post-Election Strategic Priorities for the United States. Remarks at the Chatham House Conference on Matching Capabilities to Commitments—Can Europe Deliver? London, United Kingdom. U.S. Department of State, December 6. https://2001-2009.state.gov/t/pm/rls/rm/39737.htm.

Bush, George H.W. 1989. Bush Presidential Remarks, Rheingoldhalle, Mainz, May 31. Presidential Library, College Station, Texas. Box 1, White House Press Office, file OA2313 (2).

Bush, George H.W., and Margaret Thatcher. 1989. Thatcher and Bush Remarks, 10 Downing Street, June 1. Bush Library. Box 1, White House Press Office, file OA2313 (3).

Crowley, Michael. 2016. Obama's Ukraine Policy in Shambles. *Politico*, February 29. https://www.politico.com/story/2016/02/obama-ukraine-russia-putin-219783.

Deni, John R. 2019. Staying Alive by Overeating: The Enduring NATO Alliance at 70. *Journal of Transatlantic Studies* 17 (2): 157–175.

Deutsch, Karl W., Sidney A. Burrell, Robert A. Kann, Maurice Lee, Martin Lichterman, Raymond E. Lindgren, Francis L. Loewenheim, and Richard W. Van Wagenen. 1957. *Political Community and the North Atlantic Area: International Organization in the Light of Historical Experience*. Princeton: Princeton University Press.

Dobson, Andrew P. 1997. Informally Special? The Churchill-Truman Talks of January 1952 and the State of Anglo-American Relations. *Review of International Studies* 23: 27–47.

Dobson, Andrew P., and Steve Marsh. 2010. Churchill and Truman at the Summit: SACLANT and the Tone of Anglo-American Relations in January 1952. *International History Review* 32: 211–228.

Dobson, Andrew P., and Steve Marsh. 2013. Fine Words, Few Answers: NATO's Not so New, New Strategic Concept. In *NATO Beyond 9/11: The Transformation of the Transatlantic Alliance*, ed. Ellen Hallams, Luca Ratti, and Benjamin Zyla, 155–178. New York: Palgrave Macmillan.

Dumbrell, John. 2001. *A Special Relationship: Anglo-American Relations in the Cold War and After*. London: Macmillan.
Ellyatt, Holly. 2018. Is the US-UK 'Special Relationship' Still Special? *CNBC*, July 12. https://www.cnbc.com/2018/07/11/is-the-us-uk-special-relationship-still-special.html.
Gardiner, Nile, and John Hulsman. 2004. The Bush/Blair Washington Summit. Heritage Foundation, November 10. https://www.heritage.org/europe/report/the-bushblair-washington-summit-strengthening-us-british-world-leadership.
Goldgeier, James. 2019. NATO at 70: Is the United States Still in It for the Long Haul? *Journal of Transatlantic Studies* 17: 255–267.
Milloy, John C. 2006. *The North Atlantic Treaty Organization, 1948–1957: Community or Alliance?* Montreal: McGill-Queen's University Press.
Pugh, Michael C., and Phil Williams, eds. 1990. *Superpower Politics: Change in the United States and the Soviet Union*. Manchester: Manchester University Press.
Rynning, Sten. 2019. Sustaining NATO by Consultation: Hard Choices for Europe. *Journal of Transatlantic Studies* 17 (2): 139–157.
Smith, Dan. 1989. *Pressure: How America Runs NATO*. London: Bloomsbury.
Thatcher, Margaret. 1993. *The Downing Street Years*. London: Harper Collins.
Watt, Nicholas. 2014. Crimea Crisis: Cameron to Propose Range of Sanctions Against Russia. *The Guardian*, March 3. https://www.theguardian.com/world/2014/mar/03/crimea-crisis-david-cameron-sanctions-russia-ukraine.
Wilson (Lord Moran), Charles M. 1966. *Winston Churchill: The Struggle for Survival, 1940–1965 (Diaries of Lord Moran)*. London: Constable.

CHAPTER 6

The Role of NATO in European Integration

Luca Ratti and Alessandro Leonardi

Introduction

The chapter debates the impact of NATO on European integration from the beginning of the transatlantic security partnership in the late 1940s until the present day. It specifically addresses the complex issues connected to the relationship between European endeavours to secure a US defence pledge and cooperation on the continent. In the 1940s European defence cooperation pursued multiple tasks: securing a United States legally binding commitment to European security, containing the Soviet Union and crafting a series of multilateral Euro-Atlantic arrangements, that would allow the restoration of German sovereignty. The

Luca Ratti has authored the introduction, the first section and the sections on NATO and European security after the Cold War. Alessandro Leonardi has authored the sections addressing the issue of West German rearmament, the European Defence Community and the Western European Union as well as the section addressing the impact of Brexit on European defence.

L. Ratti (✉)
History of International Relations at Università of Roma3, Rome, Italy
e-mail: luca.ratti@uniroma3.it

M. de Leonardis (ed.), *NATO in the Post-Cold War Era*, Security, Conflict and Cooperation in the Contemporary World
https://doi.org/10.1007/978-3-031-06063-2_6

German question inextricably linked the transatlantic security community and European integration. In the second half of the 1940s, together with fears of Germany's revisionism, concerns about the USSR's ambitions triggered some of the first steps towards West European security cooperation, such as the 1947 Dunkirk Treaty and the 1948 Brussels Treaty Organization (BTO). Fears about Soviet intentions also convinced the United States to support the establishment of a West European security bloc as part of a wider security area, which was formalized with the establishment in April 1949 of the North Atlantic Treaty (NAT).

It is from this assumption that the chapter proceeds as follows. The first section focuses on the relationship between European integration and negotiations for a North Atlantic Treaty in the late 1940s, showing how the United Kingdom and France endeavoured to secure a US defence pledge to Western Europe rather than to foster effective integration. The second section debates the rise and failure of the European Defence Community (EDC) in the early 1950s, assessing the merits of the policies of the United Kingdom and France and US irritation at the slow pace of their initiatives until the creation of the Western European Union (WEU) in 1954 and West German membership of NATO in 1955, before debating French President Charles de Gaulle's criticism of the Alliance and West European endeavours to resume cooperation in the areas of security and defence between the late 1970s and early 1980s. The following section highlights the interaction between US endeavours to preserve NATO and European security cooperation at the Cold War's end. Then, the chapter reviews the steps leading to the establishment of the European Union's Common Security and Defence Policy (CSDP) with the treaty of Lisbon and the impact of Brexit on European defence cooperation.

Automatism and Discrimination: European Defence Before the North Atlantic Treaty: 1947–1949

In the heydays of the Cold War, a key objective of West European decision-makers was to secure a US commitment to European security.

A. Leonardi
History of International Relations from the University of Florence, Florence, Italy

However, there were some deep differences among Western Europeans and between them and the U.S about how best to proceed. These differences arose mainly over how to deal with Germany. American fears of foreign entanglements and European fears of abandonment were crucial. Already with the signing of the inter-American treaty of reciprocal assistance in September 1947 in Rio de Janeiro, Washington had encouraged cooperation among the countries of the American continent against the Soviet and communist threat, spearheading the formation of a regional security system in the Western hemisphere. The Truman administration regarded the coordination of Western Europe's most important states as a stepping stone towards a wider transatlantic security system. However, the ultimate success of the US strategy depended on the removal of animosities among Western Europeans. The Americans were wary of bilateral security agreements and reluctant to offer binding commitments to the French and the British. For this reason, they regarded the 1947 Dunkirk treaty, being directed solely against Germany, as 'unreal and inadequate' and believed that any regional agreement should be inserted within the framework of a wider initiative (TNA 1948).[1]

On the contrary, the British viewed the treaty of Dunkirk as a first step towards a broader West European security endeavour (Baylis 1982: 236–247). Eager to maintain its role as a global power, the United Kingdom endeavoured to play the role of a transatlantic 'bridge builder' between the 'declining Europe' and the United States. The United States was virtually unscathed by the Second World War but historically adverse to participate in entangling alliances. While regarding their participation in any supernational venture inconsistent with a world power status, the British skilfully promoted and backed intergovernmental cooperation with France and Benelux to lure and keep the Americans in Europe. Moreover, while lacking manpower and heavily affected by financial constraints, London did not shy away from assuring an automatic commitment to European defence. In March 1948 the UK, France and the Benelux countries concluded a mutual assistance pact that bonded them together for 50 years through the establishment of the Brussels Treaty Organization (BTO). The Brussels Treaty provided for economic cooperation, a declaration of intention on social matters, the development of cultural exchanges and mutual and automatic assistance in the event

[1] *The National Archives*. Kew, *(TNA)*, TNA: FO 371/73045, Inverchapel-Hickerson meeting, Telegram No. 324, 21 January 1948.

of attack (FRUS 1948: 9). Like the Dunkirk Treaty, the BTO entailed the British automatic commitment to European security and identified in the preamble the 'renewal of German policy of aggression' as the main source of threat in order to reassure French anxieties and avoid provoking the USSR. Although its Article 4 established a common defence pledge against any external attack, for American decision-makers and other West European countries the tight connection between its automatism and discriminatory character—against a political entity geographically within its 'sphere' of competence—made it deeply flawed to promote a thorough reconciliation and effective security cooperation among Western Europeans. Together with the Berlin blockade in late spring, however, it pushed Congress to pass the Vandenberg resolution in June, speeding the path to the signing of North Atlantic Treaty (NAT) in April and the FRG's establishment in May 1949. Through Article 5 of the NAT Washington promised assistance to the Western Europeans against Soviet aggression but stopped short of making an automatic pledge to military intervention (NATO 1949).[2] However, while lacking an automatic commitment, the NAT did not contain any discriminatory clause. The treaty did not single out any source of threat. Its defence provisions were directed against no country but against the very concept of military menace to the signatories' security and territorial integrity. On the contrary, by stating that: 'the Parties may, by unanimous agreement, invite any other European State…to contribute to the security of the North Atlantic area', Article 10 of the treaty reiterated the US preference for a wider security bloc. While not implying any 'double containment' provisions and failing to single out any country, the non-discriminatory NAT theoretically left the door open to generally unwelcomed applicants, alongside the more palatable and natural ones. On the eve of the 1952 Lisbon North Atlantic Council (NAC) Greece and Turkey were admitted into the Alliance, although the main conundrum for Western decision-makers remained the modalities of West German participation in the defence of the West.

[2] The official text of the North Atlantic Treaty is available at https://www.nato.int/cps/en/natolive/official_texts_17120.htm.

The Conditioned De-discrimination: Germany, the Failure of the EDC, and the Creation of the WEU (1950–1954)

In the following years, West German rearmament rapidly gained centre stage in US and Western defence strategies. However, while the Joint Chiefs of Staff had already reconciled themselves with this hypothesis by the early 1950s, there was no unanimous support for rearmament among US officials. Some key figures within the administration, including Secretary of State Dean Acheson and High Commissioner in Germany John McCloy were concerned about moving too fast in transforming their relationship with Germany. The 'struggle for the soul of Faust'—as McCloy labelled it—had to be carefully fought keeping in mind the dangers connected with the 'resurgence of German nationalism'. Among Western Europeans also the French perceived German rearmament as premature and potentially threatening, while the British, although in principle being in favour of West Germany's participation in transatlantic defence, feared a Europe dominated politically and economically by Germany (DBPO 1950: 81–87). Their preferred option was West Germany's participation in the Council of Europe. Furthermore, according to the British viewpoint, it would have been unthinkable 'to rearm Germany until French strength had been greatly revived' (DBPO 1950: 117).

It was the eruption of the Korean War in June 1950 which, dramatically exposing the conventional military imbalance in Europe, decisively broke the deadlock, prompting Washington to commit several divisions to the United Nations (UN) forces in Korea and strengthening in the eyes of American decision-makers the need to find an alternative solution in the form of a rapid rehabilitation of West Germany under the leadership of France or, if necessary, under the US lead (Deighton 2010: 10–12). Also West German decision-makers were in favour of rearmament, viewing it as an opportunity to strengthen their country's democratic credentials and association with the West. In March 1950, the FRG's chancellor, Konrad Adenauer, suggested the formation of a Franco-German union as a foundation for the United States of Europe (Adenauer 1966: 244–248).

West European misgivings about German rearmament caused irritation in the United States. Already in some of the NSC 68 series, US officials had remarked that to strengthen the West against Russia it may be inevitable to sanction West German rearmament (FRUS 1950: 237–292). By late spring 1950 France's prime minister, Georges Bidault, and his foreign minister, Robert Schuman, had also accepted the principle of a West German contribution to Western defence. However, they demanded as a precondition the creation of a highly integrated NATO structure, including the appointment of a supreme commander and the establishment of a combined military staff (Creswell and Trachtenberg 2003). Furthermore, in May 1950 Schuman proposed the pooling of Franco-German coal and steel production under the joint supervision of a European High Authority. However, the French government remained particularly sceptical that the Anglo-Americans would be able to control Germany after it was rearmed.

The Pleven Plan and the European Defence Community (EDC)

In the autumn of 1950 Prime Minister René Pleven's proposal for the establishment of an integrated European army, consisting of small national battalions to be merged into the international army corps triggered mixed reactions in Washington and London. The plan provided the French with a tool 'of self-protection against American pressure' (DBPO 1950). However, it also exposed deep differences among the Western Europeans, particularly between the United Kingdom and France on the modalities of Germany's contribution. Although London did not stand in the way of Paris, Whitehall feared the federalist leanings of the French proposal and its impact on NATO. The UK's reservations about the Pleven plan further increased following the Conservative Party's return to power in October 1951. The new Conservative cabinet regarded the French project as impracticable and drew a clear distinction between cooperation within Europe and a European federation. The UK's refusal to play an active role in plans for European military integration caused much disappointment across the Atlantic: Eisenhower later remarked that he used 'every resource, including argument, cajolery and sheer prayer to get Winston to say a single kind word about EDC' (Gowland and Turner 2000: 60). Other West European governments, however, also reacted cautiously to the Pleven plan, fearing a strengthening of French influence. To counter these risks, Italy's Christian Democratic Prime Minister Alcide De Gasperi boldly proposed the merging of the European Coal and Steel Community (ECSC) and the EDC together through the establishment of a European 'federal' structure. The Americans, including the first Supreme Allied Commander in Europe, Dwight D. Eisenhower, were very supportive of the Italian plan (FRUS 1951: 439). Since its approval in October 1950, the Medium-Term Defence Plan (MTDP) had endorsed a clear-cut division of labour between the conventional-armed Western European and US land forces and nuclear-equipped American heavy and medium bombers controlled by the Strategic Air Command. While the MTDP was already entailing a nuclear strategy, it was still proposing a doctrine based on territorial defence with conventional forces. However, as the Force Goals' downward revisions were already confirming, Western governments were growing sceptical over the opportunity to pay such a high economic and political price in order to reassess the European force balance. The appearance of a 'second nuclear revolution', entailing warheads miniaturization and brand-new categories of sub-strategic delivery means, was promising to make an offsetting strategy politically and fiscally feasible.

The intersection between inter-systemic, infra-systemic, and domestic pressures on the most involved Western governments. At the systemic level, by the late 1950 the Soviet Union seemed eager to balance its Cold War stance with a more cooperative attitude both in Europe with the 'politics of the Peace Notes' on Germany and in Asia. Such apparently cooperative stance had the aim to exploit the emerging rift between the United States and France. While mainly focused on the issue of German rearmament, the spat between Washington and Paris would be further exacerbated in the years between 1952 and 1954. Hopelessly embroiled in the intractable conflict in Indochina, the French grew even more unsatisfied by the American refusal to provide decisive military support while, at the same time, the US diplomacy was impolitely lobbying Paris to accept a significant German role in Western defence. The net result of such intersection of distinct dynamics in French domestic debate triggered what philosopher and political scientist Raymond Aron had labelled the 'Fourth Republic's Dreyfuss Affair' (Buton 2004: 43–59).

Under US pressures, in December 1951 the EDC's six heads of government decided to include in the text of the EDC treaty Article 38, which foresaw the formation of a democratic body with supranational powers, while in 1952 NATO's Lisbon Conference reaffirmed the need for West German rearmament, calling for 96 divisions and 7000 combat aircraft to be available at 30-day notice for deployment in Europe by 1954. In April, London agreed to enter into a technical association with the EDC and to sign a number of agreements providing for the inclusion of British army and air force units in European formations under the command of the SACEUR. In May, the signing in Bonn of the Convention on Relations between the Three Powers and the Federal Republic ended the occupation status and restored German sovereignty. On the following day, the treaty establishing the EDC between France, the FRG, Italy and the Benelux countries and a protocol for mutual military assistance between the United Kingdom and the EDC were signed in Paris. However, while the United States and its European allies had proved capable of rebuffing Soviet propaganda and moving forward on the road of securing a West German contribution to European defence, some eight months later, US Secretary of State John Foster Dulles had grown so exasperated by France's delaying attitude to threaten an «agonising reappraisal» of the American commitment to Western European defence. (FRUS 1952–1954: 463)

The Western European Union (WEU) and West German Rearmament Within NATO

The problems raised by the EDC quickly resurfaced in the first months of the ratification debate. The Americans were irked by French hesitations, while the British government remained wary of the federalist drift that was favoured by Italy and the Benelux states. The United Kingdom now endeavoured to design an alternative framework to the EDC. In March 1952 Foreign Secretary Eden had already proposed that the various Western European communities come together under the umbrella of the Council of Europe (House of Commons 1952).[3] Frustrated by West European hesitations, the Eisenhower administration did not rule out an alternative route to German rearmament. Dynamics in Western Europe played into American hands. At the end of August, the French National Assembly's decision to put off further debate on the subject allowed the British to advance a proposal for the transformation of the 1948 BTO with France, Belgium, Luxembourg and the Netherlands into the Western European Union (WEU) through its enlargement to the FRG and Italy. Suggested at first by Housing Minister Harold Macmillan and further developed by Whitehall, the 'Eden initiative' was discussed by the British Foreign Secretary during its European tour in

[3] *House of Commons Debate*, 24 March 1952, Vol. 498, Columns 32–34, available at https://api.parliament.uk/historic-hansard/commons/1952/mar/24/council-of-europe-united-kingdom.

September 1954 (Rohan 2014: 40).The UK's proposal provided a convenient compromise between American requests of West Germany's rapid rearmament and French concerns (Deighton 1998: 181–196). In a stroke of diplomacy, Eden secured US support and the FRG's participation in the new institution, by backing its automatic security commitments with the 'unprecedented' offer to deploy up to four divisions and the second tactical air force—later renamed Royal Air Force Germany—in Europe (Rohan 2014: 41).

On 23 October 1954, the signing of the Paris protocol, by amending the 1952 Bonn contractual agreements, created a treaty basis for the continued, long-term presence of foreign forces stationed in Germany.[4] At the same time, the new arrangements modified and completed the Brussels Treaty, allowing the accession of the FRG and Italy to the WEU. On 5 May 1955, the entry into force of the Convention on Relations between the Three Powers and the Federal Republic of 26 May 1952 formally ended West Germany's occupation. On the following day, the FRG was incorporated into the Alliance.[5] However, while removing any reference to 'German aggression', the modified Brussels treaty still contained a provision aimed at singling out Bonn: West German military deployments were capped at 12 divisions and its military-related activities were severely restricted by the Agency for Control of Armaments (ASDMAE).[6]

The WEU's establishment and the FRG's integration into NATO had durable repercussions on the relationship between the Alliance and European integration. The WEU's military command structure was integrated into that of NATO, which was identified as the essential forum for transatlantic consultation. While formally tasked with the role of having an input into decision-making about maximum forces, armaments production and standardization of European armaments, the WEU's implicit

[4] The official text of the Paris protocol modifying and completing the Brussels Treaty is available at https://www.nato.int/cps/en/natohq/official_texts_17408.htm?selectedLocale=en.

[5] *Documents on Germany, 1944–1959: Background Documents on Germany, 1944–1959 and a chronology of political developments affecting berlin, 1945–1956* (Washington: US Government Printing Office, 1959), pp. 124–141.

[6] Gabinetto del Ministro (undated). Documenti Consiglio Atlantico [Appunti sui documenti che verranno in discussione alla conferenza dei nove ed al Consiglio atlantico—Documenti della Conferenza dei Nove/NPC-Paris], ASDMAE Gabinetto del Ministro 1953–1961 (Busta 26, fascicolo 1), Rome, Italy.

subordination to NATO avoided any unnecessary duplications but was also a source of concern for Western Europeans. The Eisenhower administration's 'New Look', epitomized by the strategy of massive retaliation, affirming the centrality of nuclear weapons in Western military planning, enhanced the UK's role within NATO, sparking concerns over the constitution of an Anglo-Saxon atomic directorate. On the other hand, repeated calls to give NAT's Article 2 new emphasis achieved only mixed results (ASDMAE).[7] The WEU's failure to serve as a venue for European defence integration was already apparent by the late 1950s. By then, French President Charles de Gaulle had begun his campaign for a reform of the Alliance through the creation of a three-power 'political-military directorate' of the Americans, the British and the French to discuss strategic issues. Having been rebuffed by the United States and the United Kingdom, in the early 1960s the French president briefly attempted to revive European defence cooperation through the Fouchet plans, calling for the incorporation of defence into the EEC on an intergovernmental basis.

De Gaulle's initiatives elicited mixed reactions among France's European partners. To counter French proposals and reassure its other allies, Washington proposed the establishment of a NATO Multilateral Nuclear Force (MLF). This initiative was regarded by key State Department officials as a solution, an 'egg-lying wholly milk pig', which would have been able to assuage nuclear-disappointed countries, like the FRG and Italy (Haftendorn 1996: 121). The latter had witnessed with unconcealed dissatisfaction the removal—without parallel replacement—of the Jupiter IRBMs systems in 1963. Rome's eagerness to pay a substantial price to finance its share of the MLF project was partially inspired by the country's willingness to use such a military tool to revamp European integration (ASDMAE and Nuti 2007: 272–277).[8] Furthermore, in the unlikely effort to recover the central role played by De Gasperi

[7] Gabinetto del Ministro (undated). Appunti 'Consiglio del Nord Atlantico XIX Sessione, Parigi—Dicembre 1955 [Punto IV—Applicazione dell'Art.2'], Gabinetto del Ministro 1953–1961 (Busta 26, f. 'Consiglio Nord Atlantico'), ASDMAE.

[8] Direzione generale Affari Politici, Ministero Affari Esteri (1963, March 28). Telespresso 21/627 [Discorso del Ministro degli Affari Esteri Sen. Piccioni al Consiglio Atlantico del 20 marzo 1963]. Gabinetto del Ministro 1961–1963 (B. 12, F. 3). ASDMAE.

during the negotiations on the EDC, since late 1962 the Italian government tried to include a 'European clause' within an eventual treaty on the institution of the new MLF. Under such a provision, the MLF would have progressively been transformed in a European nuclear force, while its European parties would have exercised a right to acquire the weapons and the associated delivery means from the United States. Washington would then have exercised its own right to withdraw from the MLF, leaving its European allies the control over the force (ASDMAE).[9] While Italian interest in the MLF venture was shared by the FRG, the project was deeply unpopular 'across NATO Europe'. Also the United States rapidly lost any shade of enthusiasm for it (Stoddart 2012: 60–61). When asked to weigh the eventual MLF's benefits for allied cohesion against the programme's negative impact over Arms Control talks, the special task force on non-proliferation and dissemination of nuclear weapons, headed by Deputy Secretary of Defence Roswell Gilpatric, recommended the Johnson administration to prioritize horizontal non-proliferation over the project (FRUS 1964–1968: 176).

Ultimately, the crisis of trust between the United States and its West European allies deepened following Richard Nixon's election to the White House in 1968. The new administration's paramount priorities were to extricate US troops from Vietnam and avert an excessive shift in the global balance of strength. Moreover, the Nixon administration's increasing pressures upon its European allies to share the military and economic burden of containment not only fuelled calls for a better division of labour within the Alliance and greater utilization of European military power. It also led to a new acceleration in the pace of European integration. France played a leading role in furthering them. In 1975, the creation of the European Council (EC) marked an important step to strengthen foreign policy coordination among EEC's members, although the new body did not envision a common defence. Italy and the FRG too, however, played a worthy role. In 1981 the foreign ministers of Italy and the FRG submitted to the other EEC's members a Draft European Act, which called for closer European Political Cooperation (EPC) with the aim of enabling member states to develop a common foreign policy (Bulletin of the European

[9] Direzione generale Affari Politici, Ministero Affari Esteri, Servizio NATO (1963, September 13). Telespresso 21/196. [Appunto su clausola europea per la Forza Nucleare Multilaterale]. Gabinetto del Ministro 1961–1963 (B. 12, F. 10 'Forza Multilaterale'), ASDMAE.

Communities 1981: 87–91).[10] However, neither France nor the United Kingdom were willing to contemplate steps towards supranational defence cooperation and preferred to review the WEU rather than to expand the EEC's competencies to security and defence.

NATO and European Security Cooperation at the Cold War's End: From German Unity to Maastricht (1986–1992)

At the end of the 1980s the crisis of the Soviet bloc rapidly rekindled, however, the debate about the relationship between NATO and European integration. On this issue, there were important differences between the Americans and some of their European allies. As in the early 1950s, the French were sceptical about the US blueprint for revamping NATO. Mitterrand's preference was to instil new life into the WEU in order to encapsulate a united German state into a European security framework. By contrast, the British, like the Americans, opposed French ambitions to assign European institutions a more robust security role.

London rather supported the process of NATO's transformation that was engineered by the Americans and warmly supported also by the West Germans, opposing the inclusion in the treaty of Maastricht of a specific pillar on European foreign and security policy. As a result, collective defence was downgraded, as NATO reoriented itself towards out-of-area and expeditionary missions, while Europe was assigned only a complementary security role, with limited capability, to be used only when the Americans decided not to get involved. In 1992 the Maastricht treaty sealed an imperfect compromise, formalizing the establishment of the European Union (EU)'s Common Foreign and Security Policy (CFSP) and laying the foundation for the eventual framing of a common defence policy through the WEU, which was identified as an integral part of the EU's development. However, the Maastricht treaty also acknowledged the specific character of the security and defence policies of its member states and the commitments of most of them to the transatlantic alliance. The declaration adopted by the WEU Ministerial Council in June 1992 confined Europe's operational role to the range of the Petersberg tasks, confirming NATO as Western Europe's main security provider (Hill and Smith 2000: 205–211).

[10] Draft European Act. German-Italian Initiative submitted to the European Council 26–27 November 1981. *Bulletin of the European Communities*, No. 11/1981, pp. 87–91.

However, although being unwilling to renounce its preponderant role on the continent, Washington did not oppose plans for closer security cooperation in Europe, including an expansion in the WEU's role, at the condition that these initiatives did not undermine NATO's cohesion. Nonetheless, there were conflicting strategic visions also among Western Europeans. On 5 October 1991, the United Kingdom and Italy restated the centrality of the transatlantic relationship, describing NATO's reform and the development of a European common foreign and security policy as complementary rather than alternative enterprises (Europe Documents 1991).[11] Their stance was consistent with US views and grounded in the assumption that NATO would remain an integral and fundamental component of Europe's security architecture after the Cold War. By contrast, the French, and to a lesser extent the Germans, stressed the need for the WEU to play a more robust role in the continent's security. On 14 October, in a joint letter to the president of the European Council, Mitterrand and Kohl expressed their wish that reinforced Franco-German military cooperation and a revival of the secret military clause of the 1963 Franco-German treaty, which committed both signatories to assist each other by all available means, together with closer cooperation with other WEU's members, would increase Europe's security actorness and strategic role. Furthermore, in the early 1990s Germany proved unable to wear the boots of Washington's new partner in leadership, that the Bush administration had cajoled for the Federal Republic as early as 1989. West German reluctance to assume a greater security role was on full display during the summer 1990 in the wake of Iraqi invasion of Kuwait. With the 'Two plus Four talks' moving towards a final agreement and shielded by its 'constitutional' constraints, the Kohl government shied away from playing any significant role in the embargo operations authorized by the WEU Ministerial meetings in August and September 1990 after the UN Security Council Resolutions 660 and 661 (Rohan, 2014: p. 184).

In the following year, the explosion of the interethnic conflicts in former Yugoslavia ruthlessly exposed the WEU's inadequate resources to claim a bolder role in the continent's security, triggering in 1993 the beginning of NATO's involvement in Bosnia with 'Operation Deny

[11] 'Anglo-Italian Declaration on European Security and Defence', *Europe Documents*, no. 1735, 5 October 1991.

Flight'. The Alliance's intervention in Bosnia had long-lasting repercussions on European defence cooperation, clearing any remaining doubts about NATO's role as Europe's indispensable and primary security institution. However, it also triggered new calls by some member states, as well as by the European Parliament and the Commission, to address the problems of the CFSP. Already at its 1994 Brussels Summit, NATO and the WEU reached an agreement on the concept of Combined Joint Task Forces (CJTFs) and the creation of a European Security and Defence Identity (ESDI). After the 1995 Dayton peace agreement, France's decision to participate in the NATO's led international IFOR and SFOR peacekeeping deployments in Bosnia paved the way to even closer cooperation. In 1997 the treaty of Amsterdam introduced a number of innovations in the EU's treaties and created the post of High Representative for the CFSP.[12] In the late 1990s French President Jacques Chirac's formal acceptance of a premier role for the Alliance in European security and the UK's endorsement in the Anglo-French summit in St Malo in December 1998 of a EU's security role paved the way for the creation of the European Security and Defence Policy (ESDP) at the Cologne European Council, leading to the appointment of former NATO's Secretary General Javier Solana to the post of High Representative for the CFSP.[13]

The Clinton administration supported in principle the establishment of the ESDP but presented the Europeans with the three requests spelled out by Secretary of State Madeleine Albright: first, the ESDP shall not 'duplicate' NATO assets, secondly the Union shall not 'discriminate' non-EU NATO members and ultimately, the ESDP shall not lead to a 'de-coupling' of Europe from North America. Following the events of 9/11, the Bush administration continued to step up US endorsement for the ESDP. Ongoing negotiations between the Union and the Alliance were finalized in Berlin in December 2002. The final package of agreements established the principles for the use of NATO assets and capabilities by the EU and for the creation of the NATO–EU Strategic Partnership. Arrangements were also reached about the involvement of non-EU European allies in the ESDP's missions. In the same month

[12] The text of the Treaty of Amsterdam Amending The Treaty on European Union, The Treaties establishing the European Communities and certain related Acts is available at http://www.europarl.europa.eu/topics/treaty/pdf/amst-en.pdf.

[13] Conclusions of the Presidency, Cologne European Council, 3–4 June 1999, available at http://www.europarl.europa.eu/summits/kol1_en.htm.

the NATO–EU declaration on the ESDP welcomed the strategic partnership established between the EU and NATO but also reaffirmed that the Alliance remains the foundation of the collective defence of its members.[14] In 2003 European boots went on the ground for the first time in the Union's history, as the EU started 'Operation Concordia in North Macedonia', taking over responsibilities from NATO's operation 'Allied Harmony'. In the same year, the ESDP also briefly deployed troops in Congo in the context of Operation 'Artemis' and without assistance from NATO, while in 2004 European forces replaced the Alliance at the command of the IFOR/SFOR operation in Bosnia.

Whereas following the Bush administration's decision to overthrow the Saddam Hussein regime in Iraq against the reservations that were expressed by many of Washington's European allies, France and other EU members called in a fit of rage for the establishment of separate European headquarters, in the following years the ESDP's capabilities remained limited and never exceeded the range of the Petersberg tasks. Furthermore, in the early 2000s the United Kingdom and other EU members reiterated their opposition to any process that may ultimately lead to duplicating NATO and to a de-coupling of the United States from Europe, while the EU's eastern enlargement further slowed down plans for deeper integration in security and defence, exposing a gap in member states' strategic cultures and providing Washington with a new leeway on the further development of the ESDP.

The intra-European fracture over Iraq and fears of a resurgent Russia hampered in the following years the enhancement of European military capabilities. The 2007 Lisbon Treaty introduced for the first time in the EU treaties a common defence clause, spearheading the formal disbandment of the WEU in 2011, and ushering in the creation of the Common Security and Defence Policy (CSDP). However, it did not call into question NATO's role as the cornerstone of European security. Rather, it clearly stated that the CSDP's provisions shall respect the obligations of those EU members that are also members of the Alliance. The advent of the global financial crisis in 2008, hitting hard West European economies, heavily impacted on European defence budgets, rekindling the transatlantic debate over burden-sharing, despite France's formal reintegration into NATO's military structure in 2009. In the following years, the

[14] The text of the NATO-EU Declaration is available at https://www.nato.int/cps/en/natolive/official_texts_19544.htm.

Obama administration raised significant concerns about the low level of European defence expenditures. The president himself accused the US European partners of behaving like 'free riders' (The Atlantic 2016).[15] Although the 2016 and 2018 joint NATO–EU declarations pledged to renew security cooperation between the Alliance and the CSDP, in 2016 the Trump administration's verbal attacks on the European allies raised concerns of an American abandonment of its obligations to Europe's defence, casting a shadow of uncertainty over the future of relations between the Alliance and the European Union at a time of increasing international instability.[16]

Trump's public mocking of European leaders, particularly Emmanuel Macron and Angela Merkel, his discard of national sensitivities, epitomized by his brandishing of Germany as a 'delinquent' state, and his words of admiration for 'Brexiteer' UK's Prime Minister Boris Johnson and for Russian President Vladimir Putin also stoked fears that the administration might review the American approach and reach an accommodation with Moscow that would 'decouple' the United States from European security. Despite Berlin's commitment to spend 2% of its GDP on its military by 2024, as agreed by the allies at their 2014 Newport summit, Trump repeatedly claimed that Germany owes 'vast sums' of money to NATO and the United States. While in the early 1990s Washington had restated its commitment to European security, for the first time since the days of the Nixon administration in the early 1970s a US president now questioned America's unconditional security guarantee to Europe. Since the beginning of his tenure the US president's narrative called into question American support for European integration, displaying a vehement resentment towards the failure of Washington's European allies to share the burden of transatlantic defence with the United States. However, the deepening of transatlantic frictions over

[15] The text of President Obama interview with Jeffrey Goldberg can be downloaded at https://www.theatlantic.com/magazine/archive/2016/04/the-obama-doctrine/471525/.

[16] Declaration by the Heads of State and Government participating in the meeting of the North Atlantic Council in Brussels, 11–12 July 2018 available at https://www.nato.int/cps/en/natohq/official_texts_156624.htm?selectedLocale=en and Joint Declaration on EU-NATO Cooperation by the President of the European Council, the President of the European Commission, and the Secretary General of the North Atlantic Treaty Organization available at https://www.nato.int/cps/en/natohq/official_texts_156626.htm.

burden-sharing and the prospect of the UK's withdrawal from the Union also created hope that EU leaders might be spurred to boost their support for European defence.

In response to the President's vociferous and repeated criticism of the European allies, Germany's chancellor Angela Merkel remarked that the days when Europeans could fully rely on others for the preservation of their security are finally over. Europe, she suggested, must take its destiny into its own hands (Merkel 2017, Speech by Federal Chancellor Angela Merkel at the 17th Annual Conference of the Council for Sustainable Development, available at https://www.bundesregierung.de/breg-de/aktuelles/rede-von-bundeskanzlerin-merkel-bei-der-17-jahreskonferenz-des-rates-fuer-nachhaltige-entwicklung-am-29-mai-2017-in-berlin-321118 Speech by Federal Chancellor Angela Merkel before the European Parliament in Strasburg, 13 November 2018, available at https://www.bundeskanzler.de/bk-de/aktuelles/rede-von-bundeskanzlerin-merkel-vor-dem-europaeischen-parlament-am-13-november-2018-in-strassburg-1549538) Similarly, French President Macron also remarked in a foreign policy speech that Europe 'cannot entrust its security to the United States alone'. (Speech by President Macron at the 2018 Ambassadors' conference, available at https://www.diplomatie.gouv.fr/en/the-ministry-and-its-network/news/ambassadors-week/ambassadors-week-edition-2018/article/speech-by-president-emmanuel-macron-ambassadors-conference-2018) Trump's attitude and the UK's withdrawal from the EU reignited a dormant debate among historians, political scientists and international relations theorists on the European Union's security and defence role. For a number of scholars, Trump's elections and Britain's departure from the EU family of nations should have prompted the Union to seize the opportunity to assert its moral, political and ultimately military autonomy from Washington and strengthen its security and defence policy. Their fundamental claim is that the EU may now be able to unfreeze some of the defence initiatives—such as the creation of a military headquarters—which the United Kingdom has persistently vetoed, together with the support of the United States, in the past (Biscop 2016: 431–445, Tocci 2017). Nonetheless, many of these assumptions have proven overoptimistic and partially misleading. After the Brexit referendum, France, Germany and Italy issued a joint declaration in which they acknowledged the potential of a true common foreign, security and defence policy and proposed to develop European defence through 'the necessary commitments for our joint operations, as well as for our military capacities and industry' (Joint Declaration 2016). The French and German foreign ministers also published a shared bilateral vision for 'a more coherent and a more assertive Europe on the world stage' (Ayrault and Steinmeier 2016). The French and German defence ministers then followed up with a six-page position paper in advance of the European Council in Bratislava in September 2016, in which they called among other things for triggering Permanent Structured Cooperation (PESCO). France and the European institutions also devised a number of proposals with aim of triggering closer security and defence cooperation among EU's members. Prominent among them were three major initiatives: the new Defence Action Plan that was proposed by the European Commission and by the High Representative for the Common Foreign and Security Policy; secondly, the European Council's formal establishment of the Permanent Structured Cooperation (PESCO) with the participation of 25 member states in December 2017 and third, French President Macron's European Intervention Initiative, which Paris announced in March 2018. Nonetheless, these initiatives failed to bring about visible progress and kick-start a true revival of the CSDP. By contrast, in an increasingly volatile European strategic environment, divergences and, on some occasions, open contrasts persisted among EU's member states. The inability of EU's member states to coordinate an effective response to the deteriorating security environment in Libya and the tension between Italy and France on this issue—which among others led the Italian government not to join Macron's European Intervention Initiative—crudely highlighted the practical difficulties that continue to haunt the development of a truly effective European security agency.

NATO and European Defence After Brexit

While the election in 2020 of Joe Biden to the White House bridged the rift between the two sides of the Atlantic, any initiative taken by the new administration is likely to be hampered by the impact of the UK's withdrawal from the EU on the Union's credibility as a security actor. The implementation of the withdrawal clause removes the automatic security commitment to Europe which London provided since the 1948 BT and confirmed with the creation of the WEU in 1954 and the 2007 Lisbon Treaty (Heuser 2017: 16–23, Perot 2019: 42–43). The UK's participation in all these European multilateral ventures—stretching from the conventional deployments in Europe offered alongside the WEU in 1954 until participation in the CSDP in 2007—were subject to spoken out caveats. In 1954 the credibility of Eden's unprecedented offer was to be measured against the backdrop of London's economic and security interests. The same attitude inspired the Macmillan government during the negotiations leading to the December 1962 Nassau agreement. Then, the United Kingdom formally committed its nuclear deterrent to NATO, accepting to assign it to the never materialized MLF at the condition that London could exercise a right of withdrawal when its 'supreme national interests' were at stake (Stoddart 2012: 19). While British governments were hardly enthusiastic of narrow European solutions to European security issues, nevertheless they often supported—and sometimes fostered—initiatives aimed to strengthen cooperation between London and its continental partners. In doing so, the United Kingdom was able to retain an influence over European initiatives, defend the intergovernmental method of security cooperation, and avoid any weakening of NATO's role.

The nefarious impact of the UK's disengagement from the EU's military capabilities is likely to be further augmented by the economic fallout of the COVID-19 pandemic and of Russia's aggressive conduct. The measures taken to counter the stagnation in the European economies which followed the pandemic will inevitably constraint the budget for military projects connected to PESCO (Ringsmose and Webber 2020: 11). Declining resources for the defence sector and Russia's aggressive stance might increase, rather than lessen, European reliance on the US guarantee. Within this context, calls for European strategic autonomy are likely to have little attractiveness for EU member states. While popular in principle across Western Europe, the idea of strategic autonomy would bring in the politically unbearable combination of budgetary constraints for more publicly urgent social programmes.

Germany, as the country that has committed more resources to the continent's economic reconstruction, might find the prospect of European strategic autonomy unpalatable. Berlin partnered with France in taking the lead in the further development of PESCO, supporting in 2017 the establishment of the Military Planning and Conduct Capability (Iso-Markku and Gisela Müller-Brandeck-Bocquet 2019: 12–13). However, the Federal government publicly reiterated its transatlantic commitments and NATO primacy for European security. Already in February 2017 Chancellor Angela Merkel had publicly stated that 'European defence capability cannot be alternative to NATO' (Merkel 2017). Also, the promise of closer Franco-German cooperation after Brexit, which was embedded in the 2019 Aachen treaty signed by Macron and Merkel on the very same day that Charles de Gaulle and Konrad Adenauer had signed the Élysée Treaty in 1963, is unlikely to reinvigorate European defence. Following the UK's withdrawal from the EU, Germany remains the most credible successor to the UK's historic role of a transatlantic bridge builder. It is plausible, therefore, that the new democratic administration in Washington will endeavour to repair U.S.–German ties in order both to bolster transatlantic cohesion and instil new life into the Alliance. Furthermore, while many of the European partner's concerns over Germany's security and defence role seem to be abated, the vestiges of a Cold War-minded refusal of any *Sonderposition* are still alive in Berlin (Kříž et al. 2018: 366–370). Germany's persistently cautious approach makes it highly unlikely that Berlin will reach the 2% threshold in defence spending by 2030, inevitably weakening the prospect of a 'Europeanization' of NATO, let alone, the mantra of strategic autonomy (Bergman 2021).

Conclusions

This chapter reviewed the relationship between the Atlantic Alliance and European defence cooperation from the establishment of the transatlantic security relationship in the late 1940s until the UK's withdrawal from the EU in 2020. In the heydays of the Cold War West European security and cooperation were triggered by the need to secure a US defence pledge against the Soviet threat and to create a framework for West German participation in the defence of the North Atlantic region. The Americans were wary of foreign entanglements and favoured a fast-track solution to the divisive issue of Germany's rearmament. However, France had deep reservations about a rearmed West German state, while the United Kingdom objected any development towards supranational cooperation in Western Europe. As a result, during the Cold War, while the strictly intergovernmental WEU became the formal venue for European security cooperation, NATO remained the undisputed bedrock of European defence.

While triggering a partial reassessment of those arrangements, the end of the East–West division did not undermine the transatlantic relationship. Whereas NATO remained Europe's premier security institution, the WEU was charged with the ancillary role of conducting peace-keeping and crisis management tasks. Furthermore, when at the end of the 1990s the United Kingdom and France formally acknowledged the need for an increase in European capabilities, they did not call into question the Alliance's role, portraying European security and defence policy as complementary and not alternative to NATO. Nonetheless, in the following years the EU member states failed to devote sufficient resources to the development of European capabilities, contributing to fuel US resentment towards its allies. While the Trump administration's hostile attitude highlighted transatlantic disputes over defence spending, the UK's withdrawal from the EU in 2020 cast an additional shadow of uncertainty over the EU's defence role and ambition to partner with the Alliance in the preservation of Euro-Atlantic security. For the time being no other European country seems eager or ready to fill the gap that will be opened by the UK's departure from the EU. On the one hand, France's attitude towards NATO and CSDP seems to be measured according to their valuableness for Paris immediate needs. On the other hand, a natural, albeit unintended, consequence of Brexit and of Russia's aggressive stance might be a consolidation of German leadership in Europe. While concerns about a 'hegemonic Germany' are recurrent across the EU's Southern members, the FRG remains loath to embrace a pivotal role in transatlantic security. Although Germany has been eager to bear the costs of European financial stability, expectations that Berlin might assume a more active role in European security and defence have not been fully met. For the immediate future, it appears therefore that no credible alternatives have emerged as yet to a continuing European reliance on the United States as a capability and credibility provider.

References

Primary Sources

The National Archives (TNA), Kew, TNA

Documents on British Policy Overseas (DBPO), Series II, Vol. II, The London Conferences, January–June 1950 (1987)

Foreign Relations of the United States (FRUS), 1948, 1950, 1951, 1964–1968 (Washington, DC: Government Printing Office)

North Atlantic Treaty is available at https://www.nato.int/cps/en/natohq/official_texts_17120.htm (last accessed 22 February 2021)

Archivio storico-diplomatico del Ministero degli Affari Esteri e della Cooperazione internazionale (ASDMAE), Rome, Italy. Fondi: Gabinetto del Ministro (1953–1961) and (1961–1963).

Secondary Sources

Adenauer, Konrad. 1966. *Memoirs 1945–53*. London: Weidenfeld & Nicholson.

An Anglo-Italian Declaration On European Security And Defence In The Context Of The Intergovernmental Conference On Political Union, Europe Documents, 1735, 1991.

Baylis, John. 1982. Britain and the Dunkirk Treaty: The Origins of NATO. *Journal of Strategic Studies* 5 (2): 236–247.

Biscop, Sven. 2016. All or Nothing? The EU Global Strategy and Defence Policy After the Brexit. *Contemporary Security Policy* 37 (3): 431–445.

Bergmann , Max. 2021. The EU Is the Military Ally the United States Needs: Take the Pressure Off of NATO States and Embrace the Union's Defense. *Foreign Affairs* (posted on January 6, 2021. Last accessed on February 17, 2021

Buton, Philippe. 2004. La CED, l'Affaire Dreyfus de la Quatrième République?. *Vingtième Siècle. Revue D'histoire* 84:43–59.

Creswell, Michael, and Marc Trachtenberg. 2003. France and the German Question, 1945–55. *Journal of Cold War Studies* 5:3, 5–28.

Deighton, Anne. 1998. The Last Piece of the Jigsaw: Britain and the Creation of the Western European Union, 1954. *Contemporary European History* 7: 181–196.

Deighton, Anne. 2010. Three *Ministers and the World they Made:* Acheson, Bevin and Schuman, and the North Atlantic Treaty, March–April 1949. In *The Routledge Handbook of Transatlantic Security*, ed. Jussi Hanhimäki, Georges-Henri Soutou, Basil Germond. Abingdon and New York: Routledge.

Draft European Act. 1981. German-Italian Initiative submitted to the European Council 26–27 November 1981, in Secretariat General (European Commission), *Bulletin of the European Communities* 14 (11), available at http://aei.pitt.edu/1800/1/draft_european_act.pdf

Emmanuel, Macron. 2018. Speech at the Ambassadors' Conference, 27 August 2018, available at https://www.diplomatie.gouv.fr/en/the-ministry-and-its-network/news/ambassadors-week/ambassadors-weekedition-2018/article/speech-by-president-emmanuel-macron-ambassadors-conference-2018

Goldberg, Jeffrey. The Obama Doctrine. *The Atlantic*, April 2016, available at https://www.theatlantic.com/magazine/archive/2016/04/the-obama-doctrine/471525 (last accessed 22 February 2021).

Gowland, David, and Arthur Turner. 2000. *Reluctant Europeans: Britain and European Integration 1945–1998*. Harlow: Longman.

Kříž, Zdeněk, Stanislava Brajerčíková, and Jana Urbanovská. 2018. Defense Co-operation Between Germany and the Visegrad Countries. *The Journal of Slavic Military Studies* 31 (3): 354–371.

Haftendorn, Helga. 1996. *NATO and the Nuclear Revolution: A Crisis of Credibility, 1966–1967*. Oxford and New York: Oxford University Press.

Heuser, Beatrice. 2017. Britain and the Origins and Future of the European Defence and Security Mechanism. *The RUSI Journal* 162 (2): 16–23.

Hill, Christopher, and Karen E. Smith, eds. 2000. *European Foreign Policy: Key Documents*. London and New York: Routledge.

Iso-Markku, Tuomas, and Gisela Müller-Brandeck-Bocquet. 2019. Towards German Leadership? Germany's Evolving Role and the EU's Common Security and Defence Policy. *German Politics* 29:3, 1–20.

Jean-Marc, Ayrault, and Frank-Walter Steinmeier. 2016. A strong Europe in a world of uncertainties, Auswaertiges Amt, 24 June 2016, Press Release, available at https://www.auswaertiges-amt.de/en/newsroom/news/160624-bm-amfra/281672

Joint Declaration by the Chancellor of the Federal Republic of Germany, the President of the French Republic and the President of the Council of Ministers of the Italian Republic, available at https://www.governo.it/sites/governo.it/files/dichiarazione_congiunta_ita_fra_ger.pdf

Merkel, Angela. 2017. Speech at the 53rd Munich Security Conference, available at: https://www.bundesregierung.de/bregen/chancellor/speech-by-federal-chancellor-dr-angela-merkel-on-18-february-2017-at-the-53rd-munich-security-conference-415114 (last accessed 22 February 2021).

Nuti, Leopoldo. 2007. *La sfida nucleare. La politica estera italiana e le armi atomiche 1945–1991*. Bologna: il Mulino.

Perot, Elie. 2019. The Art of Commitments: NATO, the EU, and the Interplay Between Law and Politics Within Europe's Collective Defence Architecture. *European Security* 28 (1): 40–65.

Ringsmose, Jens, and Mark Webber. 2020. Hedging Their Bets? The Case for a European Pillar in NATO. *Defence Studies* 20:4, 295–317.

Rohan, Sally. 2014. *The Western European Union. International Politics Between Alliance and Integration*. London and New York: Routledge.

Stoddart, Kristan. 2012. *Losing an Empire and Finding a Role: Britain, the USA, NATO and Nuclear Weapons, 1964–70*. New York: Houndmills.

Tocci, Nathalie. 2017. The Time for European Defence Has Come: Rome Must Step Up to the Task. available at https://www.iai.it/en/pubblicazioni/time-european-defence-has-come-rome-must-step-task, IAI Commentaries 2017, last checked 22 February 2021.

CHAPTER 7

The Origins of the Post-Cold War NATO Enlargement: Stability Projection and Factor of Crisis

Davide Borsani

The fall of the Berlin Wall in November 1989 and the dissolution of the Soviet Union in December 1991 significantly changed the international balance of power, including the European strategic environment. The Old Continent was the first and most direct battleground between the two superpowers of the Cold War era. In May 1989, once the bipolar struggle was coming to an end, the President of the United States, George H. W. Bush, declared that 'for 40 years, the world has waited for the Cold War to end', adding that 'the world has waited long enough. The time is right. Let Europe be whole and free'.

D. Borsani (✉)
Faculty of Political and Social Sciences, Catholic University of the Sacred Heart, Milan, Italy
e-mail: davide.borsani@unicatt.it

M. de Leonardis (ed.), *NATO in the Post-Cold War Era*, Security, Conflict and Cooperation in the Contemporary World
https://doi.org/10.1007/978-3-031-06063-2_7

A 'whole and free' Europe would become the US trademark phrase capturing not only forty years of American effort for European security but also labelling a US long-term policy for the next three decades on the other side of the Atlantic. From this perspective, Moscow would not have been an enemy but a partner for a common security system ranging from Vancouver to Vladivostok and encompassing the countries of the Atlantic Alliance and the members of the declining Warsaw Pact. In Bush's words, 'let us not give [the Russians] incentives to return to the policies of the past'. On the contrary, 'our goal is not to undermine their legitimate security interests. Our goal is to convince them, step-by-step, that their definition of security is obsolete, that their deepest fears are unfounded' (Bush 1989).

The new partnership between Washington and Moscow should have been the cornerstone of a 'New World Order' and a renewed dialogue between the West and the East. The newly created North Atlantic Cooperation Council (NACC), i.e. the diplomatic forum established by NATO in November 1991, would foster confrontation and collaboration between the Atlantic Alliance and the former members of the Warsaw Pact. The international situation would take another turn very soon.

The US Decision to Enlarge NATO

In January 1993, Bush's successor as US President, William J. Clinton, came to the office mainly focusing on domestic issues. In international affairs, the 'top priority' for the new Administration, as stated by the US Secretary of State Warren Christopher to British Ambassador Robin Renwick, was to foster and promote good relations with the Russian government led by President Boris Yeltsin.[1] In February, the Russian Foreign Minister Andrey Kozyrev welcomed this top priority, noting that 'the rapprochement of Russia and the NATO member states' was 'a historic chance for Europe and for the world as a whole'. Kozyrev hoped for the creation of a 'common space' in which 'everyone is interdependent and helps one another' to overcome 'the division of Europe' and initiate a process of 'mutual adaptation across the continent' (Kozyrev 1993).

Meanwhile, as early as March 1991, the Czechoslovakian President Vaclav Havel, during a visit to NATO headquarters, stated that if the

[1] See the dispatch sent by the British Ambassador to the United States, Renwick, on 14 January 1993. TNA. PREM 19/4496.

Central and Eastern European countries could not become full members of NATO at the moment, the 'doors' of the Alliance should not remain 'closed' forever (Laar 2010). The NATO Secretary-General Manfred Wörner, on a visit to the Baltic countries in March 1992, described the relationship between the former members of the Warsaw Pact and the Atlantic Alliance as a 'dynamic process' that could lead to the 'possibility' of being part of it (Cottey 1995). In March 1993, the German Minister of Defense, Volker Rühe, urged the Alliance not to act as a 'closed shop' and discuss NATO expansion towards the East through an internal debate (Arora 2006).

The US 'Russia first' priority began to fade away in the mid-1993 when the Clinton administration started an internal review process of its strategy towards Europe. The shift had two main reasons. Firstly, the members of the Visegrad Group (Poland, Hungary, the Czech Republic and Slovakia) pressed US officials and the President himself to consider NATO enlargement as a counterbalance to the traditional Russian imperialism towards Eastern and Central Europe and the tool to promote democracy in former Communist countries. Secondly, the domestic wave of bipartisan supporters in the Congress looking for new tasks and goals for the post-Cold War NATO influenced the Clinton administration. According to Senator Richard Lugar, NATO membership had to be extended to Central and Eastern Europe countries, firstly to the 'strongly Atlanticist' Czech Republic, Hungary and Poland, accelerating the process (Lugar 1993).

However, there was no strong consensus in the Clinton administration. In 1993, the Department of State concluded that the old conventional NATO task, i.e. the 'defeat' of the Soviet Union, was fulfilled. The Alliance's survival now depended on the ability to renew its commitment to promote democracy, foster liberal values in formerly Communist countries and open NATO's door to them as full members in the short-medium term. Some State Department officials, mainly the highly influential advisor Strobe Talbott, argued that a cooperative relationship with Russia was a preliminary requirement to NATO expansion (Christopher 1998). On its part, the National Security Council, led by the 'neowilsonian' Tony Lake, was firmly in favour of a rapid expansion of the full-fledged membership towards the East (Asmus 2002).

The Department of Defense had a different opinion. Both the Secretary of Defense, Les Aspin, and the Chief of Staff, formerly NATO Supreme Allied Commander in Europe (SACEUR), General John

Shalikashvilli, believed the time to expand the membership of the Alliance had not come. There were three reasons. First, NATO members were not ready to extend security guarantees to Central and Eastern European countries. Second, aspiring membership candidates would be security consumers rather than security providers, at least in the short-medium term. Third, Russia would see the enlargement as a threat to its security. The Pentagon, thus, made an alternative proposal to expansion: the 'Peacekeeping Partnership', called later 'Partnership for Peace' (PfP). This initiative envisaged close cooperation in the military field, especially in peacekeeping, between the former members of the Warsaw Pact and NATO, without contemplating a full-fledged membership. The NACC, thus, would represent the diplomatic forum for political dialogue, while the PfP would aim at increasing military interoperability.[2]

President Clinton finally took the field on October 18, facilitating a compromise between the three Administration branches. The interagency meeting attended by the President decided that at the next NATO summit there would be 'a statement of principle that NATO's membership will grow to include new democracies in Europe's east without setting criteria by which applicants are to be judged or a timetable. The statement of principle will itself be a significant step beyond anything NATO has said before and will be seen as a victory for pro-Western forces in Central Europe'. But the summit should also have called for 'a qualitatively different engagement between NATO and eastern militaries that would begin immediately' to facilitate the process of rapprochement with Eastern Europe. Therefore, the United States would immediately propose a Partnership for Peace 'open to all European states willing and able to participate' in some NATO military activities, including peacekeeping exercises. 'Active participants in the Partnership would receive a commitment to consult with NATO if they felt their security threatened, but no security guarantee'. In other words, the PfP would extend the scope of Article 4 of the North Atlantic Treaty, but not that of Article 5. Furthermore, enlargement would have been an 'evolutionary process', and the PfP represented 'the first step towards full NATO membership'.[3]

[2] Briefing Memorandum. 14 September 1993. The National Security Archives (NSA). George Washington University. https://nsarchive.gwu.edu/dc.html?doc=4390817-Document-03-Your-Deputies-Committee-Meeting-on.

[3] Memorandum to Clinton. 19 October 1993. William J. Clinton Digital Library. https://clinton.presidentiallibraries.us/items/show/101137.

The ambiguous attitude of Russia favoured the decision to start the 'evolutionary process'. In August, during a visit to Warsaw, Yeltsin and the Polish President, Lech Walesa, signed a joint declaration stating that 'the presidents raised the issue of Poland's intention to join NATO'. The Polish position 'was accepted with understanding by President Boris Yeltsin. In the event, such a decision by sovereign Poland, aiming at European integration, is not contrary to the interests of other countries, including Russia' (Zięba 2020). Russian understanding of Poland's desire was a breakthrough in the policy review process in the United States, allowing the Clinton administration to launch the first informal consultations with the four countries of the Visegrad Group for future accession to NATO. The talks took place in September, ending with no binding commitments. However, they envisaged the need to launch a 'clear and credible' message during the US Presidential trip in Europe and the NATO summit in Brussels in January 1994.[4]

Meanwhile, in a meeting held in Moscow in October with Christopher, Yeltsin defined the PfP as 'a brilliant idea, it is a stroke of a genius', dissipating 'all of the tension which we now have in Russia regarding East European states and their aspirations with respect to NATO'. However, the Secretary of State stressed that the United States 'will in due course be looking at the question of membership as a longer term eventualcty [*sic*]'.[5] In the meantime, a report prepared by Yevgeny Primakov, the Director of the Foreign Intelligence Service and future Russian Foreign Minister, stated that 'Russia has no right to tell sovereign states' whether or not they should 'join NATO'. Nevertheless, it recognized that 'in the event of [NATO] expansion by the addition of countries of the former Warsaw Pact, the principle of the balance of power is upset' and, therefore, Russian security policies and tools would require a review.[6]

President Clinton's trip to Europe was a success for the US foreign policy. In Bruxelles, NATO Heads of State and Government approved the PfP on January 11. In Prague, one day later, the US delegation,

[4] Memorandum to Lake and Berger. 23 September 1993. William J. Clinton Digital Library. https://clinton.presidentiallibraries.us/items/show/101137.

[5] Secretary Christopher's meeting with President Yeltsin. 22 October 1993. William J. Clinton Digital Library. https://clinton.presidentiallibraries.us/items/show/100538.

[6] Izvetiya Summary of Primakov/SVR Report on NATO. 26 November 1993. NSA. George Washington University. https://nsarchive.gwu.edu/dc.html?doc=4390823-Document-09-Izvetiya-Summary-of-Primakov-SVR.

including the President, met their counterparts of the Visegrad countries. According to Walesa and his colleagues, the PfP was a good idea. However, they also invited the United States to foster a fast enlargement of NATO membership to counter the Russian threat to Central and Eastern Europe. Clinton acknowledged that, at some point, Russian behaviour might make it necessary to draw a dividing line in Europe. Still, for the time being, the PfP, which represented a path on the road to full-fledged NATO membership, was trying to avoid that.[7]

In the press conference held at the end of the meetings, Clinton officially announced that NATO enlargement would happen. It was just a matter of evaluating the timeline and methods. 'While the Partnership is not NATO membership', he said, 'neither is it a permanent holding room'. Thus, 'now the question is no longer whether NATO will take on new members but when and how this will happen'. The Alliance would leave 'the door open' to new members to promote 'democracy, markets and security all across a broader Europe'. Central and Eastern Europe, thus, would be 'at the heart of a new Europe, an integrated Europe, democratic, prosperous, secure and free. That is my commitment', Clinton said. 'I think our reading of history is right', urging Russia to reframe its 'standards of greatness' (Office of the Secretary 1994). When Clinton arrived in Moscow the very next day, he reported the evolution of the enlargement affair to Yeltsin, who replied briefly that the PfP was a good proposal, supporting it.[8]

In October, the Clinton administration detailed the policy of NATO enlargement. According to the memorandum prepared by Lake and delivered to the President in October 12, the United States had the primary goal of developing 'an integrated and inclusive security system for Europe, including but going beyond NATO expansion'. The second target was in 'the medium term' to have 'an expanded NATO', including the Central European countries 'who live up to our precepts [...] democracy, market economy, responsible/good-neighborly security policies'. 'In parallel' the

[7] See the conversation memorandums in William J. Clinton Digital Library. https://clinton.presidentiallibraries.us/items/show/100538; NSA. George Washington University. https://nsarchive.gwu.edu/dc.html?doc=4390825-Document-11-The-President-s-Meeting-with-Czech; https://nsarchive.gwu.edu/dc.html?doc=4390826-Document-12-The-President-s-Luncheon-Plenary.

[8] Memorandum of Clinton-Yeltsin conversation. 13 January 1994. William J. Clinton Digital Library. https://clinton.presidentiallibraries.us/items/show/58577.

Administration would try to get 'an institutionalized relationship between NATO and Russia. This could take the form of a Treaty (an "alliance with the Alliance"). It should include a mechanism for consulting with Russia on NATO or NATO-led military operations', mainly in the peace-keeping field, 'without giving Russians a veto over NATO decisions'. The document also considered 'the prospect of further expansion to those not admitted in the first tranche'. The 'possibility of NATO membership for Ukraine and the Baltic countries should be maintained' because the United States 'should not consign them to a grey zone or a Russian sphere of influence'. The expansion of the Alliance as an '"insurance policy"/"strategic hedge" (i.e., neo-containment of Russia)' had to be 'kept in the background only, rarely articulated' in public and private.

On the contrary, the possibility of Russia joining NATO should not be ruled out. The PfP would be the tool for new members to make their Armed Forces interoperable with NATO. As for the timeline, the enlargement could not have occurred before 1998, or 'no sooner than first half of second Clinton term'. In the meantime, it was necessary to: emphasize the role of PfP; monitor the reform progress of the aspiring member countries; start consultations with Moscow; keep 'the membership door open for Ukraine, the Baltic States, Romania and Bulgaria countering Allied inclinations to "tilt" in favour of the Visegrad countries'.[9]

The Russian Thorn

Russia began its firm campaign against NATO enlargement in the second half of 1994, proposing the strengthening of the Conference on Security and Cooperation in Europe (CSCE) alternatively. The CSCE was seen in Moscow as the leading institution to foster cooperation in Europe at the highest level between NATO countries, the European Union, the former Soviet satellite states, and Russia. As a British government background paper stated, 'the Russians place great importance on developing the CSCE: it is the only European forum where they are on an equal footing with the US and Western European countries'. In the fall, not

[9] Memorandum to Clinton. 13 October 1994. William J. Clinton Digital Library. https://clinton.presidentiallibraries.us/items/show/57563.

surprisingly, Russian diplomacy had 'consistently pressed for a central, more effective role for the CSCE in European security'.[10]

On November 29, Yeltsin wrote to Clinton to 'confirm our serious interest in developing profound cooperation with NATO—both through the potential of the Partnership for Peace program and in the form of direct bilateral interaction'. He added that the Russian goal was not to make the Atlantic Alliance the heart of European security but to transform the CSCE at the upcoming Budapest summit on December 5 into 'a full-fledged all-European organization with a sound legal basis'.[11]

However, the US and Western European countries quickly rejected Yeltsin's proposal. At the NATO Foreign Ministers meeting held on the eve of the Budapest summit, Allies pushed the enlargement forward through the approval of a study to identify the criteria for admitting new members. As a protest, at the CSCE summit, Yeltsin accused the US-led plan of expanding NATO to plunge Europe 'into a Cold Peace', adding that 'history demonstrates that it is a dangerous delusion to suppose that the destinies of continents and of the world community in general can somehow be managed from one single capital'. He also said: 'We are concerned about the changes that are taking place in NATO. What is this going to mean for Russia? NATO was created during the Cold War. Why sow the seeds of mistrust? After all, we are no longer enemies; we are all partners now' (Morrison 1995). As Christopher (1998) maintained in his memoirs, the CSCE summit 'was undoubtedly the low point of U.S.–Russian relations during the first Clinton term'.

Thanks to German Chancellor Helmut Kohl's mediation and US Vice-President Al Gore's visit to Moscow, tensions between the United States and Russia decreased. On December 14, Gore told the Speaker of the Duma, Ivan Rybkin, that he would be 'personally very worried if the process of NATO expansion proceeded rapidly'. Indeed, the 'misunderstanding' in Budapest was perhaps the result of 'the inability on our part to clearly convey to the Russian side what we are talking about'. The NATO expansion would happen, but as a 'gradual, deliberate, absolutely open and transparent process, without surprises. We plan to have full and

[10] See the document with no date, but probably prepared on December 2 or 3. TNA. PREM 19\4970, part 13, October–December 1994.

[11] Yeltsin's Letter to Clinton. 29 November 1994. NSA. George Washington University. https://nsarchive.gwu.edu/dc.html?doc=4390827-Document-13-Official-informal-No-248-Boris-Bill.

frank discussions with Russia at every stage of this process'.[12] Meanwhile, Clinton chose not to interfere in the simultaneous crisis in Chechnya, considering it as a Russian domestic affair and offering Yeltsin a diplomatic olive branch (Malik 1997).

On December 21, the Clinton administration updated its policy on NATO expansion in light of the Russian stance. Despite some residual doubts by the new Secretary of Defense William Perry, the President confirmed the need for enlargement, which should no longer take place only 'in parallel' with the institutionalization of the NATO–Russia relationship, but 'in close parallel'. The impossibility of granting veto powers to Moscow on the Allied decision-making process remained a cornerstone. However, the new guidelines foresaw the possibility of establishing 'an institutional framework for consultations in the 16+1 format' (NATO countries plus Russia), including further 'guarantees' in the security field. Moreover, the United States would establish 'an increasingly serious, frank dialogue about NATO expansion' while being 'careful not to allow Russians to confuse serious dialogue with right of joint decisions or veto' or even fostering the 'perceptions of a U.S.–Russia condominium'. In conclusion, the US document hoped for the 'Russian understanding if not acceptance of package combining NATO expansion and parallel NATO–Russia relationship'.[13]

Once the United States definitively framed its policy, significant steps laid ahead. A first success materialized in May 1995, when Russia joined the PfP. However, the greatest challenge was to obtain Russian support at best or its acceptance at worst for NATO enlargement. After an almost two-year diplomatic break due to 1996 overlapping presidential elections in the United States and Russia, NATO expansion came back to the negotiating table. Still, in 1995 and 1996, several talks between Washington and Moscow clarified that the Kremlin was in principle against the enlargement.

On the eve of signing the PfP, Yeltsin said that NATO expansion was 'nothing but humiliation for Russia' because it would be 'a new form of

[12] Record of the Main Content of the Conversation between I. P. Rybkin and Vice President of the United States A. Gore. 14 December 1994. NSA. George Washington University. https://nsarchive.gwu.edu/dc.html?doc=4390828-Document-14-Record-of-the-Main-Content-of-the.

[13] See the memorandum prepared by Lake on 22 December 1994. William J. Clinton Digital Library. https://clinton.presidentiallibraries.us/items/show/101137.

encirclement', asking 'to postpone NATO expansion until the year 2000'. Clinton counter-argued that the best solution was to create 'a special relationship between Russia and NATO' in the following months to ease the enlargement issue.[14] In February 1996, the US President repeated that NATO enlargement would proceed in a 'steady, measured and transparent fashion', while 'a close, cooperative NATO–Russia relationship' was 'one of NATO's most important objectives'.[15] Eventually, Yeltsin, being reconfirmed as President like his American colleague, had to come to terms with the 'NATO problem' at the end of January 1997. On the one hand, he repeated that 'NATO expansion will seriously impair Russia's geostrategic position and will cause direct harm to our national security interests'. On the other hand, he hoped that 'our justified concern' would 'not simply be noted, but will be taken into account in a clear and precise form. It would be best if this were done' in the form of 'an official agreement between Russia and NATO'[16].

Negotiations between the two Presidents took place the following March at the historical Helsinki summit, which paved the way for the NATO–Russian agreement and the Kremlin's unenthusiastic acceptance of the expansion.[17] 'Our position has not changed', Yeltsin said, 'it remains a mistake for NATO to move eastward. But I need to take steps to alleviate the negative consequences of this for Russia. I am prepared to enter into an agreement with NATO not because I want to but because it is a forced step. There is no other solution for today. The principal issues for me are the following. The agreement must be legally binding—signed by all 16 Allies. Decisions by NATO are not to be taken without taking into account the concerns or opinions of Russia. Also, nuclear and conventional arms cannot move eastward into new members to the borders of Russia, thus creating a new cordon sanitaire aimed at Russia.

[14] See the Summary Report on One-On-One Meeting between Clinton and Yeltsin on 10 May 1995. William J. Clinton Digital Library. https://clinton.presidentiallibraries.us/items/show/57568.

[15] See the letter sent by Clinton on 8 February 1996. William J. Clinton Digital Library. https://clinton.presidentiallibraries.us/items/show/101238.

[16] See the letter sent by Yeltsin on 30 January 1997. William J. Clinton Digital Library. https://clinton.presidentiallibraries.us/items/show/101238.

[17] As a compensation, the US accepted Russia as a member of the Group of Seven (G7). Moscow joined the Group—the new Group of Eight (G8)—at the Denver summit, held in June 1997.

But one thing is very important: enlargement should also not embrace the former Soviet republics. I cannot sign any agreement without such language. Especially Ukraine. If you get them involved, it will create difficulties in our talks with Ukraine on a number of issues'. 'Regarding the countries of the former Soviet Union', Yeltsin added, 'let us have a verbal, gentlemen's agreement – we should not write it down in the statement – that no former Soviet republics enter NATO. This gentlemen's agreement would not be made public'.

Clinton strongly rejected Yeltsin's argument. 'If we were to agree that no members of the former Soviet Union could enter NATO', he stated, 'it would be a bad thing for our attempt to build a new NATO, but it would also be a bad thing for your attempt to build a new Russia. I am not naive. I understand you have an interest in who gets into NATO and when. We need to make sure that all these are subjects that we can consult about as we move forward—consult means talk about; it means making sure that we're aware of your concerns and that you understand our decisions and our positions and our thinking. But consider what a terrible message it would be if we were to make the kind of supposedly secret deal you're suggesting. First of all, there are no secrets in this world. Second, the message would be, "we're still organized against Russia – but there's a line across which we won't go." In other words, instead of creating a new NATO that helps move toward an integrated, undivided Europe, we'd have a larger NATO waiting for Russia to do something bad. Here's why it is bad for Russia, what you are proposing. Russia would be saying, "we have still got an empire, but it just can't reach as far West". Second, it would create exactly the fear among the Baltics and others that you're trying to allay and that you're denying is justified'.

With a 'neo-Wilsonian' spirit, the US President added: 'under no circumstances should we send a signal out of this meeting that it's the same old European politics of the Cold War and the same old business, we're just moving the lines around a bit. Instead, the signal here should be to tell the world and tell Russia that it's a new NATO and a new Russia'. Clinton concluded by sustaining the need of signing a 'charter' between NATO and Russia, which would be 'without precedent', 'comprehensive', 'forward looking' and 'hopeful'. It would send 'a much more powerful and positive message'. However, he admitted that 'no one is talking about a massive, all out, accelerated expansion'. Yeltsin inferred that 'the former Soviet republics will not be in the first waves' of NATO expansion, although Clinton made no formal commitment on this, stating that 'we need to find a solution to a short-term problem that doesn't create a long-term problem'.[18]

In mid-May, after a lengthy negotiation between the new Russian Foreign Minister, Primakov, and Javier Solana, the NATO Secretary-General ('supervised' by the US Undersecretary of State, Talbott), Washington and Moscow reached an agreement on the Founding Act on NATO-Russia Mutual Relations, Cooperation and Security. The Act had five parts: a preamble, which noted that 'NATO and Russia do not consider one another adversaries', plus four sections. Without entering into details, the agreed text laid out the principles governing the relationship, including formal commitments to respect the sovereignty, independence and territorial integrity and pursue the peaceful resolution of disputes. It created the NATO-Russia Permanent Joint Council that would serve as the forum for consultation and coordination between NATO and Russia, making clear that neither NATO nor Russia had a right of vetoing the other's actions.

The military dimension was the 'most contentious' part of the negotiations and 'potentially the most controversial'. Concerning nuclear deployments, the text stated NATO's 'three no's', i.e. 'no intention, no plan and no reason to deploy nuclear weapons on the territory of new members'. In the conventional field, NATO agreed to perform its activities and reinforce its positioning without creating new military infrastructures or 'additional permanent stationing', making no distinction between old and new members. As the Deputy National Security Advisor, Samuel 'Sandy' Berger, highlighted, for NATO and the United States this was 'not an absolute commitment, in case future circumstances change'.[19] Two weeks later, on May 27, the NATO–Russia Founding Act was officially signed.

Inter-Allied Negotiations

The support from NATO allies, notably the United Kingdom, Germany and France, was not automatic. Two days after signing the Founding Act, NATO Foreign Ministers met in Portugal in Sintra to discuss which

[18] See the transcript of the Helsinki summit held on 21 March 1997. William J. Clinton Digital Library. https://clinton.presidentiallibraries.us/items/show/57569.

[19] See the memorandum sent by Berger to Clinton on 15 May 1997. William J. Clinton Digital Library. https://clinton.presidentiallibraries.us/items/show/101137.

countries should be invited to join the Alliance at the next summit in Madrid in July. In September 1995, the North Atlantic Council had already approved the NATO Study on Enlargement to clarify what the 'new possible members' needed 'to do to prepare for membership'.[20] As summarized by the US Secretary of Defense, Perry, the five principles (the 'Perry Principles') to be respected for future NATO members were democratization, progress towards a market economy, civilian control of military, NATO force compatibility and stable, peaceful relations with bordering states (Mattos and Rachwald 2001).

US diplomats arrived in Portugal intending to discuss NATO enlargement for a few Central European countries, i.e. Poland, Hungary and the Czech Republic. According to the State and Defense Departments officials, these three countries were the only ones abiding by the Perry Principles, deserving the extension of US security guarantees. Further elements concurred in supporting the candidacy of the three Visegrad countries. For instance, the bipartisan support in the Congress and the influence of the American-Polish lobby. Their European counterparts, on the contrary, would consider to pursue a more extensive enlargement. The French, supported by the Italians, believed that NATO was not paying sufficient attention to its Southern flank, a threatening area as the ongoing conflicts in the Balkans were proving. Hence, they insisted that NATO enlargement had to be balanced by including some Southern European countries, such as Romania and Slovenia, as a source of stabilization.

As US Permanent Representative to NATO, Robert Hunter, stated in late March, France and Italy had already got support from Turkey, Spain and Portugal in their effort, even without being 'wedded' to this (Asmus 2002). The United Kingdom was the exception, preferring a small round of enlargement and adding Slovenia in case of consensus. France and Italy had a solid agreement: Romania and Slovenia would join NATO only together. In Sintra, the Germans remained quite ambiguous. The fragmentation among European Allies was the reason why the summit led to no conclusions on new members. However, the diplomatic debate made it crystal clear that the first admission would not be the last and that there would be a second enlargement decision sooner than later. For the moment, in the new US Secretary of State Madeleine Albright's words, the need for 'geographical balance' between the Eastern and Southern

[20] NATO Study on Enlargement. 3 September 1995. https://www.nato.int/cps/en/natohq/official_texts_24733.htm.

flanks cannot be a priority at the expense of 'the serious business of extending permanent security guarantees'.[21]

The following summit in Madrid would be decisive. On the eve of the meeting, the US diplomatic strategy aimed at solidifying support from the United Kingdom while extending it to Germany. Nordic countries would follow. Berlin was the key balancer due to its diplomatic weight, representing the geopolitical bridge between Western and Eastern Europe. In the memorandum 'Deciding Which Countries to Support for NATO Membership at the Madrid Summit' addressed to President Clinton on June 9, the new National Security Advisor, Berger, stated that there would be 'strong general advantages to limiting invitations to the three strongest candidates'. First, 'a limited initial group will underscore that the enlargement process is careful and cautious'. Second, 'the danger of dilution of the Alliance's military effectiveness will be diminished if only a limited number of countries need to be assimilated into NATO's structures at one time'. Third, 'a decision that leaves plausible, relatively non-controversial—if less well-developed—candidacies for later rounds underscores the reality that there will be later rounds, and could increase other Allies' support for a robust open-door package at Madrid'. Fourth, 'given that all Allies favour at least the three, whereas support for the other two is distributed among differing subgroups of countries, a consensus on the three should be easier to achieve as well as "deeper" than a consensus at higher numbers which could leave the damaging impression of deal-making, political compromise or log-rolling'. According to Berger, on the one hand the French President, Jacques Chirac, was 'the most difficult' to convince because he was 'determined to score a "French" victory over the Americans'. On the other hand, the German Chancellor, Kohl, could 'take a more active part' in supporting US diplomatic stance.[22]

Two days later, after lengthy consultations with the members of the Administration and the senatorial NATO Observer Group, Clinton eventually decided that the United States would support inviting only Poland, the Czech Republic and Hungary. On June 12, US diplomats officially informed Solana and NATO Allies. 'The President's decision', Talbott

[21] Asmus (2002) quoted Albright's Night Note from Sintra on 30 May 1997.

[22] Berger to Clinton. 9 June 1997. William J. Clinton Digital Library. https://clinton.presidentiallibraries.us/items/show/101137.

told them, 'was based on a decisive but straightforward criterion: on an issue as momentous as this for the Alliance, there should be the strongest and most solemn consensus. NATO worked by consensus and there was consensus in the Alliance for three; there was no consensus for four, five, or more'. After inviting the three, he added, the Allies 'needed to find the right words at Madrid to say clearly and unambiguously that the process would go forward and in a meaningful timeframe'.[23]

In a telephone call with Clinton on July 3, Kohl agreed on a minor enlargement. 'I think we can pursue it that way', the Chancellor said, 'but we simply need to give a message opening up a perspective for Romania and Slovenia', adding that 'we can come up with some kind of language'. 'I agree with that', Clinton responded, 'I think we ought to say that these three are the most ready, but that we have an interest in building NATO's southern flank, and that we'll review it in 1999'. In Clinton's words, the US goal was also 'to keep the door open to Bulgaria and Austria [A/N: a neutral country according to Austrian constitution], that doesn't create another problem for us with the Baltic states'. While somewhat sceptical about admitting the Baltics into NATO, Kohl agreed on that line, promising German mediation to mollify the French position.[24] Even Solana told Clinton that he would support the US position for a small first round of enlargement.[25]

In his opening speech at the Madrid summit on July 8, President Clinton said: 'I believe we should make our alliance broader by inviting Poland, Hungary and the Czech Republic into NATO [...] I also believe that these three countries' smooth and successful integration will create momentum for others to follow. Today, we must commit to keep the door of this Alliance open to all those ready to meet the responsibilities of membership. I believe we should exclude no European democracy. There

[23] See the cable sent by the State Department to US Embassies in Europe on 12 June 1997. William J. Clinton Digital Library. https://clinton.presidentiallibraries.us/items/show/100538.

[24] See the transcript of the Kohl-Clinton phone call on 3 June 1997. William J. Clinton Digital Library. https://clinton.presidentiallibraries.us/items/show/57651.

[25] See the transcript of the conversation between Clinton and Solana on 7 July 1997. William J. Clinton Digital Library. https://clinton.presidentiallibraries.us/items/show/101162.

are other states that are close to being fully qualified to join. When they are ready and the time is, right, I believe we should welcome them'.[26]

Chirac and the Italian President of the Council of Ministers, Romano Prodi, counter-argued that even Romania and Slovenia were on a clear path towards democracy and the free market. Moreover, Bucharest and Ljubljana were critical for stabilizing NATO's Southern flank while providing geographic contiguity and greater cohesion to the Alliance. Nevertheless, the French-Italian effort was not enough. As reported by Ronald D. Asmus, the then-US Deputy Assistant Secretary of State for European Affairs, the United States had clear support from the United Kingdom, Denmark, Norway and Iceland. Canada, Portugal and Spain underscored the need for consensus, being available only under this condition for three or five new members. Eventually, the German position closed the debate. 'One miracle has already come true', Kohl underlined, 'there is agreement on the membership of Poland, Hungary and the Czech Republic', and 'there would not be agreement on more than three countries'. Hence, he urged his counterparts to accept the three and focus on the public message on the Open Door policy the Alliance wanted to convey (Asmus 2002). France and Italy, thus, had to come to terms with it. They could accept a minor enlargement, but they also needed a public promise that a second expansion would follow.

After a lengthy debate on the language of the final communiqué, the Allies found a diplomatic solution, also thanks to Solana's mediation. 'Today', the text of the Madrid Declaration on Euro-Atlantic Security and Cooperation stated, 'we invite the Czech Republic, Hungary and Poland to begin accession talks with NATO. Our goal is to sign the Protocol of Accession at the time of the Ministerial meetings in December 1997 and to see the ratification process completed in time for membership to become effective by the 50th anniversary of the Washington Treaty in April 1999'. As for a new round of enlargement, 'We reaffirm that NATO remains open to new members under Article 10 of the North Atlantic Treaty. The Alliance will continue to welcome new members in a position to further the principles of the Treaty and contribute to security in the Euro-Atlantic area. The Alliance expects to extend further invitations in coming years to nations willing and able to assume the responsibilities and obligations of membership, and as NATO determines that the inclusion

26 See the transcript of the Clinton's speech on 8 July 1997. William J. Clinton Digital Library. https://clinton.presidentiallibraries.us/items/show/9694.

of these nations would serve the overall political and strategic interests of the Alliance and that the inclusion would enhance overall European security and stability'. More specifically, the Allies 'recognize with great interest and take account of the positive developments towards democracy and the rule of law in a number of southeastern European countries, especially Romania and Slovenia. [...] At the same time, we recognise the progress achieved towards greater stability and cooperation by the states in the Baltic region which are also aspiring members'.[27]

The final trade-off was clear: Hungary, Poland and the Czech Republic into NATO by 1999; Romania, Slovenia and the Baltics sooner than later. The United States significantly supported Baltic countries' candidacy, as the 1998 Baltic Charter—signed in Washington to strengthen political ties between the United States and Lithuania, Estonia and Latvia—would show. Poland, Hungary and the Czech Republic became full NATO members in March 1999. The following Washington summit in April 1999 reaffirmed Allies' 'commitment to the enlargement process of the Alliance'. As the final declaration stated, 'today we recognize and welcome the continuing efforts and progress in both Romania and Slovenia. We also recognize and welcome continuing efforts and progress in Estonia, Latvia and Lithuania. Since the Madrid Summit, we note and welcome positive developments in Bulgaria. We also note and welcome recent positive developments in Slovakia'.[28] Hence, the 1997 Madrid compromise did not pave the way for one round of enlargement only, but two.

At the 1999 Washington summit, NATO leaders created the Membership Action Plan (MAP), i.e. a 'programme of advice, assistance and practical support tailored to the individual needs of countries wishing to join the Alliance' (NATO March 2020). In the following three years, ten countries applied: Albania, Bulgaria, Croatia, Estonia, Latvia, Lithuania, Macedonia, Romania, Slovakia and Slovenia. In May 2000, MAP countries met in Vilnius, calling for an all-inclusive Big Bang expansion for the second round of NATO enlargement.

The new US President, George W. Bush, entered the White House in 2001, putting NATO enlargement low in his foreign policy priority list (Hendrickson and Readman 2007). Nevertheless, he was supportive

[27] Madrid Declaration on Euro-Atlantic Security and Cooperation. 8 July 1997. https://www.nato.int/docu/pr/1997/p97-081e.htm.

[28] Washington Summit Communiqué. 24 April 1999. https://www.nato.int/docu/pr/1999/p99-064e.htm.

of the Open Door policy and the Big Bang expansion. The new President made his position clear during his trip to Europe in June 2001. In 1999 'the expansion of NATO has fulfilled NATO's promise', he said, 'and that promise now leads eastward and southward, northward and onward'. Bush went on: 'All of Europe's new democracies, from the Baltic to the Black Sea and all that lie between, should have the same chance for security and freedom – and the same chance to join the institutions of Europe – as Europe's old democracies have'. He also announced: 'Next year, NATO's leaders will meet in Prague. The United States will be prepared to make concrete, historic decisions with its allies to advance NATO enlargement' (Bush 2001).

In the wake of the 9\11 terrorist attacks, the enlargement became a factor in the process of redefining and extending NATO's future political mission and military capabilities. Not only for the Allies, who already agreed de facto on a new round of enlargement four years earlier but also for Russia. The new Russian President, Vladimir Putin, surprised the West in October 2001, expressing a willingness to allow NATO's expansion even to the Baltics if Moscow would 'feel involved in the processes' of redefining the tasks of the Alliance (Daley 2001).

As a consequence, 2002 was a pivotal year for NATO. Once again, the Allies pursued a double-track policy. On the one hand, since December 2001, NATO members under British impetus launched a new initiative to improve (and renew after the 1999 Kosovo war) the relationship with Russia. Both threatened by international terrorism, NATO and Moscow revamped the consultative mechanism—now renamed NATO–Russia Council, born in May 2002—to strengthen cooperation and diplomatic exchanges on the foundations of the 1997 NATO–Russia Founding Act. On the other hand, in November 2002, the Allies met in Prague, inaugurating the new wave of NATO in the twenty-first century. Member countries agreed on developing new military capabilities to fight international terrorism, also by expanding the political role of the Alliance. Above all, the Allies invited seven countries to join NATO: the three Baltic states, Romania, Bulgaria, Slovenia and Slovakia. It was no surprise indeed.

The United Kingdom backed the United States upon the Big Bang expansion. France had no objection to expanding the Alliance southward and, most important, even to the Baltics. 'France can only express support for Estonia, Latvia and Lithuania's desire to join NATO and support their aspirations at the NATO summit in Prague,' Chirac said during a visit in Riga, 'I don't think [the Russians] have the ability, competence, or wish to stop NATO enlargement'. As for the Germans, the Minister for Foreign Affairs, Joschka Fischer, was favourable for admitting the Baltics. The new Chancellor, Gerhard Schröder, was not against the Big Bang expansion if Russia could live with it (Hendrickson and Readman 2007). Putin's words in the fall of 2001 seemed to alleviate his possible worries. Therefore, the seven countries became full NATO members in 2004.

But the enlargement was not over yet. In 2009 Albania and Croatia joined the Alliance, while Montenegro and the Republic of North Macedonia followed in 2017 and 2020. In the three decades after the Cold War, every US President—either Republican or Democratic—presided over a round of NATO expansion. According to NATO, today the 'ongoing enlargement process poses no threat to any country. It is aimed at promoting stability and cooperation, at building a Europe whole and free, united in peace, democracy and common values' (NATO May 2020). However, Moscow maintains a somewhat different view. According to Russian Foreign Minister Sergei Lavrov, the expansion of NATO remains 'a mistake, even a provocation in a way'. It is also 'an irresponsible policy that undermines the determination to build a system of equal and shared security in Europe, equal for everyone regardless of whether a country is a member of this or that bloc' (Reuters 2014).

Conclusion: The Seeds of Today's Conflict

The decision to proceed with the eastward expansion of the Atlantic Alliance profoundly influenced European dynamics. In the 1990s, NATO and the United States tried to establish a new cooperative relationship with Russia and, at the same time, to address the worries of the Eastern and Central European countries. Strategically, this proved to be contradictory.

The Allies supported the legitimacy of the principle of sovereignty, which grants each State—whether small, medium or large—the possibility of choosing its international alliances and claiming its independence from stronger powers or any other factors outside the State itself. Yeltsin apparently accepted this principle in the summer of 1993 and so did Putin in the aftermath of the 9\11 terrorist attacks. In fact, Russia did not behave consistently over the years, as the diplomatic protests in the mid-1990s show. More recently, Allies' pledge at the 2008 Bucharest summit to open NATO's door to Ukraine and Georgia made Putin draw a red line in the former Soviet geopolitical space, as the 2014 Ukrainian crisis demonstrates. After all, Yeltsin had already mentioned Ukraine as the straw that would break the camel's back. Through a historical lens, the United States has drawn the very same line in its backyard in the Western Hemisphere, particularly in the Caribbean, for security and strategic reasons.

The principle of freely choosing alliances struggles with the historical foundations of power politics. Indeed, international dynamics tend to be managed mainly by great powers, which have a different weight in global and regional affairs than small or medium powers. Not by chance, post-Soviet Russia never renounced to claim its great power status in negotiating with the United States. This happened both in the 1990s and in the following decades. Nowadays, it remains an essential goal for the Russian political leadership. According to this view, the only viable solution that Moscow would accept is exercising its power alongside the United States as an equal. NATO enlargement, thus, has been felt in Russia as an American imposition over a weakened power, representing a source of destabilization for the European balance of power. On the contrary, since the end of the Cold War, most Central and Eastern European States, particularly the Visegrad countries and the Baltics, worried about a new wave of Russian imperialism, asking the United States and NATO to be protected from their historical enemy. From this perspective, NATO's expansion made their territory more secure, rolling back Russian ambitions over a long-standing disputed strategic area.

Here lie the seeds of the conflict between NATO and Moscow we are assisting these days. One cannot exclusively see NATO expansion as a source of stabilization or as a factor of crisis. For the time being, it proved to be potentially both, depending on the points of view. Its geopolitical implications are still unclear since they involve deep historical processes, albeit today the answer is increasingly leaning towards Clinton's fear of creating a new dividing line in Europe. At the time of writing, the 2014 crisis in Ukraine and the following Russian annexation of the Crimean Peninsula represent the apex of tensions between Moscow and NATO countries in the post-bipolar era. It was no coincidence that the 2015 US National Security Strategy stated that European security and international norms that had been 'taken for granted' since the end of the Cold War were now 'in danger'.[29] In this process, NATO enlargement has proved to be both a preventive solution and one of the primary causes.

Acknowledgement The author thanks Ms Camilla Sergio (Youth Atlantic Treaty Association) for contributing to the formal review of the present essay.

Bibliography

Arora, Chaya. 2006. *Germany's Civilian Diplomacy. NATO Expansion and the Art of Communicative Action*. Palgrave Macmillan.

Asmus, Ronald D. 2002. *Opening NATO's Door. How the Alliance Remade Itself for a New Era*. Columbia University Press.

Bush, George H. W. 1989, May 31. *A Europe Whole and Free. Remarks to the Citizens in Mainz*. https://usa.usembassy.de/etexts/ga6-890531.htm.

Bush, George W. 2001, June 15. *Remarks by the President in Address to Faculty and Students of Warsaw University*. https://georgewbush-whitehouse.archives.gov/news/releases/2001/06/text/20010615-1.html.

Christopher, Warren. 1998. *In the Stream of History*. Shaping Foreign Policy for a New Era: Stanford University Press.

Cottey, Andrew. 1995. *East-Central Europe after the Cold War: Poland, the Czech Republic, Slovakia and Hungary in Search for Security*. Palgrave Macmillan.

Daley, Suzanne. 2001, October 4. Putin Softens His Stance Against NATO Expansion. *The New York Times*. https://www.nytimes.com/2001/10/04/world/a-nation-challenged-the-allies-putin-softens-his-stance-against-nato-expansion.html.

Hendrickson, Ryan C., and Kristina S. Readman. 2007. From the Baltic to the Black Sea: Bush NATO's Enlargement. In *White House Studies Compendium*, vol. 4, ed. Robert W. Watson, 283–299. Nova Science Publishers.

Kozyrev, Andrey. 1993. The New Russia and the Atlantic Alliance. *NATO Review* 1: 3–6.

Laar, Mart. 2010. *The Power of Freedom. Central and Eastern Europe after 1945*. Centre for European Studies.

Lugar, Richard G. 1993. *NATO: Out of Area or Out of Business; A Call for U.S. Leadership to Revive and Redefine the Alliance*. The Richard G. Lugar Senatorial Papers, Indiana University Library, https://collections.libraries.indiana.edu/lugar/items/show/342.

Malik, Hafeez. 1997. *The Roles of the United States, Russia and China in the New World Order*. St. Martin's Press.

[29] The National Security Strategy. 1st February 2015. https://obamawhitehouse.archives.gov/sites/default/files/docs/2015_national_security_strategy_2.pdf.

Mattox, Gale A., and Arthur R. Rachwald, eds. 2001. *Enlarging NATO*. The National Debates: Lynne Rienner Publishers.

Morrison, James W. 1995. *NATO Expansion and Alternative Future Security Alignments*. National Defense University.

NATO. 2020a, March 23. *Membership Action Plan (MAP)*. https://www.nato.int/cps/en/natolive/topics_37356.htm

NATO. 2020b, May 5. *Enlargement*. https://www.nato.int/cps/en/natolive/topics_49212.htm

Office of the Secretary. 1994. *Public Papers of the Presidents of the United States: William J. Clinton, January 1 to July 31, 1994*. U.S. Government Printing Office.

Reuters. 2014. *NATO's planned Balkan expansion a 'provocation'*. https://www.reuters.com/article/us-nato-balkans-russia-idUSKCN0HO11W20140929

Zięba, Ryszard. 2020. *Poland's Foreign and Security Policy*. Problems of Compatibility with the Changing International Order: Springer.

CHAPTER 8

NATO's Partnerships in the Mediterranean and the Greater Middle East

Antonio Marquina Barrio

Introduction

After the Cold War, the majority of NATO countries considered that the Mediterranean, as NATO southern flank, had lost relevance and interest, while the Middle East continued to be of particular relevance in view of the Arab–Israeli conflicts, Saddam Hussein's wars and weapons of mass destruction (WMD). However, the conflicts and problems of the Persian Gulf and the Arab–Israeli conflicts were outside the framework of the security guarantees set out in Articles 5 and 6 of the Washington Treaty.

In the NATO strategic concept adopted in 1991, a distinction was made between the possible risks that could affect the non-NATO states of Central and Eastern Europe and the states of the southern periphery of the Mediterranean. The risks that could affect the security of the

A. Marquina Barrio (✉)
International Security and Cooperation, Universidad Complutense, Madrid, Spain
e-mail: amarqbar45@gmail.com

M. de Leonardis (ed.), *NATO in the Post-Cold War Era*, Security, Conflict and Cooperation in the Contemporary World
https://doi.org/10.1007/978-3-031-06063-2_8

former would be the consequence of instabilities: political, economic and social difficulties, including ethnic rivalries and territorial disputes, while for the Southern and Eastern Mediterranean states, the problem was focused on the growth of military power and the proliferation of weapons technologies in missiles and weapons of mass destruction.

Asymmetry in risk management was evident. Adding to this, NATO bilateral and multilateral cooperation was connected exclusively with the Central and Eastern European states (Marquina 1993).

Projecting stability and fixing Central and Eastern Europe was the main goal. However, the crisis and internal war in Algeria induced the European members of the reactivated Western European Union (WEU) to reaffirm the importance of the Mediterranean subgroup's work on security in the Mediterranean. They focus initially on the Maghreb but the area was expanded with the later inclusion of Egypt. The agenda for a dialogue with these countries included Confidence-Building Measures (CBMs), conflict prevention, and non-proliferation of armaments, in order to deal with rising problems in southern perceptions regarding NATO and WEU military reorganization and doctrines that enhanced mobility and rapid deployment forces. The results were unsatisfactory, the WEU did not table any concrete proposals. Adding to this, the Euro-Mediterranean conference held in Barcelona in 1995 diminished the vigour of this WEU impulse. Nevertheless, the Barcelona Conference, in its first chapter entitled *Political and security partnership: Establishing a common area of peace and stability*, never developed a strategy towards the Mediterranean (Marquina 2019).

NATO Med Dialogue

In order to forge new security relationships between NATO, the non-NATO European states and the new Republics emerged after the dissolution of the Soviet Union, NATO launched in January 1994 The Partnership for Peace as a new programme going beyond dialogue and cooperation. It was a major programme of practical bilateral cooperation. Regarding the Mediterranean, once the Declaration of Principles on Interim Self-Government Arrangements was signed by the Government of Israel and the Palestine Liberation Organization (PLO) on 13 September 1993, the Peace Process in the Middle East offered a historical opportunity for launching a broader initiative between the North and South of the Mediterranean in order to promote dialogue, understanding, and confidence building. And on 8 February 1995, after overcoming significant reservations of the United States and the United Kingdom, the North Atlantic Council recommended to carry out this dialogue and cooperation with the aim of contributing to security and stability in the Mediterranean as a whole, of achieving a better mutual understanding and correcting any misperceptions between NATO and the Mediterranean partner countries on the Alliance's purposes that could lead to a perception of threat. The Dialogue was based on several principles: non-discrimination, self-differentiation, inclusiveness, two-way engagement, non-imposition, complementarity and mutual reinforcement.

Given the experience of the WEU failed dialogue, the agenda was enlarged to include some practical cooperation activities. Thus, the political dialogue meetings held with every country, at least twice a year, tried to explain to the new partners NATO's activities, its internal adaptation, and general approach to building cooperative security structures. The Med partners, for their part, presented their views on issues relating to stability and security of their own countries and the Mediterranean region. In fact, the Med partners were quite heterogeneous in their approaches to security. They did not present a common and solid approach to the Mediterranean security, facilitating the creation of a regional security forum.

The activities offered were centered on the fields of information and scientific affairs and in more specialized areas, such as participation in peacekeeping courses at NATO schools. In December 1996, NATO Foreign Ministers approved the inclusion of civil emergency planning on disaster management, opening the possibility of offering more courses at NATO schools, especially on civil emergency planning, civil–military cooperation, and examining future possibilities for increasing transparency in the field of military activities (Solana 1997).

Some expectations regarding a possible NATO contribution to democratization of Med partners, supporting the defence sector reform, were not fulfilled. And common projects on issues of common concern that would have contributed strongly to build confidence and the diffusion of misperceptions, were not adopted.

Freeing the Middle East from WMD and missile proliferation were priorities in the Western security agenda in the 1990s. However, these issues were not included in the NATO Mediterranean agenda but in the first chapter of the Euro-Mediterranean Conference of Barcelona held in 1995. Anyhow, its outcome was modest, the question of WMD was not touched in the meetings of the senior officials and the perception of risks coming from the north was not diffused in the south, and the CSBMs adopted were practically declaratory (Marquina 2019).

The Madrid NATO Summit of 8–9 July 1997 gave a new political impetus to the Mediterranean region, but the Med Dialogue was still an exercise in confidence building rather than a true partnership. The Secretary General of NATO was very clear on that before the summit: 'some caution should be exercised in trying to apply the Partnership for Peace wholesale as a model for the Mediterranean region. In the Mediterranean we can learn from PfP, but in my view, the political diversity of the region will require in time the development of separate and specific solutions appropriate to the region. Simply extending the Partnership for Peace and its activities to Mediterranean dialogue partners would lose the nuances and sensitivities on which the present dialogue is based' (Solana 1997).

Courses, research fellowships to scholars and activities such as observation of Partnership for Peace activities in the fields of search and rescue, maritime safety and medical evacuation, as well as exercises related to peace support and humanitarian relief were offered. No common military projects were on the table.[1]

Again, in the NATO Washington summit communiqué of 24 April 1999,[2] an enhanced NATO Mediterranean dialogue was emphasized. And the new Strategic Concept stated: 'The Mediterranean is an area of special interest to the Alliance. Security in Europe is closely linked to security and stability in the Mediterranean. NATO's Mediterranean Dialogue process is an integral part of NATO's co-operative approach to security. It provides a framework for confidence building, promotes transparency

[1] Egypt, Jordan and Morocco participated in both the NATO-led Implementation Force (IFOR) and the Stabilization Force (SFOR) in Bosnia and Herzegovina.

[2] At the Washington Summit Communiqué, it was stated that 'The Mediterranean Dialogue is an integral part of the Alliance's co-operative approach to security since security in the whole of Europe is closely linked to security and stability in the Mediterranean. We are pleased with the development of our Mediterranean Dialogue. The Dialogue is progressive in nature and we welcome the progress towards developing broader and deeper co-operation and dialogue with the countries in the Mediterranean region. We endorse the enhancements to the political and practical co-operation of the Mediterranean Dialogue agreed by the Council in Permanent Session and direct it to pursue their early implementation.... The Dialogue and other international efforts, including the EU Barcelona process, are complementary and mutually reinforcing and thus contribute to transparency and building confidence in the region'. In fact, there was not a division of labour with the NATO Med initiative on different topics. See Marquina (2019).

and cooperation in the region, and reinforces and is reinforced by other international efforts. The Alliance is committed to developing progressively the political, civil, and military aspects of the Dialogue with the aim of achieving closer cooperation with, and more active involvement by, countries that are partners in this Dialogue'.

But little progress was made on its substance. The main reason for this inertia was not only the fragmentation in security terms of the Southern Flank but, in particular, 'the consensus among security thinkers and planners in NATO (and the EU) that that the threat to European security in the region is not derived from the malevolent use of state power directed against Western Europe but rather from the partial, or full, collapse of the existing political authorities in the southern and eastern Mediterranean' (Whitman 1997, 1999).

The Expansion of Med Dialogue

The September 11th terrorist attacks that took place in the United States did not change the conceptual framework established in the 1999 Strategic Concept, but they fundamentally altered the aim of the Med Dialogue itself, highlighting the need for NATO and its Mediterranean partners to move closer together and to forge a genuine partnership in the face of common challenges, such as terrorism and the proliferation of weapons of mass destruction. Algeria entered the Med Dialogue in 2000.

In 2002, in the NATO Prague summit, Alliance leaders agreed a package of measures to upgrade the Med Dialogue, establishing a more regular and more effective consultation process; intensifying the political relationship through high-level contacts and the involvement of decision-makers; associating the Med partners with selected Euro-Atlantic Partnership Council (EAPC) activities; and further developing practical cooperation in security matters of common concern through more focused activities, a tailored approach to cooperation, and a continuous process of consultation at expert level. In October 2001, NATO launched the maritime surveillance operation *Active Endeavour*, focused on detecting and deterring terrorist activity in the Mediterranean.[3]

[3] The operation was terminated in October 2016 and was succeeded by Sea Guardian, a flexible maritime operation able to perform the full range of maritime security operations tasks.

In 2004, during the Istanbul summit, NATO leaders decided to elevate the Med Dialogue to a genuine partnership. Thus, the enhanced Med Dialogue will contribute to regional security and stability, by promoting greater practical cooperation, enhancing its political dimension, assisting in defence reform, cooperation in the field of border security, achieving interoperability and contributing to the fight against terrorism, while complementing other international efforts. They also launched the NATO training, mentoring and assisting the Iraqi security forces initiative.

An annual Mediterranean Dialogue Work Program (MDWP) was also established, including seminars, workshops and other practical activities in the fields of modernization of the armed forces, defence policy and strategy, defence investment, armaments and intelligence-related activities, civil emergency planning, crisis management, border security, small arms and light weapons, public diplomacy, scientific and environmental cooperation, as well as consultations on terrorism and the proliferation of WMD. The MDWP included also invitations to dialogue countries to observe—and in some cases participate—in NATO/PfP military exercises, attend courses and other academic activities at the NATO School (SHAPE) in Oberammergau and the NATO Defence College in Rome,[4] and visit NATO military bodies. The military programme also included port visits by NATO's Standing Naval Forces, on-site train-the-trainers' sessions by Mobile Training Teams, and visits by NATO experts to assess the possibilities for further cooperation in the military field. However, while 2008–2009 versions of the toolbox of activities were published for the first time in June 2010, what each country takes from it remains secret. Furthermore, NATO+7 consultation meetings were also held on a regular basis.[5]

[4] The NATO Riga Summit, held in 2006, launched the NATO Training Cooperation Initiative, complementing the Med activities, with a particular interest in interoperability, maritime cooperation, crisis management, illegal trafficking, and border security, and established a ten-week NATO Regional Cooperation Course at NATO Defense College (NDC) in Rome, on the security challenges in the Middle East. See Rademacher (2007).

[5] Consultations of the 28 Allies and 7 Med countries took place on a regular basis on a bilateral and multilateral level, at Ministerial, Ambassadorial and working level formats. That has also included three meetings of the NATO and Med Foreign Ministers in December 2004, 2007 and 2008 in Brussels. Two meetings of NATO and Med Defense Ministers in 2006 and 2007 in Taormina and Seville. Ten meetings of the Chief of Defense of NATO and Med countries took place before the Arab revolutions. The political dimension also includes visits by NATO senior officials, including the secretary-general and the deputy secretary general, to Med Dialogue countries. The main purpose of these visits

However, the multilateral level dialogue suffered ups and downs because of the Israel–Palestinian conflict. The deepening of Israel's participation in the Alliance's activities was also jeopardized. In 2006, NATO and Israel had finalized the Individual Cooperation Program (ICP) under the enhanced Mediterranean Dialogue and the modalities of Israel's contribution to the Operation Active Endeavour that NATO's Heads of State and Government decided to offer to Med Dialogue partners, but several years later, in September 2011, Turkey vetoed the Israeli request to open an official Israeli Mission at NATO headquarters as a consequence of the Gaza flotilla attack on 31 May 2010. It would also veto the inclusion of Israel in any partnership programme. NATO was unwilling to move ahead with its other Mediterranean partners in the region and leave Israel behind, but the impasse lasted until 2016.

In spite of the poor results produced by the policies adopted in the creation of a genuine partnership in 2004, again, the Lisbon summit held on 20 November 2010 mentioned that peace and stability in the Mediterranean region were essential for Euro-Atlantic security, adding that 'we intend to further develop the Mediterranean Dialogue by raising its political and practical dimensions, in order to build mutual confidence and to deal together with the common security challenges in this region'. And the new Strategic Concept reaffirmed the commitment to develop and deepen the cooperation with Med partners, being also open to include other countries of the region in the Med Dialogue.

The Istanbul Cooperation Initiative

The Istanbul Summit also launched the Istanbul Cooperation Initiative (ICI) with selected countries in the Greater Middle East with the inclusion of Bahrain, Qatar, Kuwait, United Arab Emirates, an offer to engage in practical security cooperation activities. The security and stability of the Gulf region was now considered of strategic interest to Alliance. The region apparently encompassed all the major security and defence challenges the Alliance needed to engage in: fighting terrorism, proliferation of nuclear weapons, energy security, maritime security, defence reform as well as state failure, given the situation of Iraq. Apparently, this kind of partnership did not seem as complicated as the one being

was to conduct high-level political consultations with the relevant host authorities on the way forward in NATO's political and practical cooperation under the Med Dialogue.

developed with the Mediterranean Dialogue countries, as Israel was not included, removing a major obstacle in the development of this dialogue (Jean-Loup 2012).

The issue was to achieve a practical collaboration among the militaries of the various countries having wide geopolitical differences and perceptions of threats and risks to the national and regional security and stability. This was the case when thinking about closer relations between NATO and the Gulf Cooperation Council with regard to Iran's nuclear ambitions and, on the other hand, the stabilization of Iraq and the fight against radical Islam. This explains why they sought from the beginning close bilateral relations with NATO in order to promote their own goals and strategies, ignoring their neighbour's plans without envisaging a precise regional dimension. This explains why Oman was not attracted by this initiative and preferred not to participate.

Saudi Arabia's case was different. It did not want to participate in an initiative that put the country on the same level as the small Gulf states that needed security guarantees they did not consider appropriate to its situation, size and capabilities. They preferred to establish an individual, specific relationship with NATO, outside the ICI (Jean-Loup 2012). In the first three months of 2005, three countries: Bahrain, Kuwait and Qatar formally joined the ICI. In June 2005, the United Arab Emirates also joined the Initiative.

The ICI has since developed both the political and the practical dimensions of the partnership. The political dialogue has evolved to include not only high-level meetings at ambassadorial level but also multilateral meetings starting with the first NAC+4 meeting in November 2008, followed by other annual meetings in 2009 and 2010. The practical dimension at the bilateral level was progressively enhanced through the opening of new partnership tools and activities on counter-WMD; counterterrorism; training and education; participation in NATO exercises; promoting military interoperability; disaster preparedness and civil emergency planning; tailored advice on defence reform and civil–military relations; and cooperation on border security to help prevent illicit trafficking of drugs, weapons and people.[6] This annual menu of practical activities was gradually enhanced. By 2007, the offer of cooperation to ICI countries included 328 activities/events that by 2011 increased to around 500.

[6] Fact Sheet (2014). The Istanbul Cooperation Initiative (ICI). https://www.nato.int/nato_static_fl2014/assets/pdf/pdf_2014_04/20140331_140401-factsheet-ICI_en.pdf.

At the same time, several members were active partners in NATO-led operations in Afghanistan or fighting against piracy.

However, these Med/ICI security cooperation partnerships could not manage and confront the new challenges of the twenty-first century affecting the Alliance and they did not have a significant role in stabilizing the Mediterranean and the Greater Middle East region or in helping and promoting the political evolution of participating countries. In other words, NATO was not able to move decisively from the stabilization and military and politically transformation of Central and Eastern Europe, to a new task, the stabilization and transformation of the Mediterranean and the Greater Middle East bearing in mind that the EAPC had already lost substance and interest and there was a growing feeling that the partnerships and structures created after the Cold War were becoming obsolete (Asmus 2008).

In fact, after the Warsaw summit in 2002, seven EAPC members, Bulgaria, Estonia, Latvia, Lithuania, Romania, Slovakia and Slovenia formally became members of NATO leaving behind two different groups at the EAPC, the European neutrals and the Central Asian and Caucasus states, plus Belarus, Moldova and Croatia. It was difficult to define the areas of common interest and, as a result, the practical cooperation to be developed.

In this situation, the United States tried to promote a different approach to NATO partnerships. The US Ambassador to NATO, Nicholas Burns, in 2004, presented the idea of an 'extension of the alliance of democracies' able to contribute to NATO's military missions around the world conducting military stabilization operations far beyond the borders of Europe. And in January 2006, US Ambassador to NATO, Victoria Nuland, appealed for the dissolution of the EAPC in a speech at the Oberammergau school, and asked for a global partnership forum that had to include all the partnerships (Karl-Heinz 2006). From this perspective, non-European partners were considered increasingly important, as the NATO-led mission in Afghanistan had already revealed (Asmus 2006). But this also meant muffling the issue of the expansion of the alliance of democracies and the export of democracy to the partnership regions, emphasizing the military capabilities of the partners and their possible support to NATO in fighting global threats. The future scope of NATO action and the need for cooperation now went beyond the Med Dialogue, ICI and EAPC, and implied transforming the approach of countries, seeking to contribute more to their security and obtain a reassurance, such as the ICI states wanted, than making political, operational and financial contributions to NATO-led operations.

Thus, the issue of NATO partnership configuration was soon more or less settled. On 27 April 2006, NATO foreign ministers meeting in Sofia discussed the issue and agreed to strengthen partnerships with EAPC countries and discuss the expansion of partnerships with countries such as Japan, South Korea, Australia and New Zealand. Months later at the Riga summit, the final declaration stated that: 'NATO's policy of partnerships, dialogue, and cooperation is essential to the Alliance's purpose and its tasks. It has fostered strong relationships with countries of the Euro-Atlantic Partnership Council, the Mediterranean Dialogue, and the Istanbul Cooperation Initiative, as well as with Contact Countries', outlining subsequently several measures to further develop this policy. Later, the Lisbon summit in November 2010 gave new impetus to the partnerships, making dialogue and cooperation more inclusive, effective, flexible, meaningful and strategically oriented. This resulted in a new partnership policy, which was endorsed by NATO foreign ministers at their meeting in Berlin in April 2011. Meanwhile, Med Dialogue and ICI were developed in an inertial way.

The New Strategic Concept and the Problematic Cooperation with the Med and the Greater Middle East

The new Strategic Concept, adopted at the Lisbon Summit, identified cooperative security as a key priority for NATO and tried to establish deeper partnerships for the next generation. The Strategic Concept reaffirmed the importance of dialogue and cooperation with partners establishing the framework for these relationships: 'Dialogue and cooperation with partners can make a concrete contribution to enhancing international security, to defending the values on which our Alliance is based, to NATO's operations, and to preparing interested nations for membership of NATO. These relationships will be based on reciprocity, mutual benefit and mutual respect. We are prepared to develop political dialogue and practical cooperation with any nations and relevant organisations across the globe that share our interest in peaceful international relations. NATO remained open to consultation with any partner country on security issues of common concern and committed itself to give to operational partners a structural role in shaping strategy and decisions on NATO-led missions to which they contribute'.

The EAPC continued to be seen as central to Europe and with regard to the Mediterranean and the Greater Middle East, there was again the talk of deepening and strengthening the security partnerships, as well as the inclusion of new members.[7]

Nevertheless, the central issue to be stressed here was that the outcome of this expansion and deepening of activities and dialogue in the Mediterranean and the Greater Middle East since 2001 had been quite reduced. It was almost irrelevant for dealing with the new challenges and threats and the new priorities. I can mention the main problems:

- Lack of strategic clarity in NATO over its objectives in the Mediterranean and the Greater Middle East (Asmus 2008).
- Different objectives in partner countries from those of NATO in the promotion of the bilateral dialogue and security cooperation and, in particular, non-ownership of initiatives and dialogues by the Med partners. That is a precondition for success. The countries of the Med have often considered this dialogue and initiatives almost as a favour that they made to the European and NATO countries. And given the turmoil in the Middle East and the Israeli presence, they prefer bilateral relationships with NATO members. For this reason, the launching by NATO of common projects was fundamental.
- A lack of investment of time, people and money from NATO and a profound suspicion and ignorance of NATO on the part of the countries in the region, plus the lack of those mechanisms for dialogue and cooperation on which the success of NATO and the Partnership for Peace is based.
- These partnerships did not play a significant role in stabilizing the region or in helping and promoting the evolution of participating countries (Donnelly 2004) as it happened with the partnerships with the countries of Central and Eastern Europe.

[7] Although no mention was made of global partners, the document stated that 'we are prepared to develop political dialogue and practical cooperation with any nations and relevant organisations across the globe that share our interest in peaceful international relations'.

- The inability to decouple wider regional security issues from the Israeli–Palestinian conflict (Donnelly 2004). The profound deterioration in relations between Israel and the Palestinians after the failure of the Peace agreement negotiations at Camp David prevented progress in a regional dialogue where Israel was included.
- The profound deterioration in relations between Israel and Turkey.
- Military collaboration with NATO and CBMs and CSBMs was regarded by some countries of the Med as an instrument to maintain a military *status quo* that was considered profoundly unfair.[8]
- In the case of ICI, the different perceptions of threat in particular coming from Iran and the lack of a real multilateral track.
- The military intervention in Iraq plus the pretension of regime change and the imposition of Western democratic institutions. The general feeling in the Arab countries towards NATO after what happened in Iraq and Afghanistan was very disappointing.
- As a consequence: a situation of impasse. The Arab Mediterranean countries did not know what to ask the NATO and the Alliance did not know what to offer to the Southern Mediterranean countries, with the exception of Israel. In the Greater Middle East, the ICI countries were seeking mainly their own security needs and supporting their own groups and proxies in the region.

From the NATO side, some voices openly criticized this dialogue and partnerships focused more on cooperation with the countries than on their potential transformation. All this created an insurmountable barrier and the Arab revolutions, that started in December 2010 in Tunisia, showed the illusion of the former NATO statements. NATO Med Dialogue and ICI were irrelevant for managing the revolts. Deepening cooperation and democratization was a dream.

NATO and the Arab Revolutions

However, this was not the initial official perception in NATO once the Arab revolutions started. Anders Fogh Rasmussen, on 1 June 2011, speaking on the Arab Spring said the following: 'We are prepared to

[8] Even some important military in Egypt considered this dialogue as a subtle form of NATO military espionage.

engage with partners across and beyond our existing partnership frameworks. This will allow us to discuss a broader range of issues, including those that our partners wish to raise [...] individual liberty, democracy, human rights and the rule of law. We consider these to be universal principles that apply to all peoples of the world, including in North Africa and the Middle East [...] The reform of the military and the security sector are key milestones on the road to democracy' (Rasmussen 2011).

In fact, the NATO Foreign Ministers meeting in Berlin in April 2011 approved the strengthening of the consultation mechanisms, facilitating cooperative initiatives with increased practical content and a new 'toolbox' of mechanisms and activities with partners, opening all cooperative activities and exercises offered to PfP partners and some programmes offered in the PfP 'toolbox' to all partners. The Med/ICI cooperation expanded progressively in more than 30 areas of cooperation. The 'toolbox' of the Mediterranean Dialogue passed from around 700 to more than 1600 activities and events. In the case of ICI, the activities/events passed from 328 to around 500 in 2011.

In the case of the Med Dialogue, these activities ranged from ordinary military contact to exchanges of information on maritime security and counterterrorism; access to educational programmes provided by alliance institutions; civil preparedness against CBRN attacks on populations and critical infrastructures; joint crisis management exercises and the safe destruction of arms stockpiles. A number of cooperation tools were progressively opened to Med countries.[9]

In the case of ICI, the cooperation areas included tailored advice on defence transformation, defence budgeting, defence planning and civil–military relations; Military-to-military cooperation to contribute to interoperability; the fight against terrorism, including intelligence-sharing

[9] Such as: The e-Prime database which provides electronic access to the MDWP allowing close monitoring of cooperation activities; The full package of Operational Capabilities Concept (OCC) to improve partners' capacity to contribute effectively to NATO-led Crisis Response Operations through achieving interoperability; The Trust Fund mechanism that currently includes ongoing substantial projects with MD countries such as Jordan and Mauritania; The Euro-Atlantic Disaster Response Coordination Center (EADRCC) aims at improving partners' capacity in supporting NATO's response to crises; The Partnership Action Plan Against Terrorism (PAP-T) aims at strengthening NATO's ability to work effectively with MD partners in the fight against terrorism; The Civil Emergency Planning (CEP) action plan aims at improving the civil preparedness against CBRN attacks on populations and critical infrastructures.

measures; the proliferation of weapons of mass destruction and their means of delivery; border security in connection with terrorism, small arms and light weapons and the fight against illegal trafficking; civil emergency planning, including participating in training courses and exercises on disaster assistance; joint public diplomacy activities to update governments' and opinion leaders' understanding of NATO and the evolution of the ICI; improving advice, education and training for reform on different issues affecting civil–military issues, defence and security sectors.

But NATO supply, once again, exceeded the demand of the NATO partners in the Mediterranean and the Greater Middle East and the complexity of the conflicts in the Mediterranean and, in particular, their transformation in more intricate and heterogeneous conflicts was not taken into account, considering that the successful revolutions may remove previously existing obstacles to cooperation.

Projecting stability by supporting the transformation of the political regimes, spreading the neoliberal norms and institutions, promoting democracy and human rights, was an illusion. The Arab revolutions did not mean a political transformation. The established power structures were restored in most of the countries after chaos, and countries like Libya and Syria become failed states or states profoundly divided.

The external interference of different actors in North Africa and the Eastern Mediterranean also grew. The ICI countries attended ministerial meetings held during Operation Unified Protector in 2011 but, at the end, became spoilers of the new partnership initiatives and the deepening advocated by NATO's secretary general. The external interference of Saudi Arabia and other Gulf countries, in particular Qatar, non-democratic states, putting aside the behaviour of Turkey which pursued its own policy, bypassing consultations with its NATO allies affected also by this political turmoil, hijacked the Arab revolutions somehow and the role of Turkey in projection of its Muslim model did not meet the expectations.

In this perspective, it can be stressed the short-sightedness of some experimental US policies, in order to address the 'freedom deficit' as the root cause of the extremism and terrorism existing in Muslim countries. Turkey was a good example where, at the end, the George W. Bush Administrations ended up supporting the AKP against the Kemalists. The increasing Islamization of Turkey now is a reality and Turkey has not become a model for any Arab country in the region. Turkey has also become a spoiler of NATO and Western initiatives in Libya, Syria, the Balkans and other places in the region.

The results were very regrettable, the EU and NATO lost influence in the Mediterranean and the Middle East. Russia, for her part, increased her presence in Syria, Egypt and Libya and became a solid competitor with NATO in the Mediterranean and the Middle East. It provides now some available alternatives to NATO partners, playing the interests of NATO against the interest of Russia. And Iran substantially increased its presence in the Middle East in particular in Syria, Lebanon, Iraq and Yemen.

Adding to this, the conflict in Libya created a profound instability in Mali, and the Sahel in general, broadening the space for promoting security and stability in North Africa, and the French Operation Serval, a non-NATO nor EU CSDP operation, was launched on 11 January 2013 to secure and stabilize the country. Nevertheless, the Sahel has become an increasingly ungoverned space where a good number of terrorist groups linked to al Qaeda and ISIS have been consolidated, expanding their presence in the region, exploiting the weakness of the states and accelerating the recruitment of new fighters, taking advantage of the COVID-19 pandemic.

The consequences of these revolutions are now clearer. Heterogeneity and lack of homogeneity grew between North and South. The Arab security space increasingly gravitated towards the Gulf, where the interest for the NATO Dialogue was much lower and the format was fundamentally bilateral. The values and universal principles advocated by NATO could not be developed and implemented.

In this context, some shared objectives regarding common challenges became more difficult to define, programme and plan, such as the fighting against radicalism and terrorism. For instance, in Tunisia, Ennahda, the majority party in the coalition governments formed after the fall of Ben Ali, did not condemn the radical Salafists. Radicalism and Jihadism were also spread in Libya, Syria and Egypt. Saudi Arabia and other members of the Gulf Cooperation Countries (GCC), which had financed Salafism and Wahhabism everywhere, including Asia, created a good breeding ground to increase recruitment of radical Islamists and foreign fighters in European and Muslim countries.

Another point to be stressed is the meaning of partnership and its application to the Med and the Greater Middle East. Partnership in a context of security is a very ambitious term. It means and presupposes some common values and purposes.[10] Once the heterogeneity between North and South significantly increased, NATO partnership with the Med and the Greater Middle East became a more difficult task and more precarious.

The Fight Against ISIS. The Embraced NATO Regional Order for the Med and the Greater Middle East Collapses

The Arab revolutions hit Syria in particular, generating a civil war in 2011. The fighting between factions led to the internationalization of the conflict and the financing and training of multiple Islamist groups by various countries, many of which ended up forming part of ISIS. In June 2014, Abu Bakr al-Baghdadi announced the reestablishment of the ISIS 'caliphate' in Mosul's Grand Mosque.

This announcement forced the United States to become directly involved in the conflict, starting air strikes in August. The following month, on 5 September, the Wales summit took place and discussed this profound transformation of the Syrian conflict. As a result, NATO introduced the possibility of 'enhanced opportunities' for certain partners to build a deeper, more tailor-made bilateral relationship with NATO, new goals of cooperation and a new partnership forum:

- The Partnership Interoperability Initiative that incorporated initially Jordan and, later, several regional partners: Bahrain, Morocco, Tunisia and the UAE. It was a flexible forum bringing together allies and partners. This initiative meant more connectivity with NATO, and tried to maintain and further enhance the ability of external partners to carry out joint military operations with NATO armed forces. The five partners have an enhanced political dialogue with NATO, could fill more staffing positions at NATO headquarters and could examine a broad range of issues regarding interoperability with NATO's forces for future crisis management—from command

[10] There are multiple definitions of the term and different countries apply different classifications of partners according to the importance they attribute to the bilateral relationship. See Marquina (2019).

and control, through education and training, to the participation in exercises and logistics

- The Defence and Related Security Capacity Building Initiative for projecting stability among its neighbours and beyond, without having to transfer larger NATO combat units. NATO shifted the role, from 'security provider' to 'security consultant'. This initiative was an important tool to help project stability, making it easier for partners, such as Iraq and Jordan, to make a contribution to their own security (through help in information protection; cyber defence; military exercises; counter-improvised explosive devices; communication, command and control; harbour protection; and border security) opened to other partners upon request.[11] This initiative was built upon NATO's extensive expertise in defence capacity building, including in places like Kosovo and Afghanistan and was open to other countries and organizations.

NATO announced the desire to further develop relations with relevant regional international organizations, such as the GCC and the Arab League, and be open to engaging with others, including in the context of regional crisis situations. Later, on 10 September, President Obama announced the creation of the Global Coalition to Defeat ISIS. NATO, as well as all its Med/ICI partners, with the exception of Israel and Algeria, ended up participating in the coalition.

Given the fact that NATO had recognized that ISIL constituted a grave threat to the Greatest Middle East, the North Africa region and NATO members. In 2016, the NATO Warsaw summit communiqué stated that 'the continuing crises and instability across the Middle East and North Africa region, in particular in Syria, Iraq and Libya, as well as the threat of terrorism and violent extremism across the region and beyond, demonstrate that the security of the region has direct implications for the security of NATO [...] Peace and Stability in this [...] region are essential for the Alliance'. Adding that it was fundamental to strengthen security outside the NATO territory to enhance the Alliance's role in projecting stability, adapting to the challenges and threats from all directions, confronting transnational security threats and challenges such as proliferation of WMD

[11] At the Brussels summit in July 2018, NATO allies approved a DCB package for Tunisia.

and their delivery means, criminal trafficking, reinforcing its maritime dimension, and developing a more tailor-made, individual, and flexible approach to make the partnerships more strategic, more coherent and more effective. NATO began applying a new approach to the regional partnerships called 'projecting stability'.

As practical measures, the NATO leaders decided to provide support through NATO to the fight against ISIL, contributing with several important assets such as NATO AWACS aircraft to the Global Coalition to Counter ISIL, the creation of a new division at NATO Headquarters, consisting of two pillars: intelligence (with the merged strands of military and civilian intelligence) and security (the NATO Office of Security) and improving intelligence, reconnaissance and surveillance capabilities, (drones deployed in Sicily). A maritime security operation, Sea Guardian, was launched in November 2016 in the Mediterranean Sea—non-Article 5 operation—performing three tasks: maritime situational awareness, counterterrorism at sea and support to capacity building. If decided by Allies, it could also perform other tasks such as upholding freedom of navigation, conducting interdiction tasks and protecting critical infrastructure.

The meeting of Heads of State and/or Government, on 25 May 2017 decided to add the following items: to establish a terrorism intelligence cell within the new Intelligence Division, improving the sharing of information among Allies, including the threat of foreign fighters, and greater use of NATO's Special Operations Headquarters, which already offered tailored counterterrorism training for Allies and partners. This could involve more mobile training teams deployed to countries at risk. Later, on 5 September 2017, in the Joint Force Command Naples a 'hub' to coordinate intelligence, counterterrorism and defence capacity-building activities in the southern neighbourhood was established.

The message was clear: NATO wanted to increase the support to NATO's southern partners in building counterterrorism capabilities and institutions, in building local capacity. However, it was also clear that neither NATO nor the Med Dialogue and ICI partners has taken a critical combat role in the fight against ISIS and other extremist groups in Iraq and Syria or even Libya. Adding to this, the main task in the fight against terrorism, beyond police and intelligence collaboration, contrasting the radical ideologies and narratives of the terrorist groups was absent. In this regard, the new US administration of President Donald Trump made crystal clear statements on that critical question (Marquina 2019).

Notwithstanding, in capacity-building activities with partners such as Jordan, Morocco, Egypt or Tunisia, NATO has tended to expand its relations with individual countries (Tunisia, Morocco, Egypt, Algeria, Jordan, Qatar) undermining the regional multilateral approach of the partnerships. On the contrary, the NATO-ICI Regional Centre inaugurated in Kuwait on 27 January 2017 has helped to enhance the multilateral cooperation through training courses and activities open to NATO, the GCC and their members.

Regarding non-proliferation, another traditional important item in the common agenda, it can be said that non-proliferation of WMD lost saliency after the Joint Comprehensive Plan of Action (JCPOA) was signed in Vienna on 14 July 2015 between Iran and the P5 + 1 countries. The relations with Iran continued to be a divisive element among the ICI countries that had to be nuanced as a common objective. However, the problem has remained latent as the best-case scenario in the case of Iran, a Japanese model, will be replicated in Saudi Arabia, Turkey, Egypt and even Jordan, among others. What NATO could do in this regard is very limited.

The main problem this time was to confront the new situation created once the regional order maintained after the Cold War collapsed and NATO could not present a solid alternative. The packages of specialized support in fighting terrorism, military exercises, border control, cybersecurity, harbour protection or civil protection activities contained in the Defence and Related Security Capacity Building Initiative did not constitute a solid alternative to confront the new threat and its ramifications, taking into account the perceptions of a good part of the societies of these countries, increasingly influenced by Islamism and by Islamist parties. The new initiatives in a process of reorganization were going to imply a substantial change in NATO's approach. It was no longer a matter of considering a certain dimension of cooperative security or a possible NATO crisis management in the Southern Flank but also touching the core question of collective defence. These initiatives could be perceived as a subtle way of creating advanced areas of protection in the collective defence of NATO, strengthening the existing authoritarian regimes. Heterogeneity in the activities selected by the partners meant also giving up to the ability to make a proper design for the region, acceptable to all the Med and ICI partners. Adding to this, what NATO could offer on critical issues for projecting stability such as Conflict prevention—avoiding the rising of conflicts from tensions, their spreading and their escalation—Crisis management and Conflict resolution had important limitations (Marquina 2019). Another important issue, the displacement of millions of people from the region into the European Union, induced by various causes, could not be handled by these states either, given the limited support that NATO could offer, although it tried to restraint the scandalous manipulation of migration flows by Turkey, approving the deployment of the Standing Maritime Group 2 (SNMG2) in the Aegean Sea (Marquina 2019).

Concurrently, NATO had now to deal with the implications of a strong actor like Russia that was increasing its presence and activities in the Med and Greater Middle East trying to defend its own interests that were in conflict many times with the rules, order and influence established by NATO after the Cold War and even with international agreements and international law, as was the case in Crimea and in Eastern Ukraine.

New Actors in the Med and the Greater Middle East and the Reconfiguration of the Partnerships

Today, the regional security context has changed significantly. In the Greater Middle East, important changes took place during Donald Trump's administration. On 8 May 2017, the United States announced its withdrawal from the JCPOA and on 21 May, Donald Trump visited Riyadh where he had a meeting with the GCC and afterwards participated in a summit with about 50 leaders and representatives from Muslim-majority countries where he made a significant speech urging the Arab and Islamic leaders to unite and drive out the terrorists and extremists. Trump singled out Iran as a key source of funding and support for militant groups and asked for its isolation. He also opened a new Global Center for Combating Extremist Ideology and signed an agreement to prevent the financing of terrorism (Ians 2017; Holland and Mason 2021).

But the GCC soon became fractured. In June 2017, Saudi Arabia, the United Arab Emirates, Bahrain and Egypt cut off trade and diplomatic relations with Qatar and imposed a land, sea and air embargo, accusing this country of supporting terrorism and maintaining close ties with Iran. Later, on 7 August, sanctions were imposed again by the United States to Tehran.

All this took place when Trump tried to forge a security alliance with the GCC plus Egypt and Jordan, countries with different perspectives on their own security, including the crucial question of how to deal with

Iran and its expansionism in the Middle East. Although the blockade on Qatar was a stumbling block, an attempt was made in 2018 to launch an 'Arab NATO', hoping that the initiative would become a reality in 2019, but to no avail (Behravesh 2018; Helou 2018). Afterwards, in January 2020, Trump asked for NATO's deeper involvement in the Middle East. This new initiative was quite divisive. Italy and Spain had been pushing for NATO's deeper involvement in this area but France did not consider it advisable, explaining that NATO had no experience in the region and would not be able to handle its problems successfully. In addition, Turkey was blocking NATO initiatives in the region that did not fit well in its own strategy or regional policies, such as NATO cooperation with Israel or Egypt (Jean-Loup 2020). This new proposition did not achieve practical results.

After the November 2020 general elections in the United States and in view of the foreseeable change of policies of the new administration, the GCC meeting in al-Ula decided to lift their blockade on Qatar and restored diplomatic relations with the country, but frictions have continued, especially between the UAE and Qatar, reinforced by the Turkey–Qatar strategic partnership (Ramani 2021). To all this, the impact on the GCC of the Biden administration's new policies on Iran cannot be hidden.

In addition to these profound changes, another issue of fundamental importance must be mentioned, the divisions induced by the recognition of Israel by the UAE, Bahrain, Morocco and Sudan, though Israel remains opposed to Palestinian independence. Inadvertently, all this would indirectly affect the ICI cohesion, propelling fragmentation.

In North Africa, conflicts and dissensions have also increased. Leaving aside the deep rivalry between Algeria and Morocco, the conflict in Libya has led to the formation of opposing alliances in support to two rival governments, the government of Field Marshal Khalifa Haftar in Benghazi supported by Russia, Egypt, the UAE, France, Saudi Arabia, Sudan and the backing of United States and Jordan to a lesser extent, and to the Government of National Accord in Tripoli with the impressive support of Turkey, Qatar, Algeria and sometimes Italy. These divisions have made the conflict unsolvable, inducing serious problems such as the settlement of terrorist groups, mafias and organized crime and uncontrolled migratory flows propelled by these mafias.

Added to this, the deep rivalry induced by Turkey's claims to waters, EEZ and hydrocarbon resources in the Eastern Mediterranean, clashing with the rights of Greece and Cyprus, has to be mentioned, and, above all, the growing presence and influence of Russia as previously mentioned.

Russia's intervention in Syria and the opportunities opened up by the policies implemented by the United States and the European Union in several Arab states affected by the revolutions have allowed Russia to emerge as an unavoidable external player in the Mediterranean and the Greater Middle East. Russia filled a vacuum opened by the Western democracies, and the Arab countries found in Russia an alternative support for confronting the Western policies, the case of Egypt being the most striking one (Talbot and Lovotti 2019).

Subsequently, its diplomatic and military successes in Syria have allowed it to manoeuvre in other conflicts such as Libya, Yemen, Iran, Lebanon and even to increase its influence in Saudi Arabia and Israel, creating simultaneously strong asymmetries and divisions on policies to be implemented in both the EU and NATO. Russia has become a solid competitor, complicating greatly the relations of NATO with the Med/ICI partners. It provides now some available alternatives to NATO partners, playing the interests of NATO against the interest of Russia. Russia's reappearance in the Mediterranean also requires now a new NATO deterrence and defense approach.

China, whose presence in the Mediterranean and Greater Middle East was very small at the end of the Cold War, is also a new player. Today, China is already the largest trading partner and investor in many countries in the region. In addition, its soft power has increased significantly. More than one million Chinese live, work and study in the Arab states and Beijing's cultural influence is also on the rise. The growing positive perception of China in the region is also reflected in the public opinion of the Arab countries in the face of the existing unease towards Washington (Chaolan 2021). China's military presence has also been growing in recent years, and this trend is expected to continue as US interest in the region wanes or is perceived to wane. China's cautious and increased engagement in the region, exploiting also its soft military profile, brings into play a combination of arms exports, joint military exercises, UN peacekeeping missions, counterterrorism efforts and a naval presence, contributing to a broader transformation of the regional order and increasingly challenging the US and European influence, fostering some tensions (Atilgan 2020; Sidło 2020).

This emerging transition to multipolarity is already affecting NATO's ability to define the objectives and security priorities in the region and to defend its own values against the forces that seek to overturn the rules-based order previously established. In this new environment, the Alliance has not become the centre for consultation on international security issues, as previously thought, and regarding democracy, human rights and the rule of law, their partners in the Med/ICI region could now select other models and alternatives provided by these new authoritarian and totalitarian regimes with growing influence in the region. The democratic transformation of the region is now a much more illusory dream.

In this more heterogeneous environment, NATO has to substantially redefine its approach to the partnerships in the region. In order to project stability and develop a more strategic approach, NATO needs to clarify first how it sees the present enlarged Mediterranean Strategic Space—suppressing at any cost the growing unilateralism and lack of consultation existing inside the Alliance—and how it wants to project its values and interests. The role of partners in the design and implementation of a new order for the Mediterranean and the Greater Middle East has to be redefined, starting with a strong ownership by partners of the initiatives to be approved in common and common projects. The possibility of multilateral approaches in the Med/ICI partnerships has faded away.

In the next coming years, the principles of the Med/ICI initiatives have to be revised. Looking at the evolution of these partnerships, this dialogue, while maintaining the principle of non-discrimination, has fostered singularity, and this differentiation will increase. Dialogue with partners can no longer maintain as one of its objectives the fostering of south–south cooperation, something which has proved difficult to develop and will become even more difficult in the future.

To conclude, dialogue and cooperation will be essentially bilateral and case-by-case. It is likely that the goals of strengthening political engagement, sustaining capacity building and resilience can be prevalent. However, bearing in mind the new competition among states, NATO has to start the evaluation of possible reassurances to be provided and what new contributions to the objectives of the Alliance partners should make. This will create new asymmetries in NATO's southern flank and the Greater Middle East.

Bibliography

Agnes, Helou. 2018. What's standing in the way of an Arab NATO? *Defense News*.

Asmus, Ron D. 2008, March 27. Rethinking NATO Partnerships for the 21st Century. *NATO Review*. https://www.nato.int/docu/review/articles/2008/03/27/rethinking-nato-partnerships-for-the-21st-century/index.html.

Asmus, Ron D. (ed.). 2006. NATO and Global Partners: Views from the Outside. *The German Marshall Fund of the United States*.

Atilgan, Canan. 2020. Fast and Furious: China's rise in the Middle East and North Africa. *Konrad-Adenauer Stiftung*. https://www.kas.de/en/country-reports/detail/-/content/fast-and-furious-china-s-rise-in-the-middle-east-and-north-africa.

Behravesh, Maysam. 2018, August 15. Why Trump's 'Arab NATO' plan won't curb Iran. *Reuters*.

Chaolan, Wu. 2021, January 28. Arab Barometer: People in MENA region favour China over US. *Pople's Daily*. http://en.people.cn/n3/2021/0128/c90000-9813952.html#.YBOEq8ptSaE.reddit.

Donnelly, Chris. 2004. Building a NATO partnership for the Greater Middle East. *NATO Review*. https://www.nato.int/docu/review/articles/2004/01/01/building-a-nato-partnership-for-the-greater-middle-east/index.html.

Holland, Steve, and Jeff Mason. 2017, May 21. Trump Tells Saudi Arabia and Other Muslim Nations to 'Drive Out' Islamist Extremists. *Reuters*. https://www.reuters.com/article/us-usa-trump-saudi-idUSKCN18H00U.

Ians. 2017, May 21. Donald Trump-GCC leaders' summit begins in Saudi Arabia. *Financial Express*.

Jean-Loup, Samaan. 2012. NATO's dealing with a different Gulf now. *NATO Review*. https://www.nato.int/docu/review/articles/2012/12/06/nato-s-dealing-with-a-different-gulf-now/index.html.

Jean-Loup, Samaan. 2020. The Limitations of a NATO-Middle East Military Cooperation. *Carnegie Middle East Center*. https://carnegieendowment.org/sada/81740.

Kamp, Karl-Heinz. 2006. 'Global Partnership': A New Conflict Within NATO? *Analysen und Argumente aus der Konrad-Adenauer-Stiftung*, No. 29/2006.

Marquina, Antonio. 2019. NATO'S Southern Flank and the Threat of Disruption. *Journal of Transatlantic Studies* 17: 223–237.

Marquina, Antonio (ed.). 1993. *El Flanco Sur de la OTAN*. Ediciones Complutense.

Rademacher, Fritz (2007). The NATO Training Cooperation Initiative. *NATO Review*. https://www.nato.int/docu/review/2007/Reviewing_Riga/NATO_training_cooperation_initiative/EN/index.htm.

Ramani, Samuel. 2021, January 27. The Qatar Blockade is Over, but the Gulf Crisis Lives On. *Foreign Policy.* https://foreignpolicy.com/2021/01/27/qatar-blockade-gcc-divisions-turkey-libya-palestine/.

Rasmussen, Anders F. 2011, June 1. NATO and the Arab Spring. *NATO.* https://www.nato.int/cps/en/natohq/opinions_74993.htm?selectedLocale=en

Sidło, Katarzyna W. (ed.). 2020. The Role of China in the Middle East and North Africa (MENA). Beyond Economic Interests?. *Euromesco Joint Policy Study*, 16. https://www.euromesco.net/wp-content/uploads/2019/10/Report-27_The-role-of-China-in-the-Middle-East.-Beyond-Economic-Interests.pdf.

Solana, Javier. 1997. NATO and the Mediterranean. *Mediterranean Quarterly* 8: 2–13.

Talbot, Valeria, and Chiara Lovotti (eds.). 2019. The Role of Russia in the Middle East and North Africa Region. Strategy or Opportunism?. *Euromesco Joint Policy Study*, 12. https://www.euromesco.net/wp-content/uploads/2018/11/Report-23-Russia-role-in-the-MENA-region.pdf.

Whitman, Richard. 1997–1999. Securing Europe's Southern Flank? A Comparison of NATO, EU and WEU Policies and Objectives. *NATO*, Final Report, NATO Individual Research Fellowship. https://www.nato.int/acad/fellow/97-99/whitman.pdf.

CHAPTER 9

NATO and the Impact of the *Long War* in Afghanistan: Avoiding a Wrong Memory About ISAF

Andrea Carati

In early December 2020, the Reflection Group appointed by NATO Secretary General Jens Stoltenberg presented its final report on the future of the Atlantic Alliance. The report, titled *NATO 2030: United for a new era*, aims to gauge ways to strengthen NATO's political dimension, providing practical recommendations on a number of issue areas. In the chapter on peace and security, the second recommendation states that the alliance 'should conduct lessons-learned exercises from recent missions in Afghanistan' (NATO 2020). However reasonable and achievable this seems, particularly after the international withdrawal in August 2021, it is not an easy task. Not only because NATO's engagement in Afghanistan has been by far the most demanding mission in the alliance's history,

A. Carati (✉)
Department of International Studies, University of Milan, Milan, Italy
e-mail: andrea.carati1@unimi.it

M. de Leonardis (ed.), *NATO in the Post-Cold War Era*, Security, Conflict and Cooperation in the Contemporary World
https://doi.org/10.1007/978-3-031-06063-2_9

but because a superficial appraisal of what happened during the *long war* could easily lead to incorrect conclusions.

This chapter aims to contribute to a broader and critical understanding of NATO-ISAF between 2003 and 2014. It sheds light on three main underexplored aspects of that mission that allow us to appreciate the difficulties NATO has faced in Afghanistan and, in turn, prevent us from drawing hasty conclusions. Indeed, ISAF is often compared to other NATO (and non-NATO) peacekeeping operations, while at least three exceptional circumstances that affected its limited successes are overlooked. First, unlike in any other NATO military operations, ISAF intervened late, almost two years after the United States launched its own military campaign. Second, contrary to what occurred in the Balkans, ISAF had to share the battlefield with another robust and autonomous military mission, *Enduring Freedom*. Third, over the years, ISAF had to significantly change its approach, both strategically and tactically. All these crucial aspects made ISAF a unique case of 'peacekeeping'. It is important to bear in mind its exceptionality to avert inappropriate interpretations and ill-conceived lessons.

Accordingly, the chapter argues that recognising the exceptional circumstances that NATO faced in Afghanistan should invite to avoid clear-cut generalisations, especially those that devalue the alliance's resilience and overstate past failures. It is organised as follows. The next section briefly summarises NATO's involvement in Afghanistan. The three sections that follow delve respectively into the three distinctive features of ISAF that differentiate it from other NATO missions: late involvement, uneasy coexistence with *Enduring Freedom* and the difficult transformation it underwent. Finally, the concluding section recaps the main argument and suggests that lessons-learned exercises should start preventing a 'wrong memory' of ISAF.

The *Long War* in Afghanistan and the Narrative of Failure

NATO's engagement in Afghanistan has been by far the most challenging in its history. Compared to all other operations conducted by the alliance, the NATO-led ISAF (International Security Assistance Force) operation was the longest, broadest and most ambitious. With the exception of KFOR, deployed in Kosovo since 1999, ISAF is the lengthiest mission (2003–2014). However, if we focus exclusively on combat operations, the alliance's involvement in Afghanistan has been its longest military endeavour ever. The *long war* alongside the United States was also the most extensive, in terms of both force contributions by member states and military commitment—ground, air and naval troops—and assets (Hanagan 2019). Moreover, it was also the most wide-ranging because of its unprecedented array of global activities for what, until then, had been a Euro-centric security organisation. Lastly, NATO's operations in Afghanistan have been the most ambitious due to its multiple strategic goals and activities. They range from peace support after the Taliban were defeated to state-building, from counterterrorism to counterinsurgency, from military training of Afghan security forces to humanitarian assistance (Bird and Marshall 2011).

Not surprisingly, the war in Afghanistan has been exceptionally costly. To provide what is a complicated and always approximate estimate of the costs of war, the US budgets for post-9/11 wars are a reliable source of information. The most recent papers, issued in 2019 and 2021, for the 'Costs of War Project' by the Watson Institute (Brown University, US) establishes that, since late 2001, the United States has spent an estimated $6.4 trillion in costs related to and caused by post-9/11 wars (Crawford 2018; Davidson 2021). The lion's share of those costs concerns the wars in Afghanistan and Iraq. In the Af-Pak region, the annual costs of war have fluctuated and are recently declining, but the 'total estimated appropriations for the Afghanistan and Pakistan war by the DOD and State Department are about $978 billion from FY [Fiscal Year] 2001 through FY 2020' (Crawford 2018). If the US financial expenditure in Afghanistan is any indication, it is easy to extrapolate the massive costs that NATO had to bear. In addition to financial costs, the human cost has also been considerable. The coalition has experienced casualties in Afghanistan that cannot be compared with any other NATO intervention. With the deaths of over 3500 coalition soldiers (and over 110,000 Afghan casualties), this mission has been the deadliest in NATO's history (Doucet 2020).

At its peak in 2011, NATO-ISAF dwarfed all other missions combined. That year saw NATO exceptionally engaged in several grounds, naval and air operations around the world: KFOR in Kosovo; two maritime operations in the Horn of Africa and in the Mediterranean basin (*Ocean Shield* and *Active Endeavour*); the training mission in Iraq; and the air campaign *Unified Protector* in Libya. Yet, ten years later, the mission in Afghanistan was still the largest and most significant in military terms. Indeed, in 2011 ISAF reached its maximum size of more than 131,000 troops; it was the only mission in which all twenty-eight members participated, alongside over twenty other non-NATO nations (Hanagan 2019).

Despite being such a long and massive undertaking, the general perception was that the NATO intervention in Afghanistan was failing. After the defeat of the Taliban in 2001 the prevailing mood in NATO headquarters and in Western capitals was optimistic (Bird and Marshall 2011). However, when the Taliban insurgency gained momentum in 2007, pessimism started to prevail. Since then, the general perception of it having been a failure has been on the rise (Rynning 2012) and even increased after the withdrawal of ISAF at the end of 2014 (ICG 2014). Both the persisting worsening of security conditions in the country and the inescapable negotiations with the Taliban confirmed the narrative of failure.

Even though some would not call it a failure, it is undeniable that the US-NATO intervention in Afghanistan has been largely unsuccessful in many ways (Carati 2015). After twenty years of war, state-building and humanitarian assistance, Afghanistan remains a fragile state, plagued by political instability, poverty and insecurity (UN 2020). The strategic goal of keeping Afghanistan far from returning to being a safe haven for Islamic terrorism has been accomplished only partially. Having been ousted from Afghanistan, al-Qaeda efficiently regrouped in Pakistan after a few years. The Taliban were defeated but they recently regained political sway thanks to negotiations with the United States (Nasrat 2020) and eventually they took power in Kabul in Summer 2021 concurrently with the international withdrawal. The liberal agenda to build functioning state institutions and promote basic human rights has been left largely unachieved. Of course, there have been several improvements in humanitarian conditions, compared to conditions under the Taliban regime before 2001, but they are weak, limited and reversible. More generally, they are hardly satisfying in light of such a long and extensive international effort.

However, it is probably incorrect to draw the conclusion that ISAF and its multiple tasks are of no use for future NATO peacekeeping missions, or to use the alliance's experience in Afghanistan exclusively as an example of what we should avoid in the future. Many scholars have already identified the key elements that led NATO to such a poor result in Afghanistan. The multitude of operative tasks and their ambition inevitably led to inefficiency (Bird and Marshall 2011). The heterogeneity of, and poor coordination between, national contributions to ISAF played their part in making matters worse (Auerswald and Saideman 2014). Even the doctrinal stance of NATO as a liberal 'benevolent alliance' set the stage for a mismatch between ends and means, which is always a hindrance to consistent strategies (Bird 2013; Rynning 2012). Several pundits have pointed out the scant or non-existent knowledge of the regional and cultural context (Gall 2014). While others blame the lack of political will and military resolve in the US and among European allies (Johnson 2011).

However, in the huge body of literature investigating the roots of NATO's lack of success in Afghanistan, one aspect is commonly neglected: the exceptional circumstances in which NATO was initially involved and engaged. Compared to other NATO missions, NATO-ISAF is a unique case in many regards, but three features are particularly important in correctly framing the difficulties it faced. The next three sections deal with each in turn.

NATO as the Late Comer in Kabul

When the US–NATO intervention in Afghanistan is debated, we generally assume that NATO was part of the story from the very beginning. All historical accounts and experts are accurate enough to report that ISAF was initially an UN-mandated multinational mission and NATO was not involved in 2001, neither in the US-led intervention nor in the UN peacekeeping mission. Those accounts are precise in recounting how the alliance was called to lead ISAF in August 2003. Yet, this crucial aspect of the late involvement in Afghanistan, although well known, is neglected or regarded as unimportant. The very fact that NATO took command of ISAF in Afghanistan almost two years after the beginning of the US military campaign appeared devoid of consequences for NATO. Indeed, in the overall assessment of the alliance peacekeeping missions after the end of the Cold War—especially when those missions are investigated comparatively—this unique circumstance is hardly considered.

However, NATO's belated engagement is in fact a decisive element in understanding what went wrong for the alliance in Afghanistan. It was not only an accidental or limited delay—like in Libya in 2011 when the NATO operation *Unified Protector* centralised and coordinated, after a few days, the *Odyssey Dawn* early air campaign launched by France, the UK and the United States (Chivvis 2013). In Afghanistan, NATO entered one of the most problematic theatres of war of the post-Cold War era when the battlefield had already been shaped (and had in many ways deteriorated) by the US-led military operation *Enduring Freedom* (Coll 2018; Rashid 2009). That is to say that NATO was not in the lead from the start, which is in itself problematic, but was literally inheriting a problematic situation in Afghanistan, where the country was already experiencing all the repercussions, transformations and uncertainties produced by an external military intervention that toppled the previous regime. The degree of instability and insecurity were not only the result of previous local conflicts but were part of the political void produced by the US external intervention. Focusing on some aspects of the US-led campaign before NATO's engagement and on the situation in Afghanistan in 2002 can help to reemphasise the importance of that crucial delay.

When the Bush administration launched the operation *Enduring Freedom* in late 2001, after the 9/11 terrorist attacks, the United States led a small coalition of countries with two objectives: to overthrow the Taliban regime and hunt down al-Qaeda militants (Ripley 2011). At the time, the US-led operation in Afghanistan was significantly different from both previous interventions (Iraq in 1991, Somalia and the Balkans) and the one that followed in Iraq in 2003. Unlike previous military operations, it was less planned, unilateral and a lighter type of war. Unlike *Iraqi Freedom*, it was not a large-scale invasion of the target country. The 'light footprint' approach, as the Secretary of Defence Donald Rumsfeld named it, was the framework that inspired the campaign (Salt 2018). In the early stages, *Enduring Freedom* was more a paramilitary war, with CIA operatives playing a prominent role, and almost devoid of ground troops (Coll 2018). More precisely, the strategy envisaged helping the so-called Northern Alliance (a motley aggregation of local Taliban enemies) to let them win the creeping civil war and oust the Taliban from Kabul, and possibly from the whole Afghan territory (Biddle 2006). When the Northern Alliance, thanks to decisive American air support, defeated the Taliban, which left Kabul in November 2001, *Enduring Freedom* transitioned slowly to a more familiar military campaign with a counterterrorism approach. By the end of 2002, US forces had achieved their early (and fairly focused) goals: they had overthrown the Taliban regime and dismantled the al-Qaeda network in Afghanistan.

This type of war left the country in an uncertain situation. The political vacuum in Kabul, the lack of wide-ranging control of the territory and the narrow focus on counterterrorism turned out to be the worst conditions for facilitating the country's stabilisation (Dobbins 2008). When, under the auspices of the United Nations, the delegations of prominent

Afghan representatives gathered in Bonn in December 2001, the general feeling in the international community was that the war was over and the peacekeeping/state-building missions could start, as they had in Bosnia and Kosovo after NATO military campaigns. The quick victory led to optimism about the possibility of rebuilding the country. Among other ambitious goals, one element of the roadmap to bring back stability and security in Afghanistan was the international peacekeeping mission. The original ISAF mandate was actually very limited in scope. Deployed only in Kabul and its surroundings, the UN-mandated multinational mission was clearly undersized for the vast territory of Afghanistan; it was not comparable to previous NATO peacekeeping operations in Kosovo and Bosnia. In those much smaller countries, NATO had sent around 40,000 troops to Kosovo (KFOR) and 60,000 to Bosnia (IFOR-SFOR), while in Afghanistan in late 2001/early 2002, ISAF comprised around six thousand troops (Chandler 2002; Kay 2005). In other words, in the aftermath of the *Enduring Freedom's* victory over the Taliban, in Afghanistan, there was neither a wide-ranging peacekeeping deployment nor full international control of the territory, nor at least of key strategic areas beyond Kabul.

In addition, when *Enduring Freedom* slowly turned into a larger military campaign in late 2001 and then throughout 2002, it remained focused on counterterrorism, hunting down the remnants of al-Qaeda and Taliban fighters. State-building was not among its goals and the tactical aspect of the operations (night raids in suspected houses and target killings) was completely insensitive to the social context in which they were carried out (Coll 2018). Not surprisingly, the Afghans' feelings towards the foreign soldiers gradually shifted from expectations of freedom and social improvement to scepticism and eventually disappointment (Rashid 2009). To make matters worse, in late 2002, the Bush administration was in the process of refocusing its military priorities on the forthcoming war in Iraq. As a result, the waning of US engagement in Afghanistan heightened an abandonment syndrome at the local and regional level, while increasing the perception in Western capitals that the war in Afghanistan was really over.

Until then, UN-mandated ISAF had been manned on a voluntary basis, but at the beginning of 2003 the international community started running out of volunteers and NATO offered to contribute (Schmitt 2017). Taking responsibility for the command of ISAF in August looked like stepping into a relatively easy mission. However, that perception was based on an incorrect assessment of the conditions in Afghanistan. Furthermore, NATO's mandate was immediately expanded to provide security throughout the country. The expansion, starting from the north and following a counterclockwise territorial enlargement, was long and a great deal more challenging than initially assumed. It was achieved only in 2006. In those three years, NATO faced the truth about Afghanistan. First, it realised that peacekeeping had to start from scratch—i.e. even assuming that peace was achieved in 2001—a proper mission to keep that peace had not started yet. Second, when the expansion reached the Helmand and Kandahar provinces in the south—i.e. where the Taliban still had strongholds—NATO troops faced fierce military resistance. In those provinces, there was no peace to keep, no peace to enforce. Instead, a new military campaign was starting, almost five years after the first *Enduring Freedom* operations. Third, at that point, the Afghan population was already tired of war and wary, if not distrustful, of foreign troops. The window of opportunity for peacekeeping and state-building, which experts measure in months after military intervention, not years, had expired (Rashid 2009). Thereafter, (re)conquering the hearts and minds of the local population was indeed a daunting task.

Thus, the late involvement is a crucial aspect in understanding the difficulties that NATO faced in Afghanistan. The alliance inherited a situation that had already deteriorated, and entered the target country without the opportunity to shape, from the very beginning, its military presence, the way of warfare and its relationship with the local population. When the UN-mandated mission passed the baton to NATO-ISAF, the latter did not take over any preexisting control of territory, either from the United States or from the UN. Moreover, when NATO expanded throughout the national territory, the confidence of the Afghan population in international intervention was already gone. Their hearts and minds, a key ingredient for resilient peacekeeping and state-building, had for the most part been lost. Taking these exceptional circumstances into account—which have no equivalent in any other NATO mission—is one of the fundamental reasons for avoiding hasty conclusions about the alliance's failure. Ascribing the entire responsibility for unsuccessful peacekeeping to NATO would be wrong, but it also would risk underestimating the alliance's resilience in future operations.

Peacekeeping and State-Building During War: NATO-ISAF Alongside *Enduring Freedom*

The presence, since 2003, of two large-scale international military missions is another exceptional feature of the intervention in Afghanistan. NATO-ISAF and the US-led *Enduring Freedom* continued to coexist until 2014, when both were converted into two smaller missions, NATO into *Resolute Support* and the United States into what was referred to as *Freedom Sentinel*, both concluded in August 2021. In principle, they focused on separate tasks, with ISAF engaged predominantly in peace-keeping and stability operations and *Enduring Freedom* chiefly involved in counterterrorism. Yet, that distinction frequently blurred and soon the separate missions were often engaged in the same enterprises (Auerswald and Saideman 2014). This type of situation—in which NATO and the United States participated in the same international intervention but in two separate, autonomous missions—is exceptional in post-Cold War interventionism. It is not comparable with any other NATO mission, which usually either saw the United States contributing *within* NATO (e.g. in Bosnia, Kosovo and Libya) or intervening unilaterally *outside* of NATO (e.g. in Iraq in 2003 and initially in Afghanistan until 2003). In this regard, the Iraqi case should not be misunderstood; indeed, in Iraq NATO has lately been engaged in a training operation (NMI—*NATO mission in Iraq*) but this has been a non-combat advisory mission that has remained completely marginal and separate from the American military campaign.

As a result, the military intervention in Afghanistan between 2003 and 2014 ran on a tricky double track. On the one hand, the unilateral side of the intervention was fully under US control. *Enduring Freedom* was particularly wary of the risk of being constrained by allies and multilateral deliberations (Kay 2005). More specifically, the Bush administration was wary to avoid the sort of 'war by committee' that NATO had experienced during the air campaign in Kosovo two years earlier (Sperling and Webber 2012). Moreover, as already noted, it focused chiefly on counterterrorism and disregarded the crisis management dimension of the intervention (paying no attention to state-building, confidence building, stabilisation or reconstruction). On the other hand, the multilateral side of the international engagement in Afghanistan, as established at the International Conference on Afghanistan in Bonn in 2001, aimed to gather anti-Taliban Afghan leaders and help them to fill the political void in Kabul to stabilise the country. Originally, the international community conceived ISAF as a traditional peacekeeping mission assisting the new government institutions; this is why it was deployed only in Kabul. Fighting the Taliban and al-Qaeda militants was not among its goals.

The result, supposedly, was that *Enduring Freedom* and ISAF were fulfilling two separate aims according to an apparent division of labour. However, the deterioration of security and the increasingly hostile environment NATO-ISAF faced during the expansion in the south-eastern regions jeopardised that easy division of jobs and challenged the relationship between ISAF and *Enduring Freedom*. Three aspects are worth noting in this regard. First, the problem of coordination between the two missions, with the United States being part of both. Second, the delusion of keeping peace while war was still raging. Third, the fact that neither the counterterrorism of *Enduring Freedom* nor the peacekeeping of ISAF were ready and equipped for counterinsurgency, which was what actually needed to be adopted against the Taliban insurgency.

Many scholars have already investigated problems of coordination in Afghanistan and, more generally, in other missions (Chandler 2002; Kreps 2008). These types of difficulties are specific to multilateral missions in which many international organisations contribute to the intervention. However, in Afghanistan, the problem was more prominent because the complex relationship between ISAF and *Enduring Freedom* was not shaped exclusively by conflicting views of different contributing nations or the complexity of decision-making in a multilateral environment. In Afghanistan, two huge military missions were present side by side; as a result, they suffered not only from the traditional problems of coordination *within* a multinational mission but from problems *between* missions. Furthermore, while in other contexts (e.g. in Somalia, Bosnia, Iraq or East Timor) several international organisations engaged in different tasks, with a clear division of jobs and hierarchy, in Afghanistan ISAF and *Enduring Freedom* were more similar, in many respects almost equals, and their enterprises increasingly blurred. The stubborn attitude adopted by the Bush administration, demanding to preserve wide freedom of action for US military forces and mistrusting the half-hearted multilateral engagement in ISAF, further complicated the relationship between the two missions. In this respect, it should be noted how the heterogeneity of the rules of engagement among contributing nations made the multilateral effort even more difficult. In many cases, national caveats restricted the use of force and the scope of the military's delegated authority, limiting in this way what a single national contingent could do on behalf of its nation (Auerswal and Saideman 2014). Eventually, caveats diminished the ISAF's overall effectiveness and generated resentment within the coalition. The US and NATO member states that were engaging with the most demanding offensive operations—e.g. the UK, Canada—in the southern part of the country were particularly disappointed by the 'caveats gap' among allies (Gallis 2007; Kreps 2008). Consequently, the American command, beyond keeping *Enduring Freedom* operations completely separate, did not share plans, decisions and intelligence with NATO allies. As a result, ISAF suffered from that unique circumstance that limits an easy comparison with other NATO operations.

The second aspect, which had considerable consequences for the role of NATO in Afghanistan, concerns the ambiguous post-conflict environment that has emerged since 2003. Unlike in Bosnia in 1995 or in Kosovo in 1999, when ISAF expanded throughout the Afghan territory, there was no actual peace to keep. While NATO succeeded in the Balkans with the division of two separate phases of military intervention—i.e. the military phase carried out through an air campaign, followed by a post-conflict phase involving peacekeeping (Chandler 2002)—in Afghanistan that blueprint did not work. In other words, in 2003 NATO headquarters framed the decision to take the ISAF command in terms of peacekeeping, based on the assumption that the conflict was over. In fact, the conflict was still raging in two ways: on the one hand, as NATO troops soon discovered, in the Southern and Eastern regions the Taliban were still present and easily regrouped through the porous border with Pakistan; on the other hand, *Enduring Freedom* was continuing with its own counterterrorism campaign. This is another exceptional circumstance; it distinguishes the intervention in Afghanistan from other contexts. Indeed, in no other target state was NATO (or any other security organisation) called to implement peacekeeping while a conflict was still active. More specifically, the American forces engaged in *Enduring Freedom* were jeopardising the basic premises of effective peacekeeping. Due to its priority of hunting high-value targets in both al-Qaeda and the Taliban, US forces carried out invasive house searches and air power attacks, often with dramatic side effects in terms of civilian casualties. This attitude clearly collided with the long-term reconstruction activities performed by ISAF (Boyle 2010). Obviously, the overlapping tasks of peacekeeping and counterterrorism put NATO in an exceptionally awkward situation.

The final aspect worth pointing out is paradoxical. Despite the presence of two large-scale missions, neither ISAF nor *Enduring Freedom* were strategically prepared, equipped or organised to provide what was actually needed in the face of the evolving security environment in Afghanistan, namely counterinsurgency (Reinheart 2010). The wide-ranging insurgency launched by the Taliban against the international troops made clear how security was deteriorating in Afghanistan, due not only to terrorism but also to a more insidious threat. It became increasingly apparent that the international community engaged in the country was confronting a far greater challenge. Indeed, the Taliban insurgency—like any insurgency and unlike mere terrorism—was a political struggle (Branch and Wood 2010). The military dimension of the battle (guerrilla warfare and terrorism) was only one side of the coin, the other being the political ambition to free the country from occupiers and reestablish theocratic rule (Eikenberry 2013). In their efforts to seek the population's support, accompanied by constant attempts to undermine local confidence in the international intervention, the Taliban were setting the stage for a wider battle. In this context, the aims of narrowly focused counterterrorism and peacekeeping without real peace left NATO largely unprepared for the actual challenge. In this new context, two combined developments ended up undermining ISAF peacekeeping in an exceptional way. On the one hand, the Taliban's *political* struggle seriously hampered the social and economic basis of confidence building, which is a key ingredient in effective stabilisation. On the other hand, the persistent counterterrorist approach of *Enduring Freedom*—the night raids, overreliance on air firepower, disregard for civilian casualties and local perceptions—made ISAF stability operations even more complicated.

From Peacekeeping to Counterterrorism: ISAF's Strategic and Tactical Adjustments During the Mission

The experience of NATO-ISAF is a unique case in post-Cold War interventionism in another important way. No other missions have experienced an overall change in tasks and activities in the field like that which ISAF experienced in Afghanistan. The strategic and tactical shift from peacekeeping operation to vast counterinsurgency campaign has no comparison. Initially trained and equipped for peacekeeping, after a few years, national contributions deployed to Afghanistan had to completely revise the rules of engagement, equipment, tactical posture and their range of activities. In other words, a mission designed for peacekeeping and assistance had to engage very quickly in a far more difficult task (Roberts 2009).

Predictably, the shift towards counterinsurgency brought about many difficulties. First, it demanded more kinetic and offensive operations. While peacekeeping is somewhat static and defensive, counterinsurgency requires a proactive approach. Second, counterinsurgency entails the involvement of extensive military manpower. The need for capillary territorial control against the insurgents involves the wide-ranging deployment of troops, especially infantry. Third, counterinsurgency campaigns are long and open-ended. Time is extremely important, because insurgents do not realistically expect to defeat foreign troops on the open battlefield but aim to survive until occupiers grow tired of war (Eikenberry 2013). The Taliban are no exception in this regard. They strove to survive until US and NATO military resolve waned. In this view, when ISAF started framing its role in Afghanistan in terms of counterinsurgency it was asking NATO member states to engage in an extraordinary, prolonged endeavour. The huge impact on the mission of that exceptional strategic shift suggests that assessing the role of NATO in Afghanistan cannot easily lead to generalisable conclusions.

The problems due to the overall adjustment toward a counterinsurgency campaign were particularly acute during the first years of the Obama administration. During the second term of the Bush administration, at the Pentagon and within the military establishment, a new focus on the virtues and necessities of counterinsurgency was already emerging (Branch and Wood 2010). Yet, it was with the so-called *Af-Pak Strategy* adopted in 2009 that the Obama administration refocused the US and NATO intervention in Afghanistan on counterinsurgency in earnest. The Obama review was the result of a clash of two visions within the administration and the military establishment: those who advocated the merits of counterterrorism, and argued for maintaining a 'light footprint' in Afghanistan, and those who asked for a reengagement framed within a new counterinsurgency scheme. During the policy review process, Obama eventually leaned towards the counterinsurgency option, strongly advocated by General Stanley McChrystal (on his way to being appointed ISAF commander in 2009) and Defence Secretary Robert Gates (Bird and Marshall 2011). The new strategy ended up launching a military *surge* that reached a peak of 100,000 American troops in mid-2011 (Hoffman 2009). The strategy introduced important revisions to the American military approach in the direction of more people-centred operations. The tactical approach of 'clear, hold and build' aimed to compensate for all the limits of counterterrorism—i.e. clearing a village or urban area of terrorists was not enough, it had to be followed by a longer military presence to guarantee security and, finally, help in improving and consolidating rebuilding (Strachan 2010).

The American strategic shift immediately had a huge impact on NATO. At the Lisbon Summit in 2010, President Obama urged European allies to send more troops to Afghanistan, following the United States in the strategic and tactical adjustments necessary for the counterinsurgency campaign. Eventually, key allies followed suit. The shift was not only strategic and tactical but had political significance. Indeed, the new American engagement ended up changing ISAF's composition profoundly because Obama's strategy turned out to be a 're-Americanisation' of the war in Afghanistan. That re-Americanisation put formidable pressure on NATO allies to react to the new approach and readapt their commitments.

It was not an easy task. Although the efforts NATO countries made in Afghanistan were huge and eventually contributed to improving security conditions in the country in the period 2011–2013, the strategic shift put the alliance under stress. The point here is not to evaluate the merits and limits of the new counterinsurgency engagement; instead, what is worth noticing is that this change during the mission was an exceptional event. No other NATO mission has undergone such a profound revision after being deployed. Thus, alongside ISAF's other unique features—i.e. late deployment and coexistence with another large mission on the ground—the vast strategic adjustment should be considered a limit in making clear-cut comparisons with other NATO interventions.

Conclusion: Avoiding a Wrong Memory

Since the end of the Cold War, NATO has been a particularly active multilateral organisation. It has intervened in a number of crises, from Bosnia-Herzegovina to Kosovo, from Afghanistan to Libya. It has engaged in many other operations around the world, from disaster relief to training missions, from counterpiracy to air patrolling. Peacekeeping is just one of the tasks in which NATO has proved its resilience following its wide-ranging transformation in the post-bipolar era. Thirty years after the collapse of the USSR, however, it is plain that peacekeeping is a task that entails multiple challenges. The idea that has prevailed since the 1990s—that the international community and its key institutions should be prepared for crisis management at a global level—is well established but has also changed meaning. After three decades' worth of experience in many civil wars and failed states, it is now plain that peacekeeping is not an easy formula or the silver bullet for every major crisis. More importantly, there is no 'one size fits all' recipe when the international community intervenes in war-torn countries. Even the so-called 'post-conflict' stage does not offer a guarantee that intervening in the situation will be an easy undertaking, amenable to being managed through prearranged tasks.

The variety of experiences in the field suggests caution in learning the right lessons and extrapolating from these. That is particularly true for a mission like NATO's ISAF in Afghanistan, which is seen as a *test* of the military capabilities, its political resolve and ability to go global (Gallis 2007). As the first mission 'out-of-area' out of Europe and in the middle of the American pressure to turn NATO into a global alliance, the intervention in Afghanistan represented a crucial moment of transformation. Consequently, reflections upon the outcome of the mission exacerbated many expectations about the alliance's cohesiveness and future prospects. Eventually, too many expectations, accompanied by a neglect of the exceptional circumstances in which NATO intervened in Afghanistan, contributed to overstate the value of the lessons learned.

Drawing the correct lessons to be learned from a military campaign with initial peacekeeping goals is always difficult, but this is particularly true for ISAF in Afghanistan. Indeed, the temptation to make straightforward comparisons with common standards of international peacekeeping could lead us to overlook the uniqueness of that mission and could eventually lead to incorrect assessments. If, while investigating the role of ISAF in Afghanistan, we neglect its distinctiveness within NATO interventions, we risk underestimating the alliance's resilience in the present and, more importantly, for the future. The way the alliance was involved, the tricky coordination with *Enduring Freedom* and the overall strategic adjustment after years of war, make ISAF an inimitable case. In conclusion, these exceptional circumstances invite us to abstain from oversimplifications, hasty comparisons and simplistic lessons. In other words, they suggest to avoid a wrong memory about ISAF.

Bibliography

Auerswald, David P., and Stephen M. Saideman. 2014. *NATO in Afghanistan. Fighting Together, Fighting Alone*. Princeton University Press.

Biddle, Stephen D. 2006. Allies, airpower, and modern warfare: The Afghan model in Afghanistan and Iraq. *International Security* 30: 161–176.

Bird, Tim. 2013. 'Perennial Dilemmas': NATO's post 9/11Afghanistan 'crisis'. In *NATO Beyond 9/11. The Transformation of the Atlantic Alliance*, ed. Ellen Hallams, Luca Ratti, and Benjamin Zyla, 118–139. Palgrave-MacMillan.

Bird, Tim, and Alex Marshall. 2011. *Afghanistan, How the West Lost its way*. Yale University Press.

Boyle, Michael J. 2010. Do Counterterrorism and Counterinsurgency Go Together? *International Affairs* 86: 333–353.

Branch, Daniel, and Elisabeth J. Wood. 2010. Revisiting Counterin Surgency. *Politics and Society* 38: 3–14.

Carati, Andrea. 2015. No Easy Way Out: Origins of NATO's Difficulties in Afghanistan. *Contemporary Security Policy* 36: 200–218.

Chandler, David. 2002. *From Kosovo to Kabul. Human Rights and International Intervention*. London: Pluto Press.

Chivvis, Christopher S. 2013. *Toppling Qaddafi. Libya and the Limits of Liberal Intervention*. Cambridge University Press.

Coll, Steve. 2018. *Directorate S. The C.I.A. and America's secret war in Afghanistan and Pakistan, 2001–2016*. Allen Lane.

Crawford, Neta C. 2018. *United States Budgetary Costs of the Post-9/11 Wars Through FY2019: $5.9 Trillion Spent and Obligated*. Costs of war project—Watson Institute, Brown University. November 2018. https://watson.brown.edu/costsofwar/files/cow/imce/papers/2018/Crawford_Costs%20of%20War%20Estimates%20Through%20FY2019%20.pdf. Accessed 5 February 2021.

Davidson, Jason W. 2021. *The Costs of War to United States Allies Since 9/11*. Costs of war project—Watson Institute, Brown University. May 2021. https://watson.brown.edu/costsofwar/files/cow/imce/papers/2021/Davidson_AlliesCostsofWar_Final.pdf.

Dobbins, James. 2008. *After the Taliban. Nation-building in Afghanistan*. Washington DC: Potomac Books.

Doucet, Lyse. 2020. *Taliban Conflict: Afghan Fears Rise as US Ends its Longest War*. BBC News—Asia, 20 October 2020. https://www.bbc.com/news/world-asia-54600781. Accessed 5 Feb 2021.

Eikenberry, Karl W. 2013. The Limits of Counterinsurgency Doctrine in Afghanistan: The Other Side of the COIN. *Foreign Affairs* 92: 59–74.

Gall, Carlotta. 2014. *The Wrong Enemy: America in Afghanistan, 2001–2014*. Houghton Mifflin Harcourt.

Gallis, Paul. 2007. Nato in Afghanistan: A Test of the Transatlantic Alliance. *Connections* 6: 10–32.

Hallams, Ellen, Luca Ratti, and Benjamin Zyla (eds.). 2013. *NATO beyond 9/11. The transformation of the Atlantic Alliance*. Palgrave-MacMillan.

Hanagan, Deborah. 2019. *NATO in the Crucible: Coalition Warfare in Afghanistan, 2001–2014*. Hoover Institution Press.

Hoffman, Bruce. 2009. A Counterterrorism Strategy for the Obama Administration. *Terrorism and Political Violence* 21: 359–377.

ICG. 2014. Afghanistan: The Long, Hard Road to the 2014 Transition. International Crisis Group—Asia Report No. 236. https://www.crisisgroup.org/asia/south-asia/afghanistan/afghanistan-long-hard-road-2014-transition. Accessed 5 Feb 2021.

Johnson, David E. 2011. What Are You Prepared To Do? NATO and the Strategic Mismatch Between Ends, Ways, And Means in Afghanistan—and in the Future. *Studies in Conflict and Terrorism* 34: 383–401.

Kay, Sean. 2005. What Went Wrong with NATO? *Cambridge Review of International Affairs* 18: 69–83.

Kreps, Sarah. 2008. When Does the Mission Determine the Coalition? The Logic of Multilateral Intervention and the Case of Afghanistan. *Security Studies* 17: 531–567.

Nasrat, Qaisar. 2020. Negotiating with the Taliban: How will it affect the future of Afghanistan? *Journal of Academic Perspective on Social Studies* 1: 19–27.

NATO. 2020. *Nato 2030: United for a New Era*. Analysis and Recommendations of the Reflection Group appointed by the NATO Secretary General. https://www.nato.int/nato_static_fl2014/assets/pdf/2020/12/pdf/201201-Reflection-Group-Final-Report-Uni.pdf. Accessed 5 Feb 2021.

Rashid, Ahmed. 2009. *Descent into Chaos: The U.S. and the Disaster in Pakistan, Afghanistan, and Central Asia*. Penguin Books.

Roberts, Adam. 2009. Doctrine and Reality in Afghanistan. *Survival* 51: 29–60.

Ripley, Tim. 2011. *Operation Enduring Freedom: The Seeds of War in Afghanistan*. Barnsley: Pen and Sword Books.

Rineheart, Jason. 2010. Counterterrorism and Counterinsurgency. *Perspectives on Terrorism* 4: 31–47.

Rynning, Sten. 2012. *NATO in Afghanistan. The liberal disconnect*. Stanford University Press.

Salt, Alexander. 2018. Transformation and the War in Afghanistan. *Strategic Studies Quarterly* 12: 98–126.

Schmitt, Olivier. 2017. International Organization at War: NATO Practices in the Afghan Campaign. *Cooperation and Conflict* 52: 502–518.

Sperling, James, and Mark Webber. 2012. NATO's Intervention in the Afghan Civil War. *Civil Wars* 14: 344–372.

Strachan, Hew. 2010. Strategy or Alibi? Obama, McChrystal and the Operational Level of War. *Survival* 52: 157–182.

Suhrke, Astri. 2008. A Contradictory Mission? NATO from Stabilization to Combat in Afghanistan. *International Peacekeeping* 15: 214–236.

UN Report of the Secretary General. 2020. *The Situation in Afghanistan and its Implications for International Peace and Security*. https://unama.unmissions.org/sites/default/files/sg_report_on_afghanistan_december_2020.pdf.

CHAPTER 10

NATO from the Balkans to Libya: Dynamics and Renewal of a Wilsonian Alliance

Jean-Sylvestre Mongrenier

At the end of the Cold War, NATO's future seemed quite uncertain. Despite the member countries' announced intention to perpetuate and to renew the Transatlantic Alliance, and due to the efforts of the enemy—the USSR and the countries of the Warsaw Pact—to make peace, the disappearance of NATO was not impossible. With the adoption of the Maastricht Treaty (1992), the EEC and its member countries were supposed to become a new protagonist of international relations, at least in the long run. The Common Foreign and Security Policy (CFSP) of the European Union was designed as a basis for a future common defence

This essay has been translated by Nicolas Montagne

J.-S. Mongrenier (✉)
Department of Geography, Institut Français de Géopolitique, Université Paris VIII, Paris, France
e-mail: jeansylvestre.mongrenier@sfr.fr

M. de Leonardis (ed.), *NATO in the Post-Cold War Era*, Security, Conflict and Cooperation in the Contemporary World
https://doi.org/10.1007/978-3-031-06063-2_10

policy. The European Union was supposed to take greater diplomatic and military responsibilities in its geographical environment, in Central and Eastern Europe, including the Balkans, as well as in the Mediterranean region, and even in its border areas, i.e. the Black Sea basin, the Middle East and the Red Sea basin—the 'larger Mediterranean' as described by Fernand Braudel and Yves Lacoste. That is not what happened. While the 'Europe of Defence' was struggling to take shape, NATO led a fourfold expansion. Following the increase in partnerships and the broadening of cooperation with non-member countries, the countries of Central and Eastern Europe (CEECs)—including the Balkan countries—joined the NATO. The enlargement was also functional, with the addition to the collective defence based on Article 5 of the North Atlantic Treaty of 'non-Article 5' missions relating to collective security. Finally, NATO led large-scale combat missions and military operations between the Adriatic Sea and the Libyan coast while remaining involved in defence activities as far as the Hindu Kush mountains (Afghanistan). Events such as the 'new Balkan wars', the Arab Spring and the commitment of the Allies in other regions had major impacts on NATO's 'renewal' and 'transformation' process, with some detrimental effects. However, it would be wrong to conclude that such unfavourable circumstances ruined all the work done. The post-Cold War era highlights the Wilsonian aspect of the Atlantic Alliance, an essential component of the 'liberal international order' on the agenda of the United States and its allies after World War II. Nevertheless, NATO's military engagement abroad also revealed the limits of transatlantic multilateralism.

The Atlantic Alliance Beyond Neorealism

According to the neorealist theory of international relations, the result of alliances among countries facing the 'security dilemma'—each country making its best to survive in a zero-sum international political game—depends solely on the configuration of the power balance. Alliances thus adopt defence and reaction strategies, the challenge being to neutralise virtual or actual threats by accumulating elements of power and rallying other countries (what is referred to as *bandwagoning*) to rebalance forces. This Newtonian model of interaction between the active units of the international system suggests that alliances are continuously disbanded and reformed, depending on the evolution of the power balance. In the case of NATO, the victorious alliance was not supposed to outlive the Cold

War and the need to contain the USSR and the Soviet bloc. The situation back then did not require the United States to form a multilateral alliance between North America and Western Europe (North Atlantic Treaty, 4 April 1949). Let us remember that George F. Kennan, one of the creators of the 'policy of containment', would have preferred the United States to grant unilateral security guarantees to the Western European countries without heavy obligations and binding multilateral mechanisms. If everything could be explained by the cold logic of self-serving interests, it is hard to understand how the situation and the balance of power justified the continued presence of the United States in Europe. The United States could choose a position somewhere between armed entrenchment and market-oriented internationalism, as they did in the 1920s, before the depression of the next decade led to a form of political-economic isolationism (see the Smoot-Hawley Tariff Act and the Neutrality Acts of the 1930s). In short, whether we consider the beginning or the end of the Cold War, neorealism shows some serious limits.

As Jean-Yves Haine puts it, a radiologist cannot only take into account the state of a patient's skeleton, that is in this instance, the abstract systemic structure of relations between countries. The practitioner must also be a cardiologist, because 'humans are all about blood flow and life', and a psychologist in order to 'figure out patients and better understand their ambitions and failures' (Haine 2004). The medical metaphor suggests that we should take into account not only the power balance but also the historical background of the stakeholders, their geopolitical situation and representations, their objectives, the diversity of the issues at stake, and the concrete and differentiated nature of the geographical areas involved in the armed, political or economic conflicts. In short, geopolitics as a discipline goes far beyond the mere analysis of the balance of power. The way Western leaders considered the early twentieth century and the conclusions they drew from it were essential in the founding process of NATO. Raymond Aron summarised it as follows: 'Just as France required Anglo-American guarantees after World War I because the involvement of both the United Kingdom and the United States had been necessary for victory, Western European countries asked for the commitment—even in peacetime—of the United States that had decisively contributed to the liberation of the Old Continent. (…) From this moment on, the United States became an integral part of the European system. After the two World Wars, the United States understood that they had a vital interest in preventing the establishment of either a communist or far-right domination over Europe. Governments were worried about the future and wanted to believe that the Atlantic Alliance would avoid a new war. After all, had the alliance existed in the early twentieth century, the previous wars would probably have been avoided' (Aron 1984). In the 1930s, the 'rise of perils' and the 'March to war' led to reconsider Wilson's legacy.

Let us here summarise the theories of US President Woodrow Wilson, unfairly portrayed in France as an inflexible purist. Broadly speaking, Wilson had the vision of an 'imperial cooperation' which, under the leadership of the United States, would bring together Western European countries in an alliance based on collective security, freedom of the seas, and an 'open door' policy to the wider world—including colonial empires. Wilson believed that these empires were intended to acquire the status of 'free association' at various paces depending on their geopolitical context. In many ways, such concepts go far beyond Wilson's rigorous ideology and refer to the various projects of perpetual peace developed by many philosophers during the European Enlightenment. The US president, who was a lawyer, a political scientist and a historian, had Immanuel Kant's works as bedside readings. Besides, in a world turned upside down by the ruination of Europe, the Great War and the Great Socialist Revolution, Wilsonism was a liberal alternative to Leninism. We know what happened next, as the 'prophet was disavowed by his people' (Artaud 1985). Later, Franklin D. Roosevelt initiated a careful rehabilitation of these theories, and the Wilsonism of the Truman administration inspired the North Atlantic Treaty. The Atlantic Alliance was not developed on the model of the European alliances of the nineteenth century, based on the balance of power, but on that of the Rio Treaty (2 September 1947). The Alliance was not supposed to aim at a specific attacker but at aggressions themselves, and the treaty, as a reference to the United Nations, encouraged signatories to settle their disputes by peaceful means to develop friendly relations among nations (Articles 1 and 2). A security community was founded, some 'Jeffersonian' prudence tempering the Wilsonism aspect of the text.[1] By its very nature, NATO was conceived as the North Atlantic pillar of the European integration initiated by the Marshall Plan (5 June 1947).

[1] Article 5 of the North Atlantic Treaty does not imply an automatic commitment to a common military response.

From Bosnia to NATO's Enlargement

At the time of war in Bosnia, and despite its victory during the Cold War, NATO had not yet engaged in combat operations. Along this conflict, we have to keep in mind that the middle of Europe was the main theatre; the Adriatic Sea and the Mediterranean region were strategic but not so much important than the 'Center-Europe' theatre.[2] The 'new Balkan wars', that first took place in Bosnia and Herzegovina and then in the Serbian province of Kosovo, raised very specific questions about the Alliance's role outside its responsibility area (the Euro-Atlantic area) and, consequently, of crisis management beyond collective defence. Quickly, NATO's peace-keeping—not to say peace-enforcing—operations in its near or distant geographic environment were referred to as 'non-Article 5' missions. At the London Summit of 6–7 July 1990, the Allies unanimously expressed their will to perpetuate and renew NATO. They decided to take into account the new strategic realities, including the need to build a Pan-European security architecture with the USSR and Warsaw Pact countries (the Pact would be dissolved the following year), and possible risks and threats in the Mediterranean area, especially in the South and the East. The Gulf crisis that led to the Gulf War (1991) confirmed these concerns: the Mediterranean Basin and Middle East, including the Arabian-Persian Gulf, were entering the scope. In the framework of the Strategic Concept adopted the following year (Rome Summit, 7–8 November 1991), the Allies ratified a broader security concept, crisis prevention and management requiring flexibility and responsiveness, i.e. the ability to project forces and power beyond the Euro-Atlantic area (see articles 12 and 46 of the Concept). Following the breakup of Yugoslavia, NATO and its member countries had to take practical steps. The contradictory implications of the crisis divided the Allies for four long years. At the time of the declaration of independence, and during the first phase of the armed conflict in 1991 and 1992, the Bush senior administration considered this

[2] However, let us remember that a possible extension of the membership to Egypt was evoked in the beginning of NATO. Later on, the Middle East Treaty Organization ('METO') was formed by Iran, Iraq, Pakistan, Turkey and the United Kingdom through the Baghdad Pact (24 February 1955). It has been compared to a 'Middle East NATO'. After a revolution in Iraq, the end of the Hashemite monarchy and the implementation of an anti-Western government (the Baath regime), Iraq left the METO (1958). This one became the Central Treaty Organization (CENTO). The CENTO was dissolved after the Iranian Revolution (1979).

crisis to be a European matter, especially that France, reunited Germany and the other Member States of the EEC were pursuing their diplomatic and military ambitions. It was not until the Dayton Agreement (21 November 1995) that the United States could reassert its leadership, thereby strengthening NATO's role in the Pan-European security architecture.

From January 1993, the Clinton administration was more explicitly Wilsonian than the previous one, but the practice did not immediately follow theory. Bill Clinton, who favoured national issues, was unwilling to jeopardise his political capital by getting involved in Bosnia[3] (the US president was impressed by the spectre of the Vietnam war). In addition to these domestic concerns, the United States followed a 'Russia first' policy, embodied by Deputy Secretary Strobe Talbott, seeking to spare Boris Yeltsin's Russia which was hostile to NATO's presence in former Yugoslavia. The political stand-off of November 1993 between the Russian president Yeltsin and the State Duma, followed by the rise of Vladimir Zhirinovsky and the Liberal Democratic Party of Russia (LDPR), suggested to proceed cautiously with Russia, which was seen as a 'Weimar on the Volga'. Due to the situation, it was considered necessary to postpone *sine die* NATO's enlargement to the CEECs, despite the influence of the study *Out of Area, Out of Business* published by the RAND Corporation in the same year.[4] For their part, European countries were divided. With strong US reluctance making it impossible to resort to NATO, France advocated the intervention of the Western European Union (WEU). However, the United Kingdom ruled out this option, arguing that an intervention in a civil conflict with ethnic roots would lead to a dangerous escalation. Although Germany would not oppose the project, it announced that, because of its Basic Law, it would not take part in it. Beyond legal and constitutional imperatives, Bonn's interpretation of the conflict was very different from that of Paris and London that, since the Yalta Conference, viewed with concern the 'Europe of Versailles' falling apart. Because of these disagreements, the European Troika, which

[3] It seems that Bill Clinton had read Robert Kaplan's book: *Balkan Ghosts. A Journey Through History*. 1993. In his first opinion, it was vain and even dangerous to interfere into an ethnic war.

[4] Republican Senator Richard Lugar later echoed the expression 'out of area or out of business'. Because of its scope, the study by the RAND Corporation was sometimes compared to George Kennan's Long Telegram (22 February 1946).

was supposed to resolve the conflict by diplomatic means, soon had to hand over the responsibility to Cyrus Vance and the United Nations, that negotiated a ceasefire and deployed the UN peacekeepers (UNPROFOR) in Bosnia and Herzegovina. However, due to Serbian acts of violence, it was impossible to safeguard an illusory peace, let alone enforcing it without taking part in the conflict.

Gradually, the United States and NATO behind them engaged in Bosnia and Herzegovina. The divisions among Allies and the risks they implied for NATO played an important role in the change in the position of the United States. As of 1992, the NATO Ministers of Foreign Affairs confirmed their readiness to support the CSCE and UN missions. In order to control the arms embargo, NATO dispatched a naval force to the Adriatic Sea, where ships previously deployed by the WEU were operating. AWACS and later fighters were used to control the no-fly zone (Operation Deny Flight, April 1993–December 1995). In January 1994, the Allies declared that they were ready to launch air strikes to protect Sarajevo and the proclaimed security zones. Following an ultimatum, artillery positions around Sarajevo were struck and five Serbian fighters were shot down (28 February 1994). However, the US commitment remained limited to naval and air operations, with only European soldiers deployed on the ground under the supervision of UNPROFOR. As the situation deteriorated, Washington accepted to deploy US troops in accordance with NATO's plans. After the Srebrenica massacre (11 July 1995) and a mortar attack on a market in Sarajevo, a major US air offensive (Operation Deliberate Force, 30 August–2 September 1995) supported the French and British soldiers deployed on the ground within the scope of the NATO Response Force. The ceasefire on 5th October marked the start of negotiations that led to the Dayton Peace Agreement (21st November 1995). NATO deployed the Implementation Force (IFOR) on the ground, later replaced with the Stabilisation Force (SFOR), both made up of forces from other countries, including Russia. NATO being officially a major player in collective security and cooperation with Russia, it was possible to reexamine the question of enlargement that, until then, had been postponed and replaced with a Partnership for Peace (1994), a poor solution for the CEECs.[5] Even with the 'new NATO' as a tool

[5] Strobe Talbott adhered to the principle of NATO's enlargement eastwards and tried to convince Boris Yeltsin. The negotiations, which began after the re-election of Yeltsin as President in July 1996, led to the signing of a Founding Act and the establishment of a

for integration on Europe, the EU countries considered it necessary for the European Union to have a real diplomatic and military function. Furthermore, NATO put into place a 'dialogue' with Southern and Eastern countries of the Mediterranean Basin (1995). During the Istanbul Summit (28–29 June 2004), this Mediterranean Dialogue was supplemented by an 'initiative' opened to the Arabian Gulf countries, without any great success[6] (NATO's Istanbul Initiative Cooperation, 2004).

NATO at War: The Limits of Multilateralism

US reluctance to get involved in Bosnia and the subsequent momentary paralysis within NATO partly explains why, on the occasion of a Franco-British summit in Saint-Malo, Jacques Chirac and Tony Blair agreed on a compromise on European Defence supplementary and subordinate to the Atlantic Alliance[7] (Saint-Malo Declaration, 4 December 1998). Afterwards, this agreement between the two main European military powers—which paved the way for the future European Security and Defense Policy (ESDP)—was extended within the European Union (Cologne European Council, 3–4 June 1999), the situation was deteriorating between Serbs and Kosovo Albanians. In the summer of 1998, fights between the Kosovo Liberation Army (KLA) and the Serbian forces triggered population movements. This time, NATO reacted much faster. In September 1998, the Allies declared that they were ready to strike in Serbia, should mass murders be perpetrated in Kosovo. The following month, Slobodan Milošević accepted an OSCE verification mission, supported by troops dispatched by the Allies in Macedonia, as well as a NATO air verification mission. Yet, abuses continued and negotiations that took place in Rambouillet and Paris in February and March 1999 failed. From 24 March to 6 June, NATO conducted the non-Article 5 Operation Allied Forces to compel the Serbian power to

NATO-Russia Permanent Joint Council (27 May 1997). The first enlargement eastwards—involving Poland, Hungary, and Czech Republic—was effective two years later. See D. Borsani, *NATO's Enlargement: Stability Projection and Factor of Crisis* (in this book).

[6] See A. Marquina, *NATO's Partnerships in the Middle East and the Mediterranean* (in this book).

[7] See L. Ratti-A. Leonardi, *The Role of NATO in European Integration* (in this book).

accept Kosovo's autonomy, with a NATO force as a guarantee.[8] Slobodan Milošević surrendered control of Kosovo. The Kosovo Force (KFOR) was deployed along with the United Nations Interim Administration Mission in Kosovo (UNMIK) responsible for civil administration. However, this political and military success left a bitter taste for European Allies. The obvious inferiority of the means they could deploy encouraged the countries to speed up the consolidation of the ESDP. The United States, that were responsible for most of the targeting and the strikes, did not appreciate the political constraints inherent in multilateralism, even though the latter was tempered by the decision-making process by a group of four countries, i.e. the Euro-Atlantic Quad (United States, United Kingdom, France and Germany). While the Kosovo War can be described as the pinnacle of the US Wilsonian ambitions, it marked an important turning point, US political and military officials starting to question NATO's relevance.

The US scepticism towards NATO echoed the initial reluctance of proponents of unilateralism to establish a multilateral alliance.[9] This distrust became obvious after 9/11, when the Bush Jr. administration created the 'coalition of the willing' to fight the Taliban. On 7 October 2001, the Operation *Enduring Freedom* was launched. The United States chose to sideline NATO to recover their full decision-making autonomy and keep the widest possible sphere of action. The idealistic, Wilsonian approach of the 'War on Terror' was going hand in hand with a resurgence of former US political reflexes, such as a preference for unilateral action and, by extension, a mistrust of existing alliances (Coutau-Bégarie 2009). However, the International Conference on Afghanistan (5 December 2001) overseen by the UN secretary general, led, among other things, to the creation of an International Security Assistance Force (ISAF) placed under the command of different countries in turn, on a voluntary basis. In 2003, the Allies decided that NATO's military structures and headquarters would assume the

[8] The question arising as to whether the Allies needed a new UN resolution as a legal basis for this military intervention. It was finally considered that previous resolutions, the spirit of the law as well as humanitarian emergency were sufficient.

[9] They could not prevent the passing of the Vandenberg resolution (11 June 1948) allowing the US government to form military alliances in peacetime. However, the mutual defence clause of the Washington Treaty (Article 5) does not have the automatic nature of that of the Brussels Treaty (Article V) establishing the Western Union (17 March 1948), later called the Western European Union (1955).

command of the ISAF. In the meantime, the Allies met and decided to extend the scope of the 'out-of-area' principle beyond the Euro-Atlantic area and adjacent regions (Reykjavik 14–15 May 2002). Six months later, the Prague Summit led to the concept of 'transformation', i.e. reorganising the Allied Forces on an expeditionary model. It was soon decided to extend to all of Afghanistan the ISAF's stabilisation operation[10]—different from Operation *Enduring Freedom*—focused on Kabul (December 2005). The fight against the Taliban and the necessary counterinsurgency missions led to a new functional enlargement, and NATO got involved in domains related to military action, such as the fight against terrorism, the war on drugs, and the training of the Afghan police and border guards. A global approach was needed. It was also time for NATO to enter global partnerships with Asia–Pacific Nations, such as Australia, New Zealand, Japan and South Korea. In other words, NATO became a global alliance. However, because of European and Western divisions, NATO was sidestepped in Iraq where another US-led 'coalition of the willing' took military action (20 March 2003). The following year, NATO's members agreed to establish a Training Implementation Mission in Iraq (Istanbul 28–29 June 2004). The goal was to provide assistance to the new Iraq and to the interim Iraqi government.[11]

The prospect of a Global NATO worried many members of the Alliance. Most European Allies shared this concern and doubted the advantages of a NATO cut from its historical and geographical ties, possibly becoming a 'toolbox' of the United States. For that reason, in the months before the Lisbon Summit (19–20 November 2010), Allies strived to achieve a balance between the regional security requirements and the need to deploy power in out-of-area theatres of operations. The new Strategic Concept officially adopted in the Portuguese capital was meant to refocus the efforts on collective defence and on Article 5. The following year, NATO got involved in the Libyan Civil War (19 March–31 October 2011), in which Gaddafi's regime had begun to repress the early signs of a Libyan Arab Spring. The specificity of the conflict is that the Obama administration, reluctant to get involved in a battlefield in

[10] See A. Carati, *NATO and the impact of the long war in Afghanistan: Avoiding a wrong memory about ISAF* (in this book).

[11] In fact, the implementation of this small mission required many months of difficult negotiations. Such countries as France and Germany refused to deploy men on Iraq's ground.

addition to Afghanistan and Iraq, used it to assess the capability of NATO and European Allies to plan and take charge of operations despite the limited US involvement, the so-called 'leadership by behind'. Initially, French President Sarkozy refused the involvement of NATO and the United States. In this context, his goal was to build an ad hoc coalition (i.e. a 'coalition of the willing') led by Paris, London and a Franco-British general staff. This manoeuvre would have been an operational extension to the Lancaster House Treaties signed five months earlier (2 November 2010). It appeared that politically, strategically and tactically, the United States and NATO were essential. Although France was the first country to get involved in the fights in Libya on 19 March 2011, the United States was in charge of the destruction of the entire Libyan air defence (Operation Odyssey Dawn, 19–22 March 2011). NATO headquarters in Naples took over the command of the operation, as most countries involved did not want to operate under Franco-British command. In fact, the United Kingdom itself was against this option. At France's request, the political leadership was handed over to a 'contact group' made up of 15 countries, NATO being in charge of Operation Unified Protector (19 March–31 October 2011). However, this group can hardly be considered as the mere 'secular arm' of the international community (as described by French Minister Alain Juppé). No EU intervention was conceivable, and Germany had not even voted in favour of the United Nations Security Council Resolution 1973.[12]

Conclusion

The two decades following the end of the Cold War undoubtedly established NATO as an alliance of democratic countries, a political and military pillar of European integration—concept of 'Europe as a whole'—, and a collective security organisation made to push the boundaries of *Pax Americana*. In this respect, the wars in former Yugoslavia (Bosnia and Herzegovina, Serbia and Kosovo) were real crash tests. Despite all the obstacles, the test was successful. Under the leadership of the United States, NATO became the embodiment of a liberal-democratic model and

[12] The Resolution 1973 adopted on 17 March 2011 established a no-fly zone over Libya and authorised all necessary means to protect civilians and civilian-populated areas. Russia, China and Germany, a non-permanent member of the UN Security Council, abstained from voting.

a democratic peace theory (democracies being supposed not to wage war). We could argue that the US and NATO involvement in former Yugoslavia merely crystallised geopolitical issues and front lines. Let us imagine a counterfactual series of events: what would have happened without the US intervention? Would the European Union have turned into a 'Europe Power'—i.e. a full-fledged geostrategic actor—any quicker? Given the divisions between the countries at the time, we can reasonably believe that the withdrawal of the United States and the subsequent collapse of NATO would have ruined the European efforts towards unity. Actually, NATO and the EU are both pillars of a whole, free and peaceful Europe.

If we consider NATO's commitment in Afghanistan as a *sui generis* case—although NATO's 'China turn' and its implications could invalidate the theory—the operation in Libya raises other questions. Despite their initial will to remain in the background, the United States had to rally France and the United Kingdom, the forces driving this diplomatic and military initiative. From a political and military perspective, the 'leadership by behind' showed its limits. Had the United States not taken the initiative—no matter how unwillingly—few countries would have joined France and the United Kingdom. In truth, the United Kingdom would have renounced its commitment in the absence of the United States and NATO. The fast results of Operation *Enduring Freedom* are opposed to the consequences of the fall of the Gaddafi regime on Libya's stability and its perverse effects in the Sahel. Here again, what would have been the results of a long Libyan civil war with no Allied intervention? The current situation of Syria, under the control of the Damascus regime and at the mercy of the ambitions of its neighbours, illustrates the consequences of non-interference. From the Adriatic Sea to the Libyan coast, history proves the usefulness of a NATO capable of acting remotely to anticipate risks and threats. Beyond disappointments and detrimental effects inherent to history, it is the failure of the European Allies to share the military burden, or even the predominance of industrial and commercial interests over the 'strategic assessment', that are compromising NATO's future. To conclude, the disintegration of values and representations at the base of that Wilsonian alliance and pillar of a liberal international order could be fatal to it.

Bibliography

Aron, Raymond. 1984. *Paix et guerre entre les nations*. Calmann-Lévy.

Artaud, Denise. 1985. *La fin de l'innocence*. Armand Colin.

Coutau-Bégarie, Hervé. 2009. *L'Amérique solitaire? Les alliances militaires dans la stratégie des États-Unis*. Economica.

Haine, Jean-Yves. 2004. *Les États-Unis ont-ils besoin d'alliés?* Payot.

CHAPTER 11

NATO and the Fight Against International Terrorism

Kris Quanten

Introduction

The end of the Cold War fundamentally changed the international security environment. Whereas, until then security was mainly dominated by the deterrence of state actors, new threats suddenly emerged. Terrorism in particular, with the spectacular attacks of 9 September 2001, quickly took a prominent place. Of course, this was linked to the perception of the Western population, who suddenly felt threatened in their daily lives. Since then, the fight against terrorism has continuously determined the international security agenda. NATO, which traditionally focused on the military security of its member states, also had to adapt to this new reality and seek an appropriate response (Seth 2017). However, the development of the Counter-Terrorism Strategy did not proceed without problems, and much still remains to be finalised. The July 2018 Brussels summit

K. Quanten (✉)
Department of Conflict Studies, Royal Military Academy, Brussels, Belgium
e-mail: kris.quanten@mil.be

M. de Leonardis (ed.), *NATO in the Post-Cold War Era*, Security, Conflict and Cooperation in the Contemporary World
https://doi.org/10.1007/978-3-031-06063-2_11

report clearly shows that counterterrorism is still high on the political agenda and, above all, that NATO wants to play an important role in this respect.[1] Nevertheless, the Alliance is struggling to put this strategy into practice.

In this chapter, the reasons for this will be analysed. Before doing so, we must first look more closely at the phenomenon of terrorism itself, focusing on its main characteristics and exactly what these imply for the way in which to tackle it. We will then give a brief overview of the establishment of NATO's Counter-Terrorism Strategy. The influence of the various member states on this process cannot be left out of the equation. Finally, we consider whether the current strategy can provide an adequate answer to the new emerging challenges, and what its constraints and shortfalls are. In conclusion, we propose a number of recommendations for improvement.

Conceptual Analysis

To develop an effective Counter-Terrorism Strategy, it is important to first identify the opponent and establish an unequivocal understanding of terrorism. However, there is a fundamental problem here: the term 'terrorism' is politically and emotionally highly controversial. What one person considers a terrorist, someone else might call a freedom fighter. Internationally, it is therefore extremely difficult to reach consensus on a precise definition of terrorism. This explains why, despite repeated attempts, there is still no globally accepted definition of terrorism in the UN (Chase 2013). Even within NATO, the member states are clearly not on the same wavelength. A very telling example is the ongoing debate on the PKK. Turkey is determined to brand the latter as a terrorist organisation, while most Western European member states don't. Consequently, it took until 2016 for the Alliance to reach consensus on the general definition of terrorism: 'The unlawful use or threatened use of force or violence, instilling fear and terror, against individuals or property in an attempt to

[1] Brussels Summit Declaration, issued by the Heads of State and Government participating in the Meeting of the North Atlantic Council in Brussels. 11–12 July 2018. https://www.nato.int/cps/ic/natohq/official_texts_156624.htm.

coerce or intimidate governments or societies, or to gain control over a population, to achieve political, religious or ideological objectives'.[2]

Terrorism has many facets. However, it is always based on the use of illegal violence to achieve a political effect among a specific target population. The ultimate goal is to obtain change, which is often situated on a governmental or religious level. The approach is clearly asymmetrical, with the terrorists organised in a scattered and highly decentralised network (Moghadam 2017). For their fight, terrorists increasingly use commercial off-the-shelf technologies such as drones, sophisticated weaponry and potentially even chemical, biological, radiological and nuclear (CBRN) means. The financial resources are crucial for these terrorist organisations, which is why their spectrum of operations is often linked to international criminal networks or they are involved in kidnapping, drug or human trafficking. Finally, they need safe havens in which to train and organise themselves. For this purpose, they prefer to focus on areas beyond government control and failed states.

With its globalised, hybrid structure, terrorism cannot be tackled in a classical, conventional way. This brings us to the deeper nature of the phenomenon of terrorism: it is not monolithic, but layered and multifaceted. Terrorism is therefore not primarily a military problem (Van Leeuwen 2017). Tackling the underlying causes requires much more than solely military means. It demands a holistic, multipronged approach, involving many—mostly civilian—actors (Shea 2013). The military contribution plays an important, but only secondary role in this global approach. Former US President Obama rightly commented on this: 'Force alone cannot make us safe' (Obama 2013). As a mainly military organisation, NATO can therefore only make a limited contribution to the fight against terrorism. Other actors, like the EU, UNO, World Bank, IMF, Interpol, World Health Organization and IAEA, are better suited to address the underlying causes. However, it must be clear that none of these approaches can work in isolation. Only a well-coordinated multilateral approach can lead to success in the joint fight against terrorism: highly networked threats need highly networked responses.

[2] AAP-06, NATO Glossary of Terms and Definitions (2017). https://standards.globalspec.com/std/10275442/aap-06.

NATO's Response to Terrorism

Until 2001, NATO considered the terrorist threat as a secondary phenomenon with a limited impact on the Alliance. In the 1991 Strategic Concept, it was still completely at the bottom of the list of possible threats: 'Alliance security interests can be affected by other risks of a wider nature, including proliferation of weapons of mass destruction, disruption of the flow of vital resources and actions of terrorism and sabotage'.[3] With a little change, this formulation was repeated in the Strategic Concept of 1999: 'Alliance security interests can be affected by other risks of a wider nature, including acts of terrorism, sabotage and organised crime, and by the disruption of the flow of vital resources'.[4] In the nineties, one could therefore hardly speak of a Counter-Terrorism Strategy (Bird 2015; Pastori 2015; Satloff 2000).

Neither there was any specific attention to the rise of Islamic fundamentalism. In February 1995, Secretary General Willy Claes identified Islamic fundamentalism as having replaced Communism as the major threat to NATO. Although, he was immediately compelled to recant, saying that NATO had no quarrel with Islam (Claes 1995a, b; Sanguineti 1995). In September 1999, US Deputy Assistant of State Ronald Neumann stated that there was no intrinsic conflict between Islam and the West and that: 'The USA does not have a policy towards Islam and should not have such a policy. In our decision-making [...] religion is not a factor' (Neumann 1999).

The 9/11 attacks marked a radical turnaround: suddenly terrorism was top of the security agenda. This was also the only time in NATO's history that Article 5 was invoked ... and that for a terrorist attack. Initially, the reaction was purely military. On 4 October 2001, NATO decided upon eight specific measures (Reichard 2006). First of all, the deployment of the Standing Naval Force Mediterranean (STANAVFORMED) in the Eastern Mediterranean in an antiterrorism role (operation *Active Endeavour* and its successor operation *Sea Guardian*) and, as requested by Washington, the deployment of five NATO AWACS (Airborne Warning and Control System) aircrafts on the US Eastern

[3] The Alliance's New Strategic Concept. Part I, n. 12. https://www.nato.int/cps/en/natohq/official_texts_23847.htm.

[4] The Alliance's Strategic Concept. Part II, n. 24. https://www.nato.int/cps/en/natolive/official_texts_27433.htm.

Coast in order to let the Americans deploy their own assets elsewhere (operation *Eagle Assist*). Other measures were: the strengthening of cooperation in the field of intelligence; assistance to states, even non-members of NATO which risked reprisals for their commitment in the fight against terrorism; the strengthening of specific resources necessary to antiterrorism operations; granting nocturnal overflight rights to American and other countries' aircrafts engaged in operations against terrorism and finally the access to ports and airports for refueling during these operations.

However, it soon became painfully clear that behind these initiatives at the operational level, there was no strategic vision at the political level. Hence the hasty approval, at the Prague Summit in 2002, of a Military Concept for Defence Against Terrorism.[5] This envisaged numerous new initiatives, such as intelligence sharing, CBRN measures, the establishment of a Terrorist Threat Intelligence Unit, and prioritisation of Civil Emergency planning. Again, however, all these separate initiatives lacked coordination and a real overarching strategic vision.

In 2006, the UN took a major initiative with the adoption of its Global Counter-Terrorism Strategy.[6] This action created a framework within which nations and international organisations could coordinate their actions. The UN strategy starts from a holistic approach and is based upon four pillars. Two of these—'measures to prevent and combat terrorism' and 'measures to build state's capacity to prevent and combat terrorism'—are areas in which NATO, with its military assets, could offer added value. Nevertheless, the Alliance realised that, as the UN had already shown, it first had to come up with a vision document.

This was initiated with the new Strategic Concept of 2010. For the first time terrorism was explicitly mentioned as 'a direct threat to the citizens of NATO countries and to the international stability and prosperity'[7]—no longer a purely operational-tactical threat, but a strategic challenge at the political level. It also implied working out a clear view of how

[5] Military Concept for Defence Against Terrorism. 2012. MC-472. https://www.nato.int/cps/en/natolive/topics_69482.htm.

[6] UN Global Counter-Terrorism Strategy. 2012. *United Nations*. https://www.un.org/counterterrorism/ctitf/un-global-counter-terrorism-strategy.

[7] Active Engagement, Modern Defence: Strategic Concept for the Defence and Security of the Members of the North Atlantic Treaty Organization. 2010. https://www.nato.int/cps/en/natolive/official_texts_68580.htm?selectedLocale=en.

to wage this fight against terrorism. This resulted in the Policy Guidelines on Counter-Terrorism in 2012, marking an important step forward (Santamato 2013). For the first time, the Alliance had a commonly agreed policy, clearly defining its role and mandate for the fight against terrorism. The focus was on three key areas[8]:

- Awareness: ensure the shared awareness of the terrorist threat and vulnerabilities, strategic analysis and assessment, information and intelligence sharing;
- Capabilities: develop adequate capabilities in order to prevent, protect and respond to terrorist threats;
- Engagement: engage with partner countries and international actors to enhance their ability to combat terrorism at a local level.

The fact that NATO had taken so long to develop a strategic vision had a lot to do with member states' divergent political and ideological views. Opinions differed quite considerably on the specific division of tasks between the police and the military, the exchange of intelligence between the member states and the practical application in the field of counter-terrorism measures ... to name but a few. A compromise could ultimately be reached by explicitly putting three general principles at the forefront of the fight against terrorism (Santamato 2013):

- Compliance with international law (such as the United Nations Charter, the Universal Declaration of Human Rights, the UN Counter-Terrorism Strategy) which is not just a firm legal commitment, but also a strong political statement of values;
- Support to allies: NATO sees itself in a supportive, subsidiary role. The primary responsibility lies with the member states, who dispose of more appropriate instruments such as law enforcement and judicial authorities;
- Non-duplication and complementarity: focus on targeted programmes and specific areas. NATO has unique assets and years of experience, which can be made available to the member states.

[8] NATO's Policy Guidelines on Counter-Terrorism. 2012. https://www.nato.int/cps/ic/natohq/official_texts_87905.htm.

An Evolving Counter-Terrorism Framework

The Policy Guidelines provided the strategic framework for NATO's Counter-Terrorism approach. The next step was to translate this policy to the operational level. In May 2014 NATO published an Action Plan, which identified specific tasks within the three pillars.[9] For awareness, the emphasis was on the exchange of information and intelligence between the member states, as well as with other international organisations like the EU, the UN and the OSCE. However, the most concrete initiatives were in the capabilities domain. The aim was to use innovative technology to protect vital assets, mainly deployed troops and existing infrastructure. To this end, the Defence Against Terrorism Program was launched. This consisted of research programmes for better protection against Man-portable air-defense systems (MANPADS) and CBRN attacks, the development of biometric identification systems, detection and destruction of Improvised Explosive Devices (IEDs), clearance of explosive devices, and promotion of cultural awareness among the deployed troops. An important role herein was reserved for NATO's Centre of Excellence for the Defence Against Terrorism in Ankara (Page 2014). In the third domain, that of engagement, the Partnership Action Plan on Terrorism played a central role, with the aim of contributing to regional stability through capacity building in partner countries.

With all these measures, NATO's Counter-Terrorism Strategy took a concrete form. However, the Policy Guidelines and the Action Plan were not an end. As the terrorism environment was quickly evolving, the Counter-Terrorism Strategy also had to adapt to the changing circumstances. For this reason, numerous new initiatives were taken in the following years. This often happened in the aftermath of and as a reaction to specific events—such as the dramatic terrorist attacks in Paris, London and Brussels—or as a result of bold political statements, such as those of the American President Donald Trump, who described NATO as obsolete 'because it wasn't taking care of terrorism' (Kristensen and Schousboe 2017).

Especially, the exchange of information proved to be a tricky issue and was difficult to get off the ground. Therefore, in 2016 it was decided to set up a separate Joint Intelligence and Security Division within the

[9] The document which describes NATO's Action Plan is classified and not available for public consultation.

International Staff, focusing not only on centralising terrorism-related intelligence, but on all possible threats facing the Alliance. This Division was headed by an Assistant Secretary General for Intelligence and Security who reported directly to the Secretary General.

At the same time, the awareness grew that terrorism had to be tackled preventively in the countries of origin. To this end, the concept of 'projecting stability' was introduced in 2016 (Koehler 2018). The aim was to stabilise the external borders of the Alliance by strengthening the neighbouring countries militarily, preventing entire areas from slipping out of any form of control as ungoverned spaces provide an ideal breeding ground for criminal groups, insurgents and terrorists alike. At the same time, the concept also aimed to strengthen the local security forces, enabling partner countries to tackle terrorism themselves. As Secretary General Stoltenberg said: 'In the long run, it is much better to fight terrorism and project stability by training local forces and building local security institutions, instead of NATO deploying large numbers of our own combat troops in combat operations' (Stoltenberg 2017a). Officially, the policy was intended as a 360 degrees approach; in practice, stability projection was mainly aimed at the Middle East and North Africa, the so-called MENA region. From 2017 on, mobile training teams were sent to Iraq, Jordan, Egypt, Mauritania, Morocco and Tunisia. This was done with the consent of and in consultation with the countries involved.

However, for the United States, none of these measures went far enough. President Trump clearly stated that he expected more from the Alliance in the fight against terrorism.[10] This led to a series of additional initiatives in 2017. The most remarkable was that NATO as an organisation joined the Global Coalition to Defeat ISIS (Stoltenberg 2017b). This was a sensitive issue for a number of European countries, particularly France and Germany, which had always opposed collective participation in the coalition. France and Germany were very reluctant for NATO as an organisation to take an active role in the fight against Islamic State in Syria and Iraq (Emmot 2017). Their concern included the risk of being caught up in another costly Afghan-style deployment provoking some Arab countries and risking a confrontation with Russia in Syria. Besides that, all NATO members were at that moment—on a bilateral basis—already part

[10] Sommet de l'OTAN: une nouvelle étape dans la lutte contre le terrorisme (29 May 2017). Comprendre l'Europe. https://www.touteleurope.eu/actualite/sommet-de-l-otan-une-nouvelle-etape-dans-la-lutte-contre-le-terrorisme.html.

of this coalition. In practice, this meant that NATO would deploy AWACS planes over Syria and Iraq, while providing logistical support for the operations. However, there was no question of combat missions (Stoltenberg 2017c). The decision was therefore perceived as a political concession to President Trump, without major military consequences on the ground (Kristensen and Schousboe 2017).

Despite the progress already made, the exchange of intelligence remained difficult. In 2017, it was clear that a new initiative was needed in this area (Von Loringhoven and Arndt 2017). To this end, a separate Terrorism Intelligence Cell was set up within the newly established Joint Intelligence and Security Division. This cell was to ensure a better flow and coordination of intelligence on terrorist threats and foreign fighters, enabling a quicker and better response to new terrorist dangers.

Finally, there was the problem of increasing migration from the MENA countries, creating enormous challenges on the Alliance's Southern flank. To acquire better knowledge of this problem by collecting, analysing and assessing information relating to the MENA region, the Strategic Direction-South Hub was established within Joint Forces Command Naples. This should contribute to a better understanding of the specific challenges stemming from the region, including terrorism.

All these initiatives led to a significant expansion and deepening of the Counter-Terrorism Strategy. The Alliance had thus succeeded in presenting itself as a global security actor in the fight against terrorism. Nevertheless, it soon became evident that there were limits to this approach.

Constraints and Shortfalls of NATO's Counter-Terrorism Strategy

Political Divergences

Almost paradoxically, one of the main challenges for NATO's Counter-Terrorism Strategy is the political support of its own member states. The difficulty here is the Alliance's consensus-based decision-making process. The problem is that the terrorist threat, as well as the approach to it, is not perceived in the same way by all member states. Three fault lines can be clearly distinguished. Firstly, there is opposition between the member states that see NATO playing an important role in the fight against terrorism (e.g., the United States, UK, Turkey and Denmark) and those like France and Germany that see this as the responsibility of the individual member states. The latter believe that NATO does not have adequate instruments to tackle terrorism in its totality, and that the states must take the initiative here. In addition, there is also the so-called transatlantic divide: The United States adopts a 'war on terror' approach, in sharp contrast with the 'soft' European approach (prioritising diplomatic, legal, judicial, social, economic and cultural means). Whereas the Americans focus mainly on the military approach, the European member states concentrate more on the underlying root causes.

Also among European countries, views on the approach to follow differ. For example, some member states—especially the Baltic and the northern ones—still consider the Russian danger on the Eastern flank as the most important threat, while others—mainly the southern member states—focus more on the Southern flank with the instability in the MENA region and the resulting migration issue. The crisis in Ukraine in 2014 further exacerbated this split.

All these differences in views at the political level lead to divergent priorities and emphases in the proposed approach, and hinder consensus. This explains why NATO has such a hard time developing and implementing a coherent Counter-Terrorism Strategy. We already referred to the impact of President Trump's statements on the further implementation of the Action Plan, including the accession to the Global Coalition to Defeat ISIS. Another example is the creation of the Hub for the South, which was eventually established under pressure from—and as a political concession to—the southern member states led by Italy and Spain, which are mainly confronted with the migration problems.

Better Cooperation with Other Organisations

An effective response to terrorism requires a holistic, multipronged approach involving a wide range of actors. This necessarily involves political and diplomatic instruments, law enforcement, judicial authorities, intelligence organisations, military means, immigration control, development aid, as well as economic and financial instruments. Consequently, the military contribution is only a limited part of this global effort. It is therefore important to coordinate the various approaches. This implies comprehensive coordination between the actors involved, though this is difficult in practice: NATO and the EU, for example, have long been announcing their shared intention of closer coordination in counterterrorism. In practice, however, little has been achieved. This is often due to the persistent mutual distrust between the two organisations. In this respect, NATO could and should do more.

What Role for NATO?

This brings us to the fundamental question of what role NATO should assume in this multilateral approach. The answer is clear: as a defense organisation, it should focus on the military aspects of combating terrorism. NATO can make a difference in this domain. The non-military aspects, on the other hand, should be left to the member states or other specialised organisations. NATO simply does not possess the resources nor the expertise for this. This also implies that the Alliance has no leading role to play in the fight against terrorism. US Secretary of State Rex Tillerson hit the nail on the head when he stated: 'We do not believe that NATO has to lead in the fight against terrorism. Others will often have that role (…). But NATO must add value where it can and provide greater support' (Vincze 2017). The role of the Alliance in counterterrorism is therefore one of complementarity and support.

Nevertheless, a practical problem arises here. Since several actors are involved—military and civil, state and non-state—the approach in the field must be coordinated and steered. The question then is who should take on this task? In practice, this is a sensitive issue. After all, experience shows that NATO as a military organisation is reluctant to place itself under the lead of a (civilian) umbrella organisation.

More and Deeper Partnership

Terrorism is not limited to the Euro-Atlantic zone alone, but is global. Instability in the MENA region, in particular, is a breeding ground for many terrorist organisations. This spillover from the south poses a real threat to Europe. If NATO wants to tackle the problem of terrorism at its roots, it must therefore step up its cooperation with the countries in that region: strengthening these local regimes militarily can empower them to tackle terrorism themselves. After all, local forces are best placed to do that. They know the terrain, speak the local language and are familiar with the traditions. This enables them to win the hearts and minds of the population, which is crucial in the fight against terrorism. Moreover, these partnerships have the added advantage of only requiring a limited operational footprint. NATO has already gained considerable experience in the context of projecting stability.

However, despite the enormous potential the results remain limited. This has a lot to do with the available resources. Only 1% of the Alliance's total budget currently goes to partnership programmes (Kristensen and Schousboe 2017). In addition, there is a large shortage of specialised personnel to carry out all these partner activities. NATO must therefore free up more budget and provide staff to meet the growing demands from the partner countries. If not, the Alliance runs the risk of overpromising and underdelivering, which threatens to undermine its credibility. Partnership offers numerous advantages and is an important lever in the fight against terrorism. The message is therefore clear: NATO should invest more in its partnership programmes and do it more effectively.

Intelligence Sharing

Intelligence sharing is a major key enabler of the international response to terrorism. As a military organisation, NATO is all too aware of the importance of this. This is clearly shown by the Policy Guidelines and subsequent initiatives in the field of intelligence sharing. At the same time, the Alliance is also aware of the limitations inherent to the intelligence domain. After all, NATO as an organisation does not generate any intelligence itself and depends on the member states. Since the latter are very reluctant to share sensitive information collectively and unreservedly with all 30 partners, this is mostly done on a bilateral, case-by-case basis. What NATO can do is try to facilitate the flow of intelligence through the creation of permanent consultative bodies, such as the Joint Intelligence and Security Division and the Terrorism Intelligence Cell, by standardising security clearance procedures and by assuring overall coordination (Bernasconi 2011). This is obviously a long-term process. After all, sharing intelligence also has a lot to do with building confidence, which can only be achieved by long-term efforts. This explains why the multilateral intelligence sharing between the member states is still at an embryonic stage and bilateral relationships are still the preferred approach. But there is also positive news. As part of the outreach to the MENA region, NATO has launched an additional cooperation programme for exchanging intelligence with the partner countries. This is particularly interesting as these countries, because of their geographical proximity, are more in tune with the terrorist threat on their territory. Such initiatives clearly contribute to a better picture of the terrorist threat and constitute an added value in the fight against terrorism.

Optimising Resources

Finally, an important practical aspect is the use of NATO's resources. The implementation and follow-up of the Counter-Terrorism Strategy fall under the responsibility of the Counter-Terrorism Section, which is part of the Emerging Security Challenges Division in the International Staff. Close analysis of this structure shows that it is organised in a classic, stove-piped way. This seems contradictory to the mission of this section, namely to fight against a very diffuse, organised opponent. Heavily dependent on other sections and divisions, the Counter-Terrorism Section would, at first glance, benefit from a matrix structure. However, extensive discussions with various leading authorities showed that this is difficult to realise in practice, because of the existing complex structure. Nevertheless, efforts should be made to improve coordination and management. For example, for cooperation with the MENA countries, the Counter-Terrorism Section must contact the Partnership section, which it cannot do directly in practice because of hierarchical barriers. For the same reason, the section also has no impact whatsoever on the management of the Hub for the South. However, these are crucial instruments for a successful counterterrorism approach. To better coordinate efforts, an Assistant Secretary General with exclusive authority for counterterrorism should be designated. Officially, the Deputy Secretary General has taken care of this coordination until now. However, in practice, he lacks the time to perform this task. The same applies to the available budgets. These are very limited and the Counter-Terrorism Section mainly depends on the financial resources of other sections and divisions for its programmes, which considerably complicates its operational effectiveness. Streamlining both structure and budgets would be an important step forward in a more effective counterterrorism approach. Yet again, we should not delude ourselves. The problems faced by the Counter-Terrorism Section are very revealing in that regard, and reflect the importance that member states attach to the fight against terrorism: at the political level, grand declarations are made; in practice, however, member states are very reluctant to delegate much initiative to NATO. For many nations, counterterrorism is still primarily a national responsibility.

Conclusion

How to assess NATO's Counter-Terrorism Strategy? Counterterrorism has gained tremendous importance since 2001 and is high on the political and strategic agenda. While NATO wants to position itself as an important actor in this fight, it has difficulty with finding the right approach. This has a lot to do with the divergent political visions of the member states. The strategy followed is therefore pragmatic, mainly driven by events and developments on the ground. There is virtually no clear long-term vision. The approach adopted is thus reactive, rather than preventive.

Despite these shortcomings, NATO can play an important role in the international fight against terrorism. After all, the Alliance has outstanding assets: a solid framework for cooperation between the member states and with other partners, international legitimacy, specialised military means, experienced planning structures and a great deal of experience. Yet it is clear that NATO does not have a silver bullet for all problems. This requires a broad multilateral approach. After all, in the fight against terrorism, the narrow prism of the member states alone is not enough. This implies that the Alliance must step out of its cocoon and cooperate more actively with the other actors involved. It also means that it is not up to NATO to play a leading role in the fight against terrorism. Rather, that task should go to the member states or other specialised organisations. The Alliance must above all do what it does best: focus on the military aspects in the fight against terrorism. At the same time, it must commit more to prevention. In practice, this means making more efforts in the area of partnership, especially with the countries in the MENA region. After all, without the support and active involvement of the regional partners, any effort to tackle terrorism seems doomed beforehand.

Many of the issues and suggestions discussed above are included in the document *NATO 2030: United for a New Era*, prepared by a reflection group in November 2020 as an exercise prodromal to the approval of a new NATO Strategic Concept: 'NATO must articulate a consistent, clear, and coherent approach to the South, addressing both traditional threats like terrorism [...] Terrorism poses one of the most immediate, asymmetric threats to Allied nations and citizens. NATO should more explicitly integrate the fight against terrorism into its core tasks. This fight should be given a place within NATO structures, supported by necessary resources, commensurate with the threat that it poses. NATO should enhance the fight against terrorism as part of the hybrid and cyber conversation and ensure that the threat from terrorism figures in exercises and lessons learned'.[11]

Although the emerging counterterrorism challenges facing the Alliance remain daunting, putting them into an informed perspective makes it possible to address them purposefully and constructively.

Acknowledgements The author does thank the following interlocutors for the useful exchanges of views occurred during the elaboration of this chapter: Dr. Bird Juliette, Head of the Counter Intelligence Section at NATO; Dr. Shea Jamie, Former Deputy Assistant Secretary General for Emerging Security Challenges at NATO; Dr. Koehler Kevin, Research adviser, Middle East Faculty at NATO Defense College; Prof. Massimo de Leonardis, Senior Lecturer of History of Treaties and International Politics at the Università Cattolica del Sacro Cuore of Milan; Dr. Tardy Thierry, Head of the Research Division at NATO Defense College; Dr. Ragab Eman, MED Research Fellow at NATO Defense College.

Bibliography

Bernasconi, Claudia. 2011. NATO's Fight Against Terrorism. Where Do We Stand? *NATO Defense College*, Research Paper, No. 66.

Bird, Juliette. 2015. Nato's Role in Counter-Terrorism. *Perspectives on Terrorism* 9 (2). http://www.terrorismanalysts.com/pt/index.php/pot/article/view/419.

Chase, Eric. 2013, January 24. Defining Terrorism: A Strategic Imperative. *Small Wars Journal*. http://smallwarsjournal.com/jrnl/art/defining-terrorism-a-strategic-imperative.

Claes, Willy. 1995a, February 15. Interview. *Corriere Della Sera*.

Claes, Willy. 1995b, February 23. NATO's Agenda for a New European Order. *Financial Times*.

Emmot, Robin. 2017. France and Germany Resist US Plan for Bigger NATO Role Against Islamic State. *Reuters*. https://www.reuters.com/article/us-usa-trump-nato-idUSKCN18E15S.

Koehler, Kevin. 2018. Projecting Stability in Practice? NATO's New Training Mission in Iraq. *NATO Defense College*, Policy Brief, No. 2.

[11] NATO 2030: United for a New Era. Analysis and Recommendations of the Reflection Group Appointed by the NATO Secretary General (2020, November 25). https://www.nato.int/nato_static_fl2014/assets/pdf/2020/12/pdf/201201-Reflection-Group-Final-Report-Uni.pdf.

Kristensen, Kristian, and Schousboe, Laura. 2017. How to Step Up NATO's Fight Against Terrorism. *War on the Rocks*. https://warontherocks.com/2017/09/how-to-step-up-natos-fight-against-terrorism/.

Moghadam, Assaf. 2017. *Understanding Cooperation Among Terrorist Actors*. Columbia University Press.

Neumann, Ronald E. 1999, September 23. *Remarks Before the Center for Muslim-Christian Understanding*. Georgetown University.

Obama, Barack H. 2013, May 23. *Remarks by the President at the National Defence University*. White House Press Office. https://obamawhitehouse.archives.gov/the-press-office/2013/05/23/remarks-president-nationaldefense-university.

Page, Jacqueline. 2014. The Home Game. Countering Violent Extremism Within NATO. *NATO Defense College*, Research Paper, No. 104.

Pastori, Gianluca. 2015. L'Alleanza Atlantica e la lotta al terrorismo internazionale: Breve storia di un rapporto difficile. In de Leonardis, Massimo (Ed.), *Quaderni del Dipartimento di Scienze Politiche* (nr. 8). Educatt.

Reichard, Martin. 2006. *The EU-NATO Relationship: A Legal and Political Perspective*. Aldershot.

Sanguineti, Vittorio. 1995. La NATO e l'Islam. *Affari Esteri*, pp. 820–32.

Santamato, Stefano. 2013. The New NATO Policy Guidelines on Counterterrorism: Analysis, Assessments and Actions. *Strategic Perspectives*, No. 13, US Institute for National Strategic Studies. http://inss.ndu.edu/Portals/68/Documents/stratperspective/inss/Strategic-Perspectives-13.pdf.

Satloff, Robert. 2000. US Policy Toward Islamism: A Theoretical and Operational Overview. Council on Foreign Relations. https://cdn.cfr.org/sites/default/files/pdf/2005/08/Satloff.pdf.

Seth, Johnston A. 2017. *How NATO Adapts. Strategy and Organization in the Atlantic Alliance Since 1950*. John Hopkins University Press.

Shea, Jamie. 2013, July 25. How Is NATO Dealing with Emerging Security Challenges? *Georgetown Journal of International Affairs*. https://www.georgetownjournalofinternationalaffairs.org/online-edition/how-is-nato-dealing-with-emerging-security-challenges-by-jamie-shea.

Stoltenberg, Jens. 2017a, March 31. Doorstep Statement by NATO Secretary General Jens Stoltenberg Ahead of the Meeting of NATO Foreign Ministers. *NATO*. https://www.nato.int/cps/fr/natohq/opinions_142787.htm.

Stoltenberg, Jens. 2017b, May 25. At the Same Time, We Agreed That NATO Will Become a Full Member of the Global Coalition, in Which All 28 Allies Already Take Part. *NATO*, Press Conference. http://www.nato.int/cps/en/natohq/opinions_144098.htm?selectedLocale=fr.

Stoltenberg, Jens. 2017c, May 25. Being in the Coalition Does Not Mean That NATO Will Engage in Combat. *NATO*, Press Conference. http://www.nato.int/cps/en/natohq/opinions_144083.htm.

Van Leeuwen, Marianne. 2017. NATO and the War on Terror. *Atlantisch Perspectief*, Nr. 3. http://www.atlanticcommunity.org/AP%203%202017.pdf

Vincze, Hajnalka. 2017, April 21. NATO: Assessing the Alliance's Counter-Terrorism Efforts. *Terrorism Monitor* 15 (8). https://jamestown.org/program/nato-assessing-alliances-counter-terrorism-efforts/.

Von Loringhoven, and Arndt F. 2017, September 8. Adapting NATO Intelligence in Support of One NATO. *NATO Review Magazine*. https://www.nato.int/docu/review/2017/also-in-2017/adapting-nato-intelligence-in-support-of-one-nato-security-military-terrorism/en/index.htm.

CHAPTER 12

How Strong Is NATO's Arm: Commands, Cash, Capabilities and Contributions

Alessandro Marrone

Introduction

During the Cold War the NATO arm has been exclusively aimed to hold a shield against a Soviet invasion. Then it changed to conduct operations out of the members' territory, but after 2014 collective defence and deterrence have returned as top priority for the Alliance's militaries.

As a result of these shifts, by 2012 allies reformed and streamlined the NATO Command Structure towards expeditionary operations, including through the dismantling of several regional commands and the establishment of a unique supreme commander. Yet after 2014 they reviewed it by adding new commands to face Russian military forces in Eastern Europe while approaching cyber and space as operational domains.

In the post-Cold War period, the allies' defence spending went up and down at different paces across Europe and North America, for a

A. Marrone (✉)
Istituto Affari Internazionali (IAI), Rome, Italy
e-mail: a.marrone@iai.it

M. de Leonardis (ed.), *NATO in the Post-Cold War Era*, Security, Conflict and Cooperation in the Contemporary World
https://doi.org/10.1007/978-3-031-06063-2_12

variety of domestic and international reasons. Yet since 2015, a general, steady increase of allied military budgets has occurred towards 2% of GDP because of the Russian threat and US pressure.

While the budgetary input has augmented, the military output in terms of capabilities has been partially reoriented towards high-end conflicts, mainly through the NATO Defence Planning Process (NDPP). The Alliance's Force Structure has witnessed major changes with respect to the Eastern flank, i.e. through the establishment of the Enhanced Forward Presence (EFP) and the Very high readiness Joint Task Force (VJTF) entailing significant contributions by all members. As a whole, the current posture of NATO arms towards Russia relies upon deterrence through tripwire, and defence via reinforcements.

The Shifts of the Alliance's Command Structure

The following analysis is based on the explicit recognition that NATO is an Alliance of sovereign states with no transnational or supranational authority. The Washington Treaty allowed the creation of institutional bodies such as the command structure. But they are all in various forms under the political authority of the allied governments through the North Atlantic Council (NAC). In turn, the NAC exerts this authority by consensus among member states, relying on a well-accepted American leadership. Accordingly, the command structure reflects national threat perceptions and preferences of major allies, *in primis* the US. It goes without saying that the Alliance as such has played a certain role in influencing national decisions, yet such interaction is a dynamic two-ways street.

The Transformation of NATO Commands Until 2014

By the end of the Cold War, the NATO command structure was definitively centred on the defence against a conventional Soviet Union attack over Western Germany. The Supreme Headquarters Allied Powers Europe (SHAPE) near Mons (Belgium) was the host of the Allied Command Europe (ACE) under the authority of Supreme Allied Commander Europe (SACEUR). The only other supreme commander was in charge of Supreme Allied Command Atlantic (SACLANT) in Norfolk (Virginia, US). During the Cold War, SACEUR was in charge of military operations in the European theatre, and over NATO history he has always been a US four-star General holding also the US European Command (EUCOM). As a matter of fact, the Mediterranean was considered a secondary 'flank' with respect to the Central European 'front', and the same applied to the Nordic 'flank'. As a result, the commands in Southern members from Turkey to Portugal were largely national in terms of composition and capabilities. The most integrated structures were rather those in the Alliance's centre of gravity on the Eastern front, including the Air Command of Ramstein (Germany) and the Allied Command Central Europe in Brunssum (Netherlands). In this context, SACLANT was responsible to ensure the defence of the Atlantic Sea Lines of Communication (SLOC) and the possibility for American reinforcements to swiftly flow towards Europe in case of crisis or attack.

The end of the Cold War generated a profound and prolonged politico-military reflection over the NATO commands, leading to a series of important decisions during the 1990s and 2000s. In particular, the 2002 Prague Summit of Heads of State and Governments provided an important political mandate to significantly centralise and streamline the command structure. First, SHAPE has been endowed with the supreme command of all NATO operations, both within and outside the area covered by the Washington Treaty. In parallel, SACLANT was closed. The Norfolk command has been re-tasked and reformed to drive the transformation of allied militaries in conceptual, doctrinal and technological terms—with important industrial implications—becoming the Allied Command Transformation (ACT). Its commander has retained the supreme attribute in pair with SACEUR, but does not exert any authority on the allied armed forces committed to NATO's activities and operations. In other words, a functional division of labour has been established between SHAPE and ACT. As a result, the former has gained more political attention and resources than the latter, in light of the priority attached by member states first to crisis management operations and then to deterrence and defence measures.

A second major element of this overall reorganisation has been the concentration of regional commands in Brunssum and Naples (Italy), where two Joint Force Commands (JFC) had been established in 2004. NATO did move beyond the geographic rationale of regional commands in Northern, Southern and Central Europe. The two new JFC have the same functionality in order to provide sufficient resilience to the command structure. In other words, both Brunssum and Naples are able to plan and conduct large-scale operations—as happened i.e. in

Bosnia and Kosovo. However, the Cold War legacy makes Brunssum more oriented towards land operations and NATO's Eastern border, thus increasing its relevance since 2014 at the expense of Naples. In turn, the latter by heritage has more expertise concerning the Mediterranean region and the maritime domain.

Third, allies have been substantially merged and streamlined component commands. For example, the NATO Combined Air Operation Centres (CAOC) have been reduced from six to two, currently based, respectively, in Torrejon (Spain) and Uedem (Germany). Both CAOC are under the authority of the Allied Air Command (AIRCOM) based in Ramstein (Germany). The NATO Maritime Command (MARCOM) is based in Northwood (UK), and the Land Command (LANDCOM) is located in Izmir (Turkey). The air, maritime and land commands play an important role in preparing the forces with a view to their deployment in NATO operations and activities. One last related element of the streamlining of NATO's command structure over the 1990s and 2000s has been a drastic reduction of its size. At the end of the Cold War, NATO had roughly 22.000 staff across 33 commands, while as of 2020 the personnel employed in the command structure was about 7.000.

The end of the Soviet threat was obviously the major reason for such transformation of the Alliance's command structure. Against this backdrop, the 2008 Russia's war in Georgia did not constitute a sufficient reason for keeping collective defence as a major reference point for the ongoing reform of the commands. In retrospect, it could be argued the allies missed some signals and/or looked for the indicators they wanted instead of those they needed to see. Bottom line is that over the 1990s and 2000s most NATO members believed Russia would not be a threat anymore, and this strategic assumption drove military planning within the Alliance.

In parallel with the demise of a compelling threat on the NATO Eastern flank, the 1999 Strategic Concept[1] and, above all, its successor in 2010[2] established out-of-area operations as a core task alongside collective defence and cooperative security. This politico-strategic mandate came together with the reality of large-scale, joint and prolonged NATO

[1] The Alliance's Strategic Concept. 24 April 1999. https://www.nato.int/cps/en/natohq/official_texts_27433.htm.

[2] Active Engagement, Modern Defence. 19 November 2010. https://www.nato.int/cps/en/natohq/official_texts_68580.htm.

operational deployments, noticeably in the Balkans and Afghanistan.[3] These military commitments did not necessitate regional commands in Europe, but rather centralised JFC—exactly the logic of the transformation of the command structure. Moreover, the financial crisis affecting allies between 2008 and 2011 added further political pressure to reduce NATO costs perceived as not essential—a rationale embraced by the then Secretary General Anders Fogh Rasmussen although warning 'we must cut fat and not muscle'.[4]

The US leadership has been central in NATO's transformation. The priority attached by Washington to crisis management operations in the 1990s and, above all, to the global war on terrorism after 2001, was a compelling political factor in favour of the command structure's transformation. Indeed, the latter should have enabled allies to act as valuable partners in US-led military efforts, *in primis* in Afghanistan. The very same establishment of ACT was also meant to drive a technological and doctrinal leap forward for European allies' forces, in order to maintain them interoperable with the US in a period marked by both expeditionary operations and technology-driven revolution in military affairs.[5]

In this context, the aforementioned fact that NATO is an alliance of sovereign states plays a certain role in the commands' transformation. Indeed, national politics and relations among allies contributed to a situation where de facto each of the large members already part of the integrated military command in the end obtained major headquarters. This has been the case in Germany, Italy, Turkey, UK and the US—alongside the unmovable HQs in Belgium and the Netherlands.

As for France, the prolonged absence from the command structure led to a certain doctrinal, procedural and technical divergence between the French armed forces and the others. This in turn created interoperability problems during the NATO campaigns in the Western Balkans over the 1990s.[6] The 2009 decision to fully re-enter the Alliance's military

[3] On NATO's adaptation to out-of-area operations see, among others, Ruiz Palmer (2019).

[4] Press conference by NATO Secretary General Anders Fogh Rasmussen following the formal meeting of NATO Defence Ministers. 10 June 2010. https://www.nato.int/cps/en/natolive/opinions_64277.htm.

[5] On US drive for the transformation of allied militaries toward a net-centric warfare approach, see: Nones and Marrone (2012).

[6] Interview n. 1, 8 February 2021.

bodies led, over the following decade, to solving most of these problems. Ensuring interoperable militaries within the Alliance has always been a thorny issue, particularly in light of subsequent US technological and doctrinal leap forwards.[7] Recently, the major interoperability issues arose with NATO members previously part of the Warsaw Pact or even the Soviet Union. In particular, procedures were different, past formation and training were diverging and difficult to adjust, and much of the equipment had been produced by Russia, posing challenges in terms of maintenance, repair and overhaul. Indeed, since the 2010s the US has launched several initiatives to support the replacement of Russian equipment by European allies (Mahler 2019).

Against this backdrop, the full participation of all members to the command structure plays an important role in connecting the national defence apparatus not only in terms of doctrines, procedures and interoperability, but also at the politico-military level. First, in the 30 allied armed forces, the mid-to high-level officials have spent a large part of their careers in a NATO framework, thus working with allies has become part of their formation and mindset. At the political level, the interaction with military (and diplomatic) interlocutors that are part of the Alliance's structures, including the over 30 NATO centres of excellence[8] located in almost all members, helps to maintain a certain degree of awareness and socialisation with regard to the Alliance. As a whole, the command structure and other bodies constitute an anchor against centrifugal tendencies and a driver towards more centripetal politico-military relations among allies. Such indirect role has been very important through the post-Cold

[7] See in this regard, among others: Appathurai (2002).

[8] NATO Centres of Excellence are nationally or multi-nationally funded institutions accredited by NATO. They train and educate leaders and specialists from NATO member and partner countries, assist in doctrine development, identify lessons learned, improve interoperability and capabilities, and test and validate concepts through experimentation. Although not part of the NATO command structure, they are part of a wider framework supporting NATO Command Arrangements. Designed to complement the Alliance's current resources, Centres of Excellence cover a wide variety of areas, with each one focusing on a specific field of expertise to enhance NATO capabilities. The overall responsibility for Centres of Excellence coordination and utilization within NATO lies with Allied Command Transformation, in co-ordination with the Supreme Allied Commander Europe. See in this regard: NATO ACT. Centres of Excellence. https://www.act.nato.int/centres-of-excellence#:~:text=NATO%20Centres%20of%20Excellence%20are%20nationally%20or%20multi-nationally,capabilities,%20and%20test%20and%20validate%20concepts%20through%20experimentation.

War period when the absence of a single, compelling threat has generated greater differentiation of threat perceptions and security interests within the Alliance.

The Post-2014 Re-adaptation

The new command structure established in 2012 has been questioned already in 2014 by the Russian war in Ukraine. The effectiveness, efficiency, scale and rapidity of Russia's attack against a European country neighbouring four NATO members triggered a multi-faced Western reaction at the politico-military level. The majority of allies, from the US, the UK and Germany to Nordic and Eastern Europe have returned to perceive Russia as a threat rather than a partner. Both NATO and EU have looked at Moscow's hybrid warfare and adopted countermeasures. The priority to defend the Alliance's borders in Europe has replaced the previous emphasis on out-of-area operations.[9] While the 2010 Strategic Concept has not been updated or replaced until June 2022, a wide debate on the priority threats to be addressed by NATO unfolded after 2014.[10,11] The Alliance's military bodies have rediscovered the deeply-rooted mindset towards planning and implementing deterrence and defence measures on the Eastern flank. In the 2010s most mid-level officials had no personal memory of the Cold War, as they spent most of their careers in out-of-area operations. However, the NATO military institutions and staff as a whole were somehow familiar with going 'back to basics' on collective defence. Moreover, the tide of Western interventionism abroad was shifting back already from 2011, with the transition from ISAF to a much smaller Resolute Support mission and finally to the 2021 retreat from Afghanistan, and the US attempts to leave Iraq and not enter the Syrian conflict, thus making room for a focus on Europe's defence.

In this context, the NATO command structure has been further reviewed to assess its ability to stand against the post-2014 Russian threat. Such a review concluded that the overall posture was only partly adequate

[9] See in this regard, among others: Marrone et al. (2014).

[10] See in this regard, among others: Fassi et al. (2015).

[11] See in this regard, among others: Fassi et al. (2015).

to ensure an appropriate deterrence and defence capacity.[12] Accordingly, allies took a number of important decisions in this regard. By September 2019 NATO created a Support and Enabling Joint Force Command at Ulm (Germany), tasked with coordinating the Reception Staging Onward Movement and Integration (RSOMI) of allied forces. It aims at speeding and protecting the movement of armour and infantry across Europe, under SACEUR authority,[13] mostly through the West-East corridor. In parallel, initiatives on military mobility have been undertaken within both NATO and the EU to make European transport infrastructure fit for the transit of extremely heavy, large equipment, through both physical upgrades and bureaucratic streamlining.[14]

By September 2020 an Atlantic Joint Force Command has been re-established in Norfolk, co-located with the US Second Fleet, to ensure the security of maritime routes for reinforcements and supplies across the Atlantic covering vast geographic areas, from the American East Coast, past the Greenland-Iceland-UK (GIUK) gap and into the Arctic.[15] Day-to-day NATO maritime operations will continue to be run out of MARCOM. Allies deemed the re-establishment of an Atlantic Command crucial to ensure the feasibility and credibility of American reinforcements to Europe for deterrence and defence purpose. A third important measure, linked to the command structure review as well as to the establishment of Ulm and Norfolk bodies, has been the re-boost of the overall size of the NATO commands.

Actually, the command structure undertook two major transformations in the post-Cold War period. The first one shifted and adapted away from Europe's collective defence towards out-of-area operations. The second one has rebalanced NATO's focus on an article 5 scenario against Russian aggression: the decision taken at the 2014 Wales Summit represented an immediate reaction; those of the 2016 Warsaw Summit a mid-to long-term adaptation; and finally the 2018 Brussels Summit marked a consolidation of this process for the long run. Building on that basis, in

[12] Interview n. 1, 8 February 2021.

[13] New NATO command declared operational. 17 September 2019. https://www.nato.int/cps/en/natohq/news_168945.htm#:~:text=In%20June%202018%2C%20NATO%20Defence,Europe%20in%20a%20crisis%20situation.

[14] See in this regard: Drent et al. (2019).

[15] NATO's new Atlantic command declared operational. 17 September 2020. https://www.nato.int/cps/en/natohq/news_178031.htm.

2019 the allied Military Committee approved the new NATO Military Strategy, a capstone document supporting the ongoing wider adaptation of the Alliance (Broeks 2019). Once again, a political rationale supported military adaptation. Right after 2014, the US wanted to reassure Eastern European allies, maintain a credible Euro-Atlantic bloc to deter Russia, and defend Europe from a possible Russian attack, while increasingly focusing the bulk of American armed forces on China. Moreover, the creation of the Ulm command and the enhancement of the Szczecin one (Poland) reflected the renewed investments by Berlin and Warsaw in collective defence. The re-establishment of a maritime command in Norfolk was also meant to keep the US sufficiently engaged in Europe's collective defence. In retrospect, it could be argued that over the 1990s and 2000s the Alliance went too far into transformation at the expense of Europe's collective defence, and the pendulum had then to shift back to find a new equilibrium. The 2022 Strategic Concept solidifies the such equilibrium centred on article 5 and the Russian threat.

However, the ongoing adaptation is not simply a return to the Cold War. First, the unique supreme role of SACEUR and the enhancement of the joint level through Brunssum and Naples JFC remain in place. Second, in 2019 NATO declared outer space an operational domain alongside air, land or sea, and has adopted a Space Policy.[16] Such a decision recognises the importance of this dimension for allied military operations, the trend towards its militarisation, and the technological race in this field between the West, Russia and China. In 2020, allies decided to establish a new Space Centre at Allied Air Command in Ramstein, to help coordinate allied space activities and support NATO operations from space including information sharing about potential threats. Then in 2021, they agreed to create a Center of Excellence on Space in Tolouse (France)[17] to carry out a variety of work strands including doctrine, training and exercises. The effects of these decisions on the command structure are still unclear, as NATO has no traditions of space

[16] London Declaration. 4 December 2019. https://www.nato.int/cps/en/natohq/official_texts_171584.htm.

[17] Defence—Establishment of the NATO space centre of excellence in Toulouse. Communiqué issued by the Ministry for the Armed Forces. 4 February 2021. https://www.diplomatie.gouv.fr/en/french-foreign-policy/security-disarmament-and-non-proliferation/news/article/defence-establishment-of-the-nato-space-centre-of-excellence-in-toulouse.

activities, and crucial assets such as satellites and launchers are owned and operated only at the national level with little coordination among allies. As a result, the first step for NATO is to factor space in military operations in conceptual and doctrinal terms. At the same time, the command structure will have to make an effort in terms of related expertise, education, training and infrastructures. Having said that, NATO will rely primarily on US leadership in this regard with a minor involvement of the few members whose armed forces own and operate robust space assets—France, Germany, Italy and the UK.

Another novelty of the post-2014 NATO posture regards cyberspace. The 2016 Warsaw Summit recognised it as an operational domain and the 2018 Brussels declaration explicitly stated that cyber defence is part of collective defence.[18] Taken together, they represent an important and ambitious posture: on that basis, a cyber attack could trigger the activation of article 5 and provoke military actions across the cyber, land, sea and air domains (Marrone and Sabatino 2021). Accordingly, in 2019 allied created a Cyberspace Operations Centre (CYOC) within ACO. The Centre is responsible for NATO cyber operations in support of operational commands, primarily for monitoring cyberspace and coordinating cyber activities with those in the other domains.[19] At the technical level, the NATO Communications and Information Agency (NCIA) provides many of the capabilities necessary to the Alliance's structures in terms of cyber defence. Moreover, the NCIA directly manages some of the allied networks, interacting with the NATO Cyber Security Centre (NCSC) and the NATO Computer Incident Response Capability (NCIRC).

To sum up, the Alliance's command structure is re-adapting some Cold War elements to the post-2014 security environment, in terms of managing heavy, large, high-end forces in Eastern Europe, and it is approaching space and cyberspace as new operational domains. The 2022 Strategic Concept fully integrates space and cyberspace into NATO deterrence and defence posture. But the allies' armed forces have to adapt

[18] Brussels Summit Declaration. 11 July 2018. https://www.nato.int/cps/en/natohq/official_texts_156624.htm.

[19] The establishment of CYOC had been set forward by the 2018 Brussels Summit. For further information, please see: Brzozowski (2018). NATO Sees New Cyber Command Centre by 2023 as Europe Readies for Cyber Threats. EURACTIV.com, https://www.euractiv.com/section/defence-and-security/news/nato-sees-new-cyber-command-centre-by-2023-as-europe-readies-for-cyber-threats/.

too concerning size, equipment, organisation and skills. For instance, several allies have found it hard to adequately staff NATO structures in light of the decrease of military personnel that occurred in the last three decades,[20] as well as of the difficulties to recruit and retain the expertise required for cyber defence and thus for the CYOC.[21] In turn, the quality and quantity of allied militaries obviously depend also on the trends of defence spending at the national level.

The Issue of Allies' Defence Spending

As for the analysis of the command structure, the premise for looking at member states' military budgets is that each of them is ultimately decided at the national level. The US and NATO pressures have influenced to a certain extent European decisions, but the debate on burden-sharing remains an open issue among sovereign allies.

Military Budgets Trends Until 2014

Article 3 of the Washington Treaty states that 'in order more effectively to achieve the objectives of this Treaty, the Parties, separately and jointly, by means of continuous and effective self-help and mutual aid, will maintain and develop their individual and collective capacity to resist armed attack'.[22] The commitment to invest in military capabilities is enshrined in the NATO founding act, with a clear reference to the collective defence *raison d'être* of the Alliance. Yet the Washington Treaty does not specify any quantitative indication of the appropriate level of defence spending, leaving it to the allies' political decisions.

The changes in both the international security environment and domestic politics in the major members led to different trends in defence spending during and after the Cold War. Four structural elements have to be taken into account. First, the US has always invested in defence far more than its European allies, in both absolute and percentage

[20] Interview n. 8, 12 February 2021.

[21] Interview n. 4, 13 February 2021.

[22] The North Atlantic Treaty. 4 April 1949. https://www.nato.int/cps/en/natolive/official_texts_17120.htm.

terms, reflecting a variety of factors including American global ambi tions. These ambitions mean that only a part of the Pentagon budget is devoted to Europe's collective defence. For instance, the American military commitment is heavy, expensive and prolonged in the whole Pacific rim from Japan to South Korea and Taiwan, not to mention the Middle East. Second, among European allies, the UK and France have maintained a larger budget in terms of GDP percentage than Italy and Germany, despite the comparable economic and demographic size. This has reflected also the ambitions of two former colonial powers, endowed with a national nuclear deterrent representing per se an expensive capability. Once again, as for the US, not all British or French military investments were meant to serve NATO's purposes, particularly in the case of France. Third, Germany and Italy have constantly underinvested in defence, in terms of GDP percentage, in comparison with all other major and middle NATO allies—including Turkey and Spain—for a number of historical and political reasons. Finally, as for Central and Eastern European allies, once they joined NATO in several cases military budgets were significantly reduced, taking for granted the US security umbrella through the Alliance. Yet after 2014, almost all new members have drastically increased their defence spending.

Looking in particular to the post-Cold War period, in the early 1990s military expenditure sharply decreased across Europe and North America, as governments were eager to harvest the so-called 'peace dividend' and to shift resources to other domestic policies. In 1989, on the verge of the Berlin Wall fall, the Allies spent on average 4% of GDP on defence. Ten years later, this percentage shrinks by about two-thirds, down to 2.42%. The downward trend was present in all major NATO members. The US hit the threshold of 2.9%, for the first time below the percentage of the other two allies (Turkey and Greece) and very close to France (2.6%) and the UK (2.2%). The reduction was less robust in Germany (from 2.4 to 1.5%), while the Italian defence budget decreased only from 2.1 to 1.9% (Wołkonowski 2018). As a result, ad the end of the 1990s the gap between allies' spending was narrower than ever before in NATO's history. This reflected a shared threat assessment on the absence of a direct, compelling menace to national and collective security.

The turn of the century witnessed an inversion of the defence spending trend in the US, following the 2001 terrorist attacks on American soil and the subsequent military intervention in Afghanistan and Iraq. The Pentagon budget steadily and constantly increased from 516.6

billion dollars in 2000 to 776.6 billion in 2009, scoring an impressive plus 50% (Wołkonowski 2018). Over the same period, the defence spending of the 'NATO Europe' grouping—that is all European allies plus Turkey, including the new members from the Baltic to the Balkans—rose from 250 billion dollars to 282,3 billion dollars, a 13% increase (Wołkonowski 2018). In particular, Germany, Spain, Turkey and the UK significantly contributed to this upward trend.[23] These figures show how reactive is the US budget to changing defence policy goals, by leveraging a continental-size economy and a unified decision-making process. In comparison, the European trend demonstrates less flexibility due to economic constraints, fragmentation and to some extent divergence among allies and, above all, the lack of a shocking attack. Such an asymmetry is even more evident looking at the percentage of GDP devoted to defence. For Washington, it was on average 3.4% per year in 2000–2004 and 4.5% in 2005–2009—with a peak of 5.4 in 2009—while the group of European allies allocated 1.8% GDP to defence during the first half of the decade and 1.7% over the second one.[24]

The financial crisis spreading from the US to Europe between 2008 and 2011 constituted a watershed for NATO defence spending. The Pentagon budget fell from 776.6 billion dollars in 2009 to 618 billion dollars in 2015—a minus 20% cut. In the same period, 'NATO Europe' budgets declined from 282 to 253 billions—that is minus 10%. In other words, the whole allied spending reduced significantly, and the transatlantic gap did narrow again insofar as the US moved from 4.9% GDP to 3.4%, and European allies from 1.7 to 1.4%.[25]

[23] The figures for France and Italy show a decrease mainly due to the changes in the counting respectively of Gendarmerie and Carabinieri. While in the 1990s the expenses of those military polices devoted mainly to homeland security were entirely counted in the defence budget, currently only the portion of these forces employed abroad—i.e. as trainers within international operations—is included in NATO's official figures. This has a led to a formal decrease of French and Italian defence budgets which in reality did not regarded the Army, the Navy or the Air Force.

[24] Financial and Economic Data Relating to NATO Defence—Defence expenditures of NATO countries (1990–2010). Press Release PR/CP(2011)027. 10 March 2011. https://www.nato.int/nato_static_fl2014/assets/pdf/pdf_2011_03/20110309_PR_CP_2011_027.pdf [Figures are in 2010 current prices].

[25] Defence Expenditures of NATO Countries (2009–2016). Press Release PR/CP(2016)116. 4 July 2016. https://www.nato.int/nato_static_fl2014/assets/pdf/pdf_2016_07/20160704_160704-pr2016-116.pdf.

The 2014 Defence Spending Pledge and the Transatlantic Burden Sharing

As mentioned before, the 2014 Russian military intervention in Ukraine constituted a wake-up call for NATO regarding the very same cornerstone of the Alliance, collective defence and deterrence. The effectiveness, efficiency and readiness of Russia's armed forces prompted fears about the Baltic States and Poland and raised questions on the size of allied armies and the whole NATO military posture. On top of that, international Islamic terrorism represented a further source of concern, particularly for France, Italy and others in Southern Europe. As a result, an upward trend in defence spending began in several European countries already in 2015.[26]

Against this backdrop, the summit of Head of State and Governments held in Wales in 2014 adopted the Defence Investment Pledge, by committing to reverse the trend of declining budgets. In doing so, allies reiterated commitments expressed in various ways since 2006, with more precise wording. In quantitative terms, they solemnly pledged to move towards the 2% GDP threshold by 2024. They also promised to allocate more than 20% of their defence expenditure to major equipment, including technological research and development, with a view to meeting their NATO capability targets and filling Alliance's capability shortfalls.[27] The 2% has become the most visible parameter of defence spending, repeatedly recalled in NATO and government documents and declarations.

The 2% issue has been particularly important for the US, as the last chance to improve the burden-sharing across the Atlantic. Throughout NATO history, American Congress and administrations have frequently accused European allies to spend too little on defence and over-rely on the Washington security umbrella and the Pentagon budget. Particularly in the post-Cold War period, large sectors of both Democrats and Republicans began to perceive an increasingly unfair and unsustainable burden-sharing concerning collective security.[28] The US pressure on the

[26] See in this regard: Marrone et al. (2016).

[27] Wales Summit Declaration. Paragraph 14. 5 September 2014. https://www.nato.int/cps/en/natohq/official_texts_112964.htm.

[28] An example of such bipartisan position is the speech on the future of NATO delivered in June 2011 in Brussels by the then Secretary of Defence Robert Gates, who served in

2% target reached its apex under the Donald Trump administration, up to the extremely tense 2018 Brussels summit where many observers in Europe and the US feared the Republican President was about to tear down the Alliance (Cohen et al., 2018).

As a matter of fact, between 2014 and 2020, all allies increased their defence budgets, with the number of European members spending more than 2% augmenting from two to nine—including the UK, France and Poland.[29] Turkey got close to the target, while Germany and Italy reached, respectively, 1.6 and 1.4%. These percentages have been to a certain extent augmented by the 2020 fall of GDP across the West due to the Covid-19 pandemic. However, beyond this extraordinary circumstance, the increase of allied spending on defence has been robust and constant also in absolute terms over the last five years. The whole military budgets of NATO members rose to about 1,000 billion euro in both 2019 and 2020, which is about 12% more than 2015.[30] The upward trend has been more pronounced in the US, as already happened in the 2000s. Concerning the percentage of equipment expenditure over the entire defence budget, as of 2020 fifteen European allies already exceed the 20% threshold, including all major ones except for Germany which stands at 16.8%.

Comparing Defence Spending in NATO and Russia

The budget is an important parameter of allies' military might, however, it has to be put in the right context of deterrence and collective defence vis-à-vis Russia. According to a CSIS comprehensive comparison of defence spending data, in 2018 the group 'NATO Europe' allocated 275.9 billion dollars while Russia only 63.1 billion (Cordesman and Molot 2019). In other words, European allies alone spent about four times

this role under both George W. Bush and Barack Obama administrations. See: Text of Speech by Robert Gates on the Future of NATO. 10 June 2011. https://www.atlanticcouncil.org/blogs/natosource/text-of-speech-by-robert-gates-on-the-future-of-nato/.

[29] Defence Expenditure of NATO Countries (2013-2020). Press Release PR/CP(2020)104. 21 October 2020. https://www.nato.int/nato_static_fl2014/assets/pdf/2020/10/pdf/pr-2020-104-en.pdf.

[30] Ibidem. Meanwhile the number of European allies increased to 28 with the accession of Montenegro and North Macedonia, but their quantitative contribution to overall NATO defence spending is negligible.

the Russian Federation. By adding the US and Canada, in that year NATO combined military budgets accounted for 970.3 billion, which is about 15 times Moscow's (Cordesman and Molot 2019). The 2018 data were not exceptional in comparison with the previous three decades: over the entire post-Cold War period, Russian military spending oscillated roughly around 9–11% of the US. For sure, personnel and equipment costs in Russia had been far lower than in the West, and this has helped the Kremlin to mitigate such an unbalance. Moreover, Moscow's official figures may prove partly inaccurate, and the unstable exchange rate between roubles and US dollars further alters the comparisons. However, these three factors cannot radically change the balance of spending which remains in favour of NATO's military might. Moreover, in comparison to the 1990s, the Alliance's enlargement to 14 new members and a GDP growth higher in the West than in Russia has led the ensemble of allies to spend in 2020 nearly as much as they were spending in 1990 in absolute terms (Cordesman and Molot 2019), thus recovering from the 1990s and 2009–2014 cuts. These comparisons help to consider defence spending as an important but not sufficient parameter to assess allied capabilities for deterrence and collective defence vis-à-vis Russia.

Capabilities and Contributions to Collective Defence and Deterrence

In recent years, the debate within the Alliance has moved towards a more nuanced way to look at burden-sharing, through an approach based on three 'C': Cash, Capabilities and Contributions.[31] Cash obviously refers to the 2% GDP threshold and it is the easiest measurement across allies. The second 'C' relates to the output in terms of capabilities. It involves both quantitative parameters such as the 20% invested in major equipment, and quality parameters for instance regarding readiness, mobility and sustainability. Here the NDPP plays an important role in identifying capability targets for Allies and assessing eventual gaps. The third 'C' refers to the allies' military contribution to the Alliance's operations, activities and exercises, from the deployments in Afghanistan and the Balkans

[31] Such an approach was put forward by Secretary General Stoltenberg already in 2017. See for example: Press conference by NATO Secretary General Jens Stoltenberg following the meeting of the North Atlantic Council at the level of Defence Ministers. 29 June 2017. https://www.nato.int/cps/en/natohq/opinions_145385.htm.

to the deterrence and defence measures on the Eastern flank. Noticeably, in recent years non-US allies (and NATO partners) have provided half of the troops deployed within Resolute Support and around 80% of Kosovo Force units.

Taken together, the 'Three C' approach provides a better and more comprehensive way to assess how strong is NATO's arm than the sole 2% parameter. Yet for a variety of reasons, it is not really well-developed and implemented within the Alliance.[32] Actually, European allies like Italy have strongly supported this approach. For Rome, it serves also to mitigate the American criticism of the national budget far from reaching the 2% goal by 2024, as well as to capitalise on the robust and prolonged Italian contributions to allied operations in the Balkans and Afghanistan.[33] In contrast, Washington has systematically insisted only on the 'Cash' element also because it entails a strong and clear political message, which resonates among the American Congress and public opinion keen to have a fair burden-sharing for US taxpayers.

Against this backdrop, a comprehensive and detailed analysis of NATO's military might is beyond the scope of this chapter. An in-depth focus will rather be adopted on conventional capabilities and contributions to collective defence and deterrence,[34] through a three steps approach. First, the NDPP will be analysed as an important tool to connect the input of allies' defence spending with the output in terms of military capabilities fit for collective defence and deterrence. Second, the NATO Force structure will be discussed with respect to the Eastern flank. Third, the whole Alliance's posture will be assessed in terms of deterrence through tripwire and defence via reinforcement.

The Role of NATO Defence Planning Process

The starting point for the NDPP is the Political Guidance agreed upon by member states every four years—last time in 2019. The document derives its main assumptions from the Strategic Concept currently in place

[32] See in this regard: Mattelaer (2016).

[33] On Italy's position, see: Bitondo et al. (2017).

[34] NATO's collective defence and deterrence have always relied and continue to rely on both conventional and nuclear components. While recognising the fundamental linkage between the two, in the given length of this chapter the focus will be only on the conventional aspect in order to adequately address it.

and defines the scale and nature of the operations the Alliance should be able to conduct in the future (Fleischer 2015). On this basis, the NATO bodies elaborate collective and individual capability targets. In particular, ACT, ACO, the Defence Policy and Plans Division and the Defence Investment Division are involved in defining these targets with a view to the Alliance's operational needs in 5–10 years. For instance, ACT prepares studies on NATO Framework for Future Alliance Operations. The NDPP process draws from results of previous defence planning processes outputs, MC161 NATO agreed intelligence, lessons learned from operations and member states' capability surveys (Fleischer 2015). On that basis, a list of Minimum Capability Requirements (MCR) is prepared and then confronted with the state of the art of allies' capabilities outlined by the aforementioned surveys in order to identify shortfalls. Accordingly, NATO bodies elaborate on a proposal of tailored targets for each member through bilateral dialogue, in order to agree with the respective Ministry of Defence on the specific national targets. The agreed packages are submitted to the Defence Planning Committee, the Nuclear Planning Group and the North Atlantic Council for approval and endorsement. Allies in turn contribute to the collective elaboration of the Political Guidance, manage the respective bilateral dialogues by choosing what they commit to fulfil, and finalise the process through their participation in the decisions of NAC and other relevant committees.

The whole process is based, on the one hand, on the principle of reasonable burden sharing, whereby it is politically not acceptable to refuse the proposed targets altogether. On the other hand, lies the principle of reasonable challenge, whereby members should be encouraged to develop those capabilities which fit their security interests, e.g. in terms of maritime rather than land force projection. In theory, the general expectation is that each nation will deliver what it promised, but there is no mechanism to enforce it. NATO bodies do monitor the implementation of the agreed targets and present an annual report to the NAC and then to allied Defence Ministers, yet it is all about moral suasion and peer pressure. As mentioned at the beginning of this chapter, NATO remains an alliance of sovereign nations, and through the NDPP they are free first to select the target to reach and then to change their mind in this regard for both domestic and international reasons. According to some practitioners, in the early 1990s on average allies used to agree on about 70% of NDPP targets and respected roughly half of those on which they agreed. Since 2014, the situation has significantly improved because NATO members have increasingly recognised the importance of the Alliance's targets for collective defence.[35] However, a gap between the forces' goals and the actual acquisitions remains a quasi-permanent feature of the interaction between NATO bodies and member states.

Obviously, the NDPP has a different impact on allies' defence planning on the basis of their size, national interests, geopolitical positions, level of ambitions, etc. It goes without saying that the US has its own agenda and it exerts more influence on the NDPP than vice-versa. For different reasons, both France and Turkey have traditionally attached less priority to NATO indications than to other reference points for the development of their militaries. Italy and Germany have constantly attributed significant importance to NDPP, but still retained national preferences and room for manoeuvre. The majority of medium and smaller allies have taken it as a main and useful guideline, also because of the limited national capacity for autonomous planning. As a whole, it can be argued that capability development is very much tied in with national perspectives of threats and opportunities, as well as with competing industrial policies, and the collective footprint in this regard is limited. In this context, the added value of NDPP is to harmonise the national defence planning by achieving a certain degree of coherence and coordination.

The NDPP is complemented by other Alliance's tools meant to favour more effective and efficient investments in military capabilities. For example, the NATO Standardization Office supports the achievement of a minimum level of interoperability among allied militaries, despite the diversity of platforms in use and the variety of suppliers. Indeed, it is the repository of hundreds of NATO standards in use by allies (Grand and Gillis 2020). Moreover, the Conference of National Armaments Directors had been established already in 1966 to provide a common forum for allies to identify and pursue opportunities for cooperation in capability development (Grand and Gillis 2020). However, for a variety of reasons NATO's influence in this regard has remained limited, and commonly funded capabilities are circumscribed to a handful of examples such as the Airborne early Warning and Control Systems (AWACS). As for other aspects of NATO's posture, this reflects the reality of an Alliance of sovereign nations.

[35] Interview n. 8, 12 February 2021.

The bottom line is that the NDPP contributes to shaping allied militaries in a way that fits NATO's purposes, in terms of both collective defence and deterrence and out-of-area operation—with a growing emphasis on the former. However, as mentioned before, major member states deploy their armed forces in a variety of frameworks including the UN, the EU, ad hoc coalitions, bilateral cooperation and unilateral operations. Therefore, the portion of national capabilities allocated to NATO's force structure is extremely important to enable the Alliance's commands to draw from allies' might, otherwise, in facing the Russian threat the risk is to have an insufficient pool of resources to be mobilised by the adapted command structure.

The NATO Force Structure and the Eastern Flank

Soon after NATO's establishment, allies permanently put part of their national forces under the SACEUR authority, in order to enable a swift, coherent and massive defence in case of Soviet attack. It was the beginning of the NATO force structure, which is a distinct pool of national forces and HQs placed at the Alliance's disposal on a permanent or temporary basis. During the Cold War, the majority of these standing forces were deployed in Western Germany at the immediate disposal of ACE, and were cut by 45% already in 1993 (Young 1997).

Allies reviewed the NATO force structure in line with the aforementioned trend towards expeditionary operations as well as the adaptation of the command structure. In 2001, they announced a new setting based on rapidly deployable, mobile, sustainable and flexible multinational forces and command and control capabilities: those needed for conducting the kinds of crisis response operations NATO had undertaken in the Balkans and which military planners believed would continue to characterise future operations (Bjerg Moller 2019). Accordingly, allies created over time nine multinational deployable land HeadQuarters (HQs) based on voluntary contributions, to be activated at short notice, known as NATO Rapid Deployable Corps HQs (Deni 2004).

A landmark for the force structure transformation has been the creation of the NATO Response Force (NRF), decided at the 2002 Prague Summit. It is a multinational force made up of land, air, maritime and special forces components which can be deployed rapidly in various operational scenarios. The NRF is based on a rotational system with a different Rapid Deployable Corp HQs acting every year as Land Component

Command, on standby to be deployed in case of crisis (Bjerg Moller 2019). The rotation mechanism led allies to provide capabilities for NRF by meeting significant procedures and standards, which are required for both defensive and expeditionary operations.[36]

Against this backdrop, after 2014 a number of parallel initiatives have been undertaken on the basis of the Readiness Action Plan.[37] First, a Very high readiness Joint Task Force (VJTF) has been created. It is a multinational brigade of approximately 5.000 troops supported by air, maritime and special forces. It is led on a yearly rotational basis by framework nation providing the bulk of VJTF including a combat brigade, HQs and logistics, while others allocate plug-in capabilities.[38] It is on standby at the highest readiness level, to be deployed within a few days if needed. While theoretically available for both collective defence and crisis management tasks on both Eastern and Southern flanks, in reality it plans and exercises mainly to rapidly intervene in the East in case of a Russian attack.

The VJTF is part of the NRF, which in turn has been enhanced after 2014 to reach the size of 40.000 troops. The NRF was clearly conceived with a view to the crisis management operations prioritised in the 1990s and 2000s, but it was never used after its establishment and allies had some problems to adequately staff it (Kacprzyk 2018). As for its spearhead VJTF, since 2014 the whole NRF mainly focused on possible Russian aggression. In this contest, its readiness has been enhanced up to a situation where the VJTF is deployable in 5–7 days, the second brigade in 30 days and the third one in 45 days (Kacprzyk 2018). In 2021 the JFC Naples acted as an operational command for the NRF, under the SACEUR authority.

Readiness is a key feature of both VJTF and NRF. While during the Cold War allies were used to keep large forces ready to fight in Europe, through the 1990s and 2000s readiness levels decreased. Infrastructures

[36] NATO Allied Joint Force Command Naples. NATO Response Force. https://jfcnaples.nato.int/page6734927.aspx.

[37] Wales Summit Declaration. 5 September 2014. https://www.nato.int/cps/en/natohq/official_texts_112964.htm.

[38] The UK, Germany, Italy, Spain and Poland have acted as VJTF framework nations so far. In 2021 Turkey has taken over the lead, and units from Albania, Hungary, Italy, Latvia, Montenegro, Poland, Romania, Slovakia, Spain, the UK and the US serve on the force, currently counting 6.400 troops. See: Turkey takes charge of NATO high readiness force. 1 January 2021. https://www.nato.int/cps/en/natohq/news_180627.htm.

such as air basis were closed and forces were repatriated in North America, UK and Western continental Europe—while the overall size of European militaries decreased too. After 2014, it was not possible to simply go back to the Cold War posture, because some infrastructures and capabilities were not available anymore. Moreover, keeping a high readiness is very expensive because of the equipment, personnel, enablers, communications and logistics needed. In this context, the Allies chose first to expand and intensify exercises in Central Eastern Europe in order to both increase the readiness level of robust force packages for VJTF and NRF, and move them closer to the Eastern flank by making them more familiar with this scenario. Second, the 2018 Brussels Summit launched the NATO Readiness Initiative whereby allies commit to having 30 heavy or medium manoeuvre battalions, 30 kinetic air squadrons and 30 major naval combatants ready to use within 30 days together with enabling forces (Kacprzyk 2018). Overall, the readiness level of the NATO force structure has significantly increased with respect to 2014, but such a starting point was very low in comparison with the end of the Cold War.

Allies recognised the need to facilitate the deployment of VJTF and NRF in the Eastern members in case of crisis. Therefore, in 2015 they decided to establish nine NATO Force Integration Units (NFIU) in the Baltic States, Poland, Slovakia, Hungary, Romania and Bulgaria, charged to assist RSOMI of allied multinational forces. They provide broad planning support, particularly for collective defence; they also work with host nations to identify logistical networks, transportation routes and supporting infrastructures.[39] In other words, they serve as the linkage between the respective host nation and the NATO force structure in both peace (for exercises) and crisis time (Bjerg Moller 2019). They fall under the authority of the Headquarters Multinational Corps North-East (MNC-NE) in Szczecin, enhanced up to 400 officials from 24 NATO countries,[40] and of the newly established Multinational Division South-East (MND-SE) one in Romania. Both are land commands, with a narrower focus and smaller capacity than JFC Brunssum and Naples.

Finally, in 2016 an EFP has been established in the Baltic Republics and Poland, composed of four multinational battle groups—one per

[39] NATO SHAPE.NATO Force Integration Units (NFIU). https://shape.nato.int/operations/nato-force-integration-units.

[40] NATO MNCNE. Organisations. https://mncne.nato.int/about-us/organisation.

country—each one relying on approximately 1.000–1.2000 units. The battle groups are led by four framework nations, respectively, the US (Poland), Germany (Lithuania), Canada (Latvia) and the UK (Estonia). This was a very important move because it represented the first-ever robust built-up of NATO military presence in the new members, and entails a tactical command and control capacity on their territories. It is complemented by the establishment of a Multinational Division North-East (MND-NE) HQ in Elblag (Poland) and a Multinational Division North (MND-N) HQ in Adazi (Latvia).[41] Once again, they are built upon a framework nation, Poland in the first case and Latvia, Estonia and Denmark in the second one. These two HQs coordinate and supervise training and preparation for the EFP, which in the end falls under the MCN-NE authority in peacetime (Bjerg Moller 2019).

The Warsaw Summit also decided on the establishment of a Tailored Forward Presence (TFP) in Romania, Bulgaria and Turkey. It has been implemented mainly through a maritime component in the Black Sea, with training activities involving the NATO Standing Naval Forces with additional capabilities, and an enhanced air policing of Bulgaria and Romania by rotating allied air forces (Leuprecht 2019). The Romanian initiative to establish the MND-SE is part of this enhancement of NATO's posture in the Black Sea region. All these measures on the Eastern flank have been complemented by strengthening also NATO's cyber defence and defence against missile attacks (Broeks 2019), which obviously goes well beyond land or maritime borders with Russia.

The complex command puzzle constituted by EFP, TFP, NFIU and multinational HQ is the result of the effort to better integrate these countries into the NATO force structure, by enhancing the relatively weak military linkages built in the few years between their accession to the Alliance and the 2014 Crimea watershed. Indeed, the 1999 and 2004 enlargement did not result in a forward deployment of NATO troops on their territory, and the only military footprint was the MNC-NE in Szcezecin, a joint training centre in Bydgoszcz (Poland), and the Baltic Air policing mission set up in 2004 (Hagström Frisell et al. 2019).

Such a complex puzzle poses serious challenges to the command structure previously discussed. Indeed, the military units part of the EFP and VJTF respond to the respective national chain of command, while the

[41] NATO MNCNE. Multinational Divisions. https://mncne.nato.int/forces/divisions.

framework nation is responsible for its own battle group, i.e. in terms of force generation and strategic planning, and for the relations with the host country (Leuprecht 2019). It is not crystal clear which actions will have to be ordered by individual capitals and which ones by the command structure. Since a single national government will decide more rapidly than the Alliance's bodies acting by consensus, it may well happen that the US could bypass NATO to intervene pending a decision by the North Atlantic Council (Luik and Praks 2017). On the one hand, this increases the rapidity of reaction by Washington and other major allies, which in turn makes the deterrence posture more credible in Russia's eyes. On the other hand, it introduces an element of differentiation and entropy within the Alliance which may challenge its cohesion in case of crises.

Against this backdrop, NATO has taken steps to increase the responsiveness of its decision-making process, in order to effectively take collective political decisions in a few days. The Alliance has further developed its advance plans and regularly practices its crisis decision-making procedures (Turner 2019). These procedures involve pre-prepared response measures and steps, which can be drawn upon, or modified, as necessary (Turner 2019).

Deterrence Through Tripwire, Defence Via Reinforcements

Prior to the 2022 Russian invasion of Ukraine, the ensemble of EFP, TFP, VJTF, NRF and NFIU constituted a deterrence and defence posture based on the assumption that a small forward force on the Eastern flank serves to avoid an easy *fait accompli* by Russia. Any form of hybrid attack against any member will face the resistance of multinational forces and thus immediately generate casualties among troops of all 30 member states—including the US. Per se, this 'tripwire' mechanism should change the strategic calculus in Moscow and act as deterrence—as happened during the Cold War, *mutatis mutandis*, with the US and NATO forces in Western Berlin encircled and outnumbered by the Warsaw Pact. Deterrence through tripwire is probably the only solution at hand, since allied militaries have to defend a vast perimeter from north Norway to eastern Turkey, while patrolling the seas and running demanding out-of-area operations. As a result, they are stretched in operations far from the respective main bases. In contrast, the Russian armed forces are smaller than NATO combined ones, but they can massively and rapidly concentrate on a single entry point close to their infrastructures and HQs, such as the Baltic States—as done in Crimea.

Differently from the Cold War, a Russian attack would not aim to defeat the West. It would rather seek to break the territorial integrity of a given ally in Eastern Europe by demonstrating collective defence is a paper tiger, thus becoming able to intimidate European countries. Should this deterrence through tripwire fail and a Russian attack occur, the burden of escalation will be on the NATO side to retake the piece of land occupied by Russia and prove collective defence is real. This would happen by the rapid arrival first of VJTF and then of the rest of NRF, as well as by national reinforcements *in primis* from the US. Such a flow of Western capabilities will be facilitated by the NFIU and the commands already in place from Norfolk and Ulm to the Eastern flank. And everything should take place under the overall coordination of the NATO command structure and political bodies.

There is consensus among experts and practitioners that such a defence via reinforcements should be sufficient to halt and roll back a relatively small-scale, hybrid attack comparable to the one that occurred in Crimea in 2014. However, if Russia is willing to use the conventional weapons at its disposal in the European theatre these would pose a serious challenge to a posture mainly based on reinforcements. Indeed, Moscow has placed a number of Anti Access/Area Denial (A2/AD) capabilities in the region bordering NATO countries, including the Kaliningrad enclave—placed between Poland and Lithuania—Belarus and Crimea. These capabilities encompass first and foremost a range of missile systems, including dual-capable interceptors potentially armed with nuclear weapons, as well as air defence systems and submarines able to inflict dramatic losses to allied forces moving to the Eastern flank via land, sea or air transports.[42] Moreover, geography constitutes an advantage for Russia particularly concerning the narrow 'Suwalki Gap' connecting Poland and Lithuania, which is caught between Belarus and the Kaliningrad stronghold. In the maritime domain, the opening of new Arctic routes and the increased Russian submarine presence in the North Atlantic will challenge the security of the sea lines of communication between the US and Europe. NATO is aware of these threats. In early 2020 it decided to hold the

[42] See in this regard: Lasconjarias and Marrone (2016).

exercise Defender Europe despite the Covid-19 pandemic, in order to test and improve the ability to deliver reinforcements in a crisis scenario—with about 20.000 US troops moved across the Atlantic.[43] Several allies also increased their investments in stealth fighter aircraft, missile systems and anti-submarine maritime patrol aircraft to counter Russia's A2/AD capabilities and ultimately to hit the territory of the Russian Federation. That would mean a conventional war in Europe.

In conclusion, defence via reinforcement would only work if NATO deploys VJTF and NRF to fight Russian troops and Moscow decides that the price of an A2/AD escalation is too high—which is the preferable outcome of the current NATO posture. Implicitly, the different steps of reinforcements—first VJTF and then NRF—are meant to allow diplomatic negotiations to take place to reach a ceasefire or at least de-escalate. Such a positive outcome largely depends on two factors. First, the ability of NATO forces in Europe—mostly European ones—to hold ground and fight almost alone in the first phases of conflict.[44] Noticeably, the great majority of combat forces contributed to NRF as well as those identified by the NATO Readiness Initiative are provided by European allies and Canada (Turner 2019). The second factor is the US's ability to massively and rapidly reinforce Europe despite their military commitments in the Pacific from Taiwan to South Korea.

Should the negotiations fail in the reinforcement phase, the alternative would be a fully fledged conventional war across land, sea, air, space and cyber domains, centred on European theatre but with immediate repercussions on North American security, given for example the threat of hypersonic missiles. In this case, the combined allied military might would still defeat Russia if there will be no nuclear escalation. In other words, the Alliance's perimeter is not defendable as such after the 2004 enlargement, and Russia can indeed occupy a Baltic territory in a few days as feared by several simulations.[45] But Moscow cannot hold the conquered position if the US is willing to lead a NATO conventional rollback by accepting dramatic losses. In this scenario, there are two options left to the Russian Federation: either to retreat, or to escalate to nuclear weapons.

[43] NATO SHAPE. Defender-Europe 20. https://shape.nato.int/defender-europe.

[44] See in this regard: Posen (2020).

[45] See in this regard: Shlapak and Johnson (2016).

Against this backdrop, the reviewed NATO command structure is planning contingency scenarios in the Baltic, the Black Sea Region and broadly speaking in the Alliance's Eastern flank, preparing to implement defence via reinforcement. The force structure has adapted to make the deterrence tripwire robust and credible from the EFP to the VJTF and NRF, and multinational commands have been established from the Baltic to Romania. The NDPP has been reoriented towards the development of high-end capabilities for a possible war with Russia, and the allies' defence spending has steadily increased since 2015 in both relative and absolute terms. Finally, the 2022 Strategic Concept further focuses NATO military posture on the Eastern flank. In conclusion, the NATO arm for collective defence and deterrence looks sufficiently strong to make it probable it will never be tested—the real success of the Alliance's history.

Acknowledgments The author does thank the following interlocutors for the useful exchanges of views occurred during the elaboration of this chapter: Gen. Vincenzo Camporini, Gen. Stefano Cont, Gen. Frederic Pesme, Adm. Stefano Dotti, Dr. Andrea Gilli, Prof. Stefano Silvestri, Dr. Sten Rynning and Adm. Ferdinando Sanfelice di Monteforte. The chapter's content is the sole responsibility of the author. A special thanks to Ottavia Credi for her support in terms of literature review and editing.

Bibliography

Appathurai, James. 2002. Closing the Capabilities Gap. *NATO Review* (September): 2–4.

Bitondo, Francesca, Alessandro Marrone, and Paola Sartori. 2017. Challenges to NATO and Italy's Role: Trump, Brexit, Collective Defence and Neighborhood Stability. *Documenti IAI* 16, no. 18E.

Bjerg Moller, Sara. 2019. Building the Airplane While Flying: Adapting NATO's Force Structure in an Era of Uncertainty. *NDC Policy Brief*, no. 11, May.

Broeks, Jan. 2019. The Necessary Adaptation of NATO's Military Instrument of Power. *NDC Policy Brief*, no. 14, June.

Cohen, Zachary, Michelle Kosinski, and Barbara Starr. 2018. Trump's Barrage of Attacks 'Beyond Belief,' Reeling NATO Diplomats Say. *CNN*, July 11.

Cordesman, Anthony H., and Max Molot. 2019. NATO's 'Brain Death' Burden-sharing Blunders—Focusing on the Right Investment, Force Strength, and Readiness Needs. *CSIS Working Paper*.

Deni, John R. 2004. The NATO Rapid Deployment Corps: Alliance Doctrine and Force Structure. *Contemporary Security Policy* 25 (3): 498–523.

Drent, Margriet, Kimberley Kruijver, and Dick Zandee. 2019. Military Mobility and the EU-NATO Conundrum. *Clingendael Report*.

Fassi, Enrico, Sonia Lucarelli, and Alessandro Marrone. 2015. *What NATO for What Threats? Warsaw and Beyond*. NATO HQ.

Fleischer, Pawel. 2015. NATO Defence Planning Process. Implications for defence posture. *Securitologia* 21 (1): 103–114.

Grand, Camille, and Matthew Gillis. 2020. Alliance Capabilities at 70: Achieving Agility for an Uncertain Future. *NDC Policy Brief*, no. 1, January.

Hagström Frisell, Eva (Ed.), Robert Dalsjö, Jakob Gustafsson, and John Rydqvist. 2019. *Deterrence by Reinforcement—The Strengths and Weaknesses of NATO's Evolving Defence Strategy*. Swedish Defence Research Agency.

Kacprzyk, Arthur. 2018. Perspectives on NATO's Deterrence and Defence on the Eastern Flank. *PISM Bulletin* 125, no. 1196.

Lasconjarias, Guillaume, and Alessandro Marrone. 2016. How to Respond to Anti-Access/Area Denial (A2/AD)? Towards a NATO Counter-A2/AD Strategy. *NDC Conference Reports* 1, no. 16.

Leuprecht, Christian. 2019. The Enhanced Forward Presence: Innovating NATO's Deployment Model for Collective Defence. *NDC Policy Brief*, no. 22 (October).

Luik, Juri, and Henrik Praks. 2017. Boosting the Deterrent Effect of Allied Enhanced Forward Presence. *ICDS Policy Paper*.

Mahler, Jackie. 2019. Examining the European Recapitalization Incentive Program. *Europe's Edge*.

Marrone, Alessandro, and Ester Sabatino. 2021. Cyber Defence in NATO Countries: Comparing Models. *IAI Papers* 21, no. 5.

Marrone Alessandro, Olivier De France, and Daniele Fattibene. 2016. Defence Budgets and Cooperation in Europe: Developments, Trends and Drivers. *IAI Documents and Working Papers*.

Marrone, Alessandro, Paola Tessari, and Carolina De Simone. 2014. Italian Interests and NATO: From Missions to Trenches?. *Documenti IAI* 14, no. 12E.

Mattelaer, Alexander. 2016. US Leadership and NATO—Revisiting the Principles of NATO Burden-Sharing. *Parameters* 46 (1): 25–33.

Nones, Michele, and Alessandro Marrone. 2012. The Transformation of the Armed Forces: The Forza NEC Program. *IAI Research Papers*.

Posen, Barry R. 2020. Europe Can Defend Itself. *Survival* 62 (6): 7–34.

Ruiz Palmer, Diego A. 2019. A Strategic Odyssey: Constancy of Purpose and Strategy-Making in NATO, 1949-2019. *NDC Policy Brief*, no. 3, June.

Shlapak, David A., and Michael W. Johnson. 2016. Reinforcing Deterrence on NATO's Eastern Flank Wargaming the Defense of the Baltics. *RAND Research Report*.

Turner, Patrick. 2019. NATO at 70: What Defence Policy and Planning Priorities?. *NDC Policy Brief*, no. 23, October.

Wołkonowski, Jarosław. 2018. NATO Defense Expenditures in 1949-2017. *SHS Web of Conferences* 57.

Young, Thomas-Durell. 1997. *Multinational Land Formations and NATO: Reforming Practices and Structures*. Strategic Studies Institute, US Army War College.

CHAPTER 13

Conclusion: NATO Between Mere Survival and Strategic Relaunching

Massimo de Leonardis

NATO is at the crossroads between mere survival and strategic relaunching. The pledge of art. 5 maintains its permanent importance and it is enough to justify NATO existence. For many NATO members the threat of an attack to their territories remains an entirely hypothetical eventuality. For others, Russia is a real danger, almost as the Soviet Union was. It is not surprising that Poland and Lithuania show the highest rate of approval of NATO, respectively 82 and 77%. The problem is that 'when asked whether their country should or should not use military force to defend a NATO ally from a hypothetical attack by Russia, in only five of the 16 member states surveyed—the Netherlands, the U.S., Canada, the UK and Lithuania—do half or more say that they should use such force. Across the 16 countries, a median of 50% says that their country should

M. de Leonardis (✉)
Faculty of Political and Social Sciences, Catholic University of the Sacred Heart, Milan, Italy
e-mail: massimo.deleonardis@unicatt.it

M. de Leonardis (ed.), *NATO in the Post-Cold War Era*, Security, Conflict and Cooperation in the Contemporary World
https://doi.org/10.1007/978-3-031-06063-2_13

not defend a NATO ally in the event of an attack by Russia, while 38% say they should'.[1]

In any case, NATO cannot confine itself to being an insurance policy which probably will never require payment. After the disappearance of the Soviet Union and of the Warsaw Pact, Dean Acheson's well-known remark on Britain (Acheson 1963)[2] could be applied with a little adaptation to the Atlantic Alliance, which 'has lost an enemy and not yet found a role'. Actually, after the Cold War, NATO played many roles, but just for this it is rather awkward to state that 'the fundamental purpose of NATO is more demonstrably clear today than it has been for decades' (NATO 2030). Reviving Russia as the 'enemy' *par excellence* would be as much misleading as the lifting of an old lady in search for a new youth.

The Alliance is well aware that a thorough reappraisal of its role is necessary. In December 2019, the NATO summit in London asked the Secretary General to undertake an endeavour similar to those performed in the past, when the Alliance perceived the necessity of a long-term reflection on its role. In 1956, there was the 'three wise men' report, and in 1968 the Harmel report. Now, in December 2020 the Secretary General presented to the North Atlantic Council the report *NATO 2030: United for a New Era. Analysis and Recommendations of the Reflection Group Appointed by the NATO Secretary General*.[3] In order to redact this document, the *Reflection Group*, composed of ten scholars or former politicians, conducted extensive consultations within and outside NATO. The document is prodromal to the drafting of a new *Strategic Concept*; the same procedure was adopted to write the *Strategic Concept* of 2010, when Madeleine Albright chaired a Group of Expert to prepare it.

Once again, NATO is invited to adapt, since the next ten years will be very different from the previous decades: 'it will be a world of

[1] Pew Research Center, *NATO Seen Favorably Across Member States*, Report, 9 February 2021, p. 23. https://www.pewresearch.org/global/2020/02/09/nato-seen-favorably-across-member-states/.

[2] In a speech at West Point military academy on 5 December 1962, the former Secretary of State said: 'Great Britain has lost an Empire and has not yet found a role' (Acheson 1963).

[3] https://www.nato.int/nato_static_fl2014/assets/pdf/2020/12/pdf/201201-Reflection-Group-Final-Report-Uni.pdf. Unless specified differently, following quotes are from this document.

competing great powers, in which assertive authoritarian states with revisionist foreign policy agendas seek to expand their power and influence'. In this volume, more than once the distinction was recalled between the military role and structures of the Atlantic Alliance and the political ones, upholding the view that the former are in better shape than the latter. *NATO 2030* states that 'the Alliance could be said to be formidable in military strength; but it is far from invulnerable to such political turbulence' has 'experienced internal strains', as in various other instances during its history, and its political dimension needs strengthening. Therefore, 'NATO needs a strong political dimension to match its military adaptation'.

Notwithstanding the alleged 'clear demonstrability of NATO purpose', various measures are suggested to improve public diplomacy and a better appreciation of the Alliance's scope. Some measures follow patterns already existing within the EU. For example, it is suggested to found a NATO University; EU has the European University in Florence. The institution of a Harmel fellowship was also proposed; EU finances the Jean Monnet Chairs. It is a noticeable and welcome reversal of the policy followed by NATO Public Diplomacy Division in the last years, which no longer supported university students' visits to NATO headquarters, privileging social medias and high school students. It is unlikely that a teenager would follow NATO news on Twitter or similar platforms.

Another example of lessons that NATO tries to learn from others is the suggestion to 'consider developing a North Atlantic equivalent of the US Defence Advanced Research Projects Agency (DARPA) or European Defence Fund (EDF) charged with encouraging support for innovation in strategic areas among Allies'.

Since the diverging political perspectives among the member States are the Atlantic Alliance's major internal problem, it is suggested to soften the rule of consensus, to strengthen the powers of the Secretary General and intensify the dialogue. 'Allies should strive to hold national policies to the line of policy developed at NATO'. Is it recommended 'to hold more frequent Ministerials and, when appropriate, expand their format. It should resume the practice whereby the number of annual Foreign Ministerials matches the number of Defence Ministerials, [...] It should hold more informal meetings and institute regular consultations on issues beyond the traditional agenda, including meetings of NATO Political Directors or other senior officials'. In this last case, the historical patterns are the Treaty of the Elysée of January 1963, which originated the Franco-German Axis and the recommendations of the Harmel Report of 1967.

The approach towards collaboration with the EU in the field of European defence repeats traditional positions: 'NATO should welcome EU efforts towards a stronger and more capable European defence capacity insofar as these strengthen NATO, contribute to a fair transatlantic burden-sharing, and fully involve non-EU Allies. Ongoing European efforts should be better used to increase the share of European Allies in support of NATO capability targets'. Albeit with softer words, basically it is the same concept of the three 'd', 'no decoupling', 'no duplication', 'no discrimination', expressed by US secretary of State Madeleine Albright in 1999.[4] At that time, the NATO major ally not a member of the EU which had not to be 'discriminated' was just Turkey, now we have the United Kingdom too. It is also recommended the already experimented pattern of 'coalitions of the willing' among NATO members and partners for operations not involving everybody.

Looking to the international scenario, Russia, China, and international terrorism are identified as the major reasons of concern. Russia is the 'main challenge', China is an 'emerging challenge'. Beijing 'does not pose an immediate military threat to the Euro-Atlantic area on the scale of Russia', however, its growing power and assertiveness make China 'a full-spectrum systemic rival'. Finally, 'NATO should more explicitly integrate the fight against terrorism into NATO's core tasks'. Unsurprisingly, *NATO 2030* echoes the approach of the American *National Security Strategy* released in December 2017.[5]

NATO 2030 is a sufficiently straightforward document of 67 pages, which draws a lot from previous similar exercises and sometimes does not refrain from calling a spade a spade. For example, it talks of 'illegal mass migrations', while zealots of political correctness would require saying 'migrants'. The word 'Islamic' is mentioned for the so called 'State', so everybody may understand which are the foundations of 'international terrorism'. Since the one of 2010 is outmoded, *NATO 2030* recommends the approval in 2021 of a new *Strategic Concept*, which, however, 'is not a

[4] Press Briefing at the Conclusion of the NATO 50th Anniversary and Euro-Atlantic Partnership Council Meetings. Washington. 25 April 1999. http://www.usia.gov/topical/pol/eap/alberg25.htm.

[5] https://trumpwhitehouse.archives.gov/wp-content/uploads/2017/12/NSS-Final-12-18-2017-0905.pdf.

panacea'. Actually, a new *Strategic Concept* is expected to be approved at NATO summit in Madrid in June 2022, where a new Secretary General should also be elected. British ambitions to fill this post for the fourth time, after Lords Ismay, Carrington, and Robertson, might be frustrated by the consideration that the Secretary General should better come from a country member both of NATO and EU (Stoltenberg, a Norwegian, is not), as a token of collaboration between the two organizations. On its part, EU is currently engaged in drafting a 'Strategic Compass' to cement the foundations for a shared vision for EU security and defence among the Member States. During 2022, the two organizations, NATO and EU, should sign a joint declaration, something already done in 2016 and 2018.

NATO 2030 offers 138 recommendations, which in most cases appear wise. As the 'three wise men' remarked in 1956 on a similar occasion it will not easy 'for the member governments to carry them into effect'. In the next years it will be seen how many of these recommendations will be adopted.

Some considerations may in any case be formulated from the point of view of *Realpolitik*. Institutional shrewdness, as increased consultation and dialogue, may help but certainly cannot provide itself a solution to political divergences among the allies. Many procedures are already in place, 'but what we need is more political will to use them'.[6] French President Macron targeted explicitly Ankara, talking of 'an uncoordinated aggressive action by another NATO ally, Turkey, in an area where our interests are at stake' (Macron 2019). In this respect, French record is not certainly blameless. In the past, France behaved more than once just in the same way of Turkey: attacking Egypt in 1956 and Libya in 2011 and recalling unilaterally its troops from Afghanistan in 2012. A realist knows perfectly that in foreign policy you find always the coherence of interests, rarely the consistency of principles. Certainly Turkey's interventions in the MENA region cannot be glossed over and in a specific case the stance of Ankara set a dangerous precedent. It never happened that an ally bought armaments from a power which NATO considers a rival (Russia).[7]

[6] Press conference by NATO Secretary General Jens Stoltenberg ahead of the meetings of NATO Defence Ministers on 17 and 18 February at NATO Headquarters. 15 February 2021, https://www.nato.int/cps/en/natohq/opinions_181427.htm.

[7] Turkey bought Russia's S-400 air defence systems; in retaliation Washington blocked the transfer of F-35 fighter jets to Ankara.

Other countries, maybe less brazenly, pursue national agendas regardless of NATO policies. Germany is determined to go on with the Russian project of Nord Stream 2 gas pipeline across the Baltic. Many Europeans countries look at relations with China taking into account only their economic interests and neglecting the political and strategic implications; the main example is Belt and Road Initiative.

China and Russia are both identified by NATO as hostile actors. Confronting both Russia and China wouldn't be for NATO biting off more than it can chew? One of the pragmatic guidelines of Otto von Bismarck was that in a group of five great powers you should try to join forces with at least two (Herre 1991); this is valid also in a group of three. NATO, standard-bearer of the West, should not make the mistake of pushing Russia to embrace China.

It is stated that Russia is responsible of the 'illegitimate and illegal invasion and annexation of Crimea' from Ukraine. The two adjectives have different meanings. Illegal refers to the violation of a precise law or regulation. Indeed, international treaties may be seen as a legal transaction, based on the principle *pacta sunt servanda* (pacts must be respected) or, as diplomatic historians say, treaties are the expression of a temporary situation and of the correlation of forces among the signatories. From this perspective, the underlying principle is *rebus sic stantibus* (this being the case), which, as Bismarck (Bismarck 1898) said, is the unexpressed clause of any treaty. Even taking for granted that Russia behaved illegally, her acts were also illegitimate, that is to say unfounded, unjustified, unwarranted?

Considering Crimea's history[8] and ethnic background, Moscow can advance many reasonable claims on the peninsula. The policy of the West may take two opposing courses about Ukraine. The first was indicated by Zbigniew Brzezinski (Brzezinski 1997): The West must fully integrate Ukraine in its system of international organizations (NATO and EU), preventing Russia 'to become a powerful imperial state'. On the contrary, Henry Kissinger suggested that if 'Ukraine is to survive and thrive, it must not be either side's outpost against the other — it should function

[8] Crimea was annexed by the Russian empire in 1783. In 1954 the Soviet Union transferred the peninsula from the Russian Soviet Federative Socialist Republic to the Ukrainian Soviet Socialist Republic. According to some authors (Sakwa 2015) that decree violated the Soviet constitution. In any case, at that time the transfer from a Republic to another had little practical consequences.

as a bridge between them [...] To treat Ukraine as part of an East-West confrontation would scuttle for decades any prospect to bring Russia and the West — especially Russia and Europe — into a cooperative international system [...] Ukraine should not join NATO' (Kissinger, 2014). Actually Ukraine means border-land (Cella 2021; Kubicek 2008).

In the post-Cold War, the United States and NATO followed the first line of action. They may continue this course, being aware that it would prevent a rapprochement with Russia, without obtaining the return of Crimea to Ukraine, unless dramatic developments take place. Or they could try to strike with Russia that global deal which was never attempted in the last thirty years. Historically, the alternative patterns are that of the Congress of Vienna in 1815, including in the concert of powers the former enemy, France, or that of Peace Conference of Versailles in 1919, imposing a *Diktat* to vanquished Germany. It is a difficult choice, on which there are different views among NATO member States and inside them. A legalistic approach leads nowhere. NATO implicitly recognized that by condoning the Turkish invasion of Cyprus in 1974, with the ensuing creation of the Turkish Republic of Northern Cyprus, recognized only by Ankara. Even that was illegal, albeit Turkey, as Russia in Crimea, had arguments to justify its action.

'A shared democratic identity is what distinguishes the Alliance from the principal threats and challenges it faces'. Certainly this is an added value for NATO. Does this imply that NATO should defend human rights abroad and make their violation a key issue in its relations with other nations? This is an old question, to which also there are no easy answers. When NATO was just a military alliance could ignore this issue; now it claims a political role and taking a position is expected. Traditional diplomacy prescribed a distinction between foreign and domestic policies. States should be judged by their actions in the international arena and not according to the type of their regime. A new idealistic approach now prevails (in theory) and NATO performed 'humanitarian interventions', albeit against rather innocuous foes and with not-so-successful results. In practice, nobody dares to compromise its interests. President Macron rolled out the red carpet to the ruler of Egypt, General Abdel Fattah al-Sisi, and candidly admitted that France could not bother about democracy and human rights there, having strategic and economic interests in that country. In this respect, little has changed from the times of Bismarck, who once said that knowing about the sufferings of someone in some parts of the world he could pray for him but could not make him an object of German policy (Langer 1950). As during the Cold War, the West and NATO need to be pragmatic and selective without being and appearing cynical.

The great and new strategic factor is the impressive rise of China, that presents 'both opportunities and challenges that we need to address together as an Alliance', as the London Summit Declaration of December 2019 says. A measured statement, open to a wide range of developments. NATO could adopt a minimalistic approach, staying on guard, trying to foster a member States' common policy towards China and intervening with concrete measures only if the security of the North-Atlantic area is threatened. Otherwise, NATO could actively enter the game of 'containing' China up to the point of acting (very much) out-of-area. We may guess that the first line of action will be adopted, unless relations with China seriously deteriorate. With the exception of the United Kingdom,[9] no European NATO country seems prepared to support Washington in confronting China in its neighbourhood.

Probably the future *Strategic Concept* will mention NATO's determination to watch closely and maybe to confront China in different domains: the impact of emerging and disruptive technologies, cybersecurity, the preservation of the technological edge, the link between climate change and security. However, it is unlikely that NATO will engage out-of-area against Beijing. This task will be left to the United States and its traditional allies in the Far East and the Pacific, as demonstrated by the AUKUS agreement of September 2021 among Australia, United Kingdom and United States, with the broad meaning of containing Chinese expansionism. AUKUS continues the historical pattern of ANZUS (Australia, New Zealand, United States) signed in September 1951 and of the 'Five Eyes', an intelligence alliance comprising Australia, Canada, New Zealand, the United Kingdom, and the United States.

Talking in February 2021 at Chatham House in London,[10] NATO Secretary General Jens Stoltenberg was very prudent: 'we don't regard China as an adversary', 'NATO is and will remain a regional alliance of Europe and North America [...] But the challenges we face are more

[9] In June 2021 a British-led aircraft carrier group voyage took the HMS Queen Elizabeth to the disputed South China Sea.

[10] 'New Ideas for NATO 2030'—a youth event organized by NATO and Chatham House. 4 February 2021. https://www.nato.int/cps/en/natohq/news_180769.htm.

and more global. So we need a global outlook'. He revived the idea of working 'more closely with like-minded partners across the globe to develop a community of democracies. Like Australia, Japan, New Zealand and South Korea'; Afghanistan, Colombia, Iraq, Mongolia, and Pakistan, who are (or were in February) also in the list of the 'partners across the globe' were not mentioned; aptly so, I should say. Instead, Brazil and India are pointed out as 'potential new partners'. India is a rival of China. In the 1990s Carlos Menem's Argentina seemed willing to join NATO as a full member, now it is the turn of the other South American giant. Surely, we are witnessing the first steps of a path already taken in the 2000s and then dropped: NATO going global, if not in membership, at least in its outreach. The 'community of democracies' is reminiscent of the 'spiritual federation of the West' sketched in 1948 by Ernest Bevin.

Actually, the Atlantic Alliance is the most important institutional expression of the West, which is confronted by the 'Rise of the Rest' (Zakaria, 2012). In 1948, the future NATO secretary general Manlio Brosio, at that time Italian ambassador to Moscow, wrote in his diary: 'a higher civilization must also resist by force and impose itself by force. Historical fatalism that considers the justice of new movements to be inevitable only because they are new is the coward's philosophy. Our civilization is superior. So we have two duties: to spread it and defend it' (Brosio 1986). Today, these words would fall under the axe of political correctness. However, a prerequisite to stop the West's decline is to recover a sense of identity and pride for its historical achievements. An attitude opposed to 'Westlessness', which refers 'to a divided and in some parts increasingly illiberal West that seems to be retreating from the global stage'.[11]

As already mentioned in the Introduction, it should be noted that the entire manuscript was completed before the Russian invasion of Ukraine. This event, rather unexpected in its magnitude, adds a sense of drama to the scenario, but does not change its fundamental and long-term features.

Bibliography

Acheson, Dean. 1963. *Vital Speeches*, 29 (6).
Bismarck, Otto von. 1898. *Gedanken und Erinnerungen*. Stuttgart: Cotta.

[11] *Westlessness—The Munich Security Conference 2020*, https://securityconference.org/en/news/full/westlessness-the-munich-security-conference-2020/.

Brosio, Manlio. 1986. *Diari di Mosca 1947/1951*. Bologna: Il Mulino.
Brzezinski, Zbigniew. 1997. *The Grand Chessboard: American Primacy and Its Geostrategic Imperatives*. New York: Basic Books.
Cella, Giorgio. 2021. *Dalla Rus' di Kiev ad Euromajdan. L'Ucraina nella geopolitica dell'Europa centro-orientale*. Roma: Carocci.
Herre, Franz. 1991. *Bismarck: der Preußische Deutsche*. Köln: Kiepenheuer und Witsch.
Kissinger, Henry A. 2014. *To settle the Ukraine crisis, start at the end. The Washington Post*, March 5.
Kubicek, Paul. 2008. *The History of Ukraine*. Westport: Greenwood Publishing Group.
Langer, William L. 1950. *European alliances and alignments, 1871–1890*. New York: Knopf
Macron, Emmanuel. 2019. *Briefing. Macron's View of the World. A President on a Mission. The Economist*, November 9.
Sakwa, Richard. 2015. *Frontline Ukraine. Crisis in the Borderlands*. New York: I. B. Tauris.
Zakaria, Fareed. 2012. *The Post-American World*. New York: W. W. Norton & Company.

Index of Names

M. de Leonardis (ed.), *NATO in the Post-Cold War Era*, Security, Conflict and Cooperation in the Contemporary World
https://doi.org/10.1007/978-3-031-06063-2

L

M

N

O

P

R

S

FSC
www.fsc.org
MIX
Papier | Fördert
gute Waldnutzung
FSC® C083411

Kolibri 360 GmbH
Ferdinand-Jühlke-Straße 7
99095 Erfurt, Deutschland
produktsicherheit@kolibri360.de